Human Rights Regime
Dialogic & Debates

Human Rights Regime Dialogic & Debates

Editor

Dr Pratyush Vatsala

GYAN

ISBN : 978-81-212-1310-3

Price : ₹ 990

First Published, 2016

Published by

Gyan Publishing House
5, Ansari Road
Daryaganj, New Delhi-110002
Phones: 9811692060
E-mail: books@gyanbooks.com

Printed at: G. Print Process, Delhi.

Cataloging in Publication Data—DK
Courtesy: D.K. Agencies (P) Ltd. <docinfo@dkagencies.com>

Punjabi, Riyaz, author.
Human rights regime : debates & concerns / [Prof. Riyaz Punjabi].
pages cm

1. Human rights. I. Title.

JC571.P86 2016 DDC 323 23

Contents

List of Contributors

Riyaz Punjabi, Former Professor JNU and Vice Chancellor University of Kashmir is President, International Centre for Peace Studies. He was granted the Padma Shri, one of India's highest civilian awards in 2011 in Education.

Satish C. Aikant, Former Professor of English, H.N. B. Garhwal University, Pauri Campus. Has been Fellow at IIAS.

Raj Lakshmi Datta, Assistant Professor Dept of Economics, D.B.S. PG College, Dehradun. Earlier associated with the School of Social Sciences at Doon University Dehradun and Department of Economics HNB Garhwal (Central) University Srinagar.

Jayant Chowdhary Dr Jayanta Choudhury, Assistant Professor, Department of Rural Management & Development, Tripura University.

Reshmi Ghosh, Research Associate, Centre for Rural Studies, Tripura University.

Manjula Srinivas, Associate Professor & Head Department of Mass Media, Kishinchand Chellaram College. Mumbai.

S. K. Ahuja, Brigadier, YSM, PhD has served as Commander 109,Gurez Sector. Presently posted at Mizorum.

Ritu Sharma, Assistant Professor, Kalindi College, New Delhi.

Rekha Kaul, Associate Professor, Department of Political Science, Lakshmibai College, University of Delhi has authored several articles for academic journals and two books, *Caste, Class and Education* and *Education, Development and Underdevelopment* (ed.), both published by Sage Publications.

Tahira Khatoon, Currently a student of M.Phil (4th Semester) in Political Science in Centre for Political Studies, Jawaharlal Nehru

University, New Delhi. Also teaching in Kalindi College, University of Delhi as an adhoc Assistant Professor in Political Science Department.

Sunil Kumar, PhD Research Scholar, School of International Studies, Centre for West Asian Studies. Jawaharlal Nehru University, Delhi.

Prem Anand Mishra, Assistant Professor, Peace Research Centre, Gujarat Vidyapith, Ahmedabad, Gujarat.

Priyadarshini Sahu, PhD Scholar, Centre For West Asian Studies, School Of International Studies Jawaharlal Nehru University, New Delhi.

Abhijay Negi, Presently pursuing VIII Sem. Constitutional Law Hons. at National Law University, Jodhpur, has been awarded by NDTV (Greenathon Teens for Green Contest), Tata Nano (Student of the year Contest), Times of India (I Lead India). Founder & Chairperson, of NGO MAD.

Sangya Meena, Assistant Professor, Dept. of Pol. Science, D.A.V. PG College, Dehradun.

Richa Pandey Joshi, Assistant Professor in English, Doon University, Dehradun.

Dev Kumar Jacob, Assistant Professor, Nodal Center of excellence for human rights education, School of Law, rights and constitutional governance-TISS, Mumbai.

Aradhana Sethi, Research Scholar, Banasthali Vidyapeeth, Rajasthan.

Paritosh Singh, Assistant Professor, Dept. of Sociology, D.B.S. PG College, Dehradun.

Aparna Dixit, Research Fellow, Jamia Milia Islamia.

Preface

The book of Genesis presents the narrative of creation to understand life on earth, a complex mix of joy and woe imparting rainbow shades to human life. The Man was allowed to enjoy heaven except the tree of knowledge and was destined to live in paradise. In Abrahmic religion, God created Man out of dust and a woman to accompany him, offering him a paradise on earth to enjoy forever while Hindu thought cherished Man as son to immortality.

Moreover, if all declarations including UDHR proclaim the fact that all human beings are born free and equal with a birth right to enjoy a dignified life or at least not to be questioned by another Man, as only God could question him, why should he/she not be allowed to continue to live for ever like that as God made him to be.

Human beings, man, woman and the third gender in all religions, have always been curious to know the truth and also to develop the capabilities to discern and to sit on judgement with a knowledge of good and evil. In the pursuit of a common goal and fate, humanity is a single family, irrespective of the fact that we believe in Christianity, Judaism or Islam. We may cherish to see ourselves in the image of Adam and Eve but, Satan as our worldly attachment may bring us down from the paradise at any point of time.

However, human beings need a continuous check on their conscience to remain the image of God, 'Amritasya Putrah' and not to fall a prey to their greed and ego which is as natural as weeds in a beautiful garden. Since time immemorial, work has been the defining issue of the creator as well as the creation. 'Karma' voluntary or involuntary, is the most prominent theory which reflects the life matrix and provides a logical explanation to human life.

The synergy of work and development is the real achievement which transcends beyond the job and earning a livelihood, which may culminate in a life of satisfaction and fulfilment in 21st Century. It may be giving care to the needy or social networking or involving people for a social cause. HDR 2015 enunciates the importance of work for human development. All kinds of work, including care giving to a child or aged to the devotion of a painter to his work, have been the prime focus, though, remained neglected for a long time.

Human development, in modern terms, is defined as enhancing the skill of a person by providing technical support, safety and security measures, well being and problem solving initiatives which might be taken up as a remedial measure by the humanity keeping in view the quality, sustainable development and creation of opportunities for present and future generations. Human development is not something to be seen in void. It has to uphold human rights and values which are building blocks of a sustainable world which takes along everyone and does not leave anyone behind. Inclusive and holistic development is the ultimate agenda which has to be at work through innovations in the field of building peace, igniting hopes and providing conducive work environment to the masses.

The start ups, freelancing from home, surrogacy, single mothers, Gay and Lesbian marriages are a major breakthrough in the area of human freedom, progress and work. The idea of world citizenship as an emerging trend of the day gives an opportunity to think big and grow big but ultimately leaves us without home, struggling hard to live the present moment in the real sense. In a state of fusion and confusion, growth and development remain the most cherished goals to be accomplished by the society.

Economic growth alone can not guarantee satisfaction, giving equal access to public goods and quality services. Income growth and the GDP rate do not guarantee human well being. The most challenging issue is how to tap the potential resources and growth, with a human development approach in present world dynamics. All efforts of removing poverty and inequality are often captured by elites who defy all kinds of reforms creating structural barriers to sustainable development.

Human Rights Regime is a sensitive human world which encompasses all kinds of social cohesion, dialogic and debates since UN declaration on Human Rights and beyond, extending it to all inhabitants of the earth. All human actions, aspirations are covered under one vast umbrella of human rights with a humanist attitude. UNESCO declaration of taking up Peace as the top priority and responsibility of present generation to future generation brings it close to the agenda of new world order which has changed the dynamics of the world, as it can not be controlled by the political forces alone.

The perception of well being, work and employment has drastically changed. It is not only livelihood, a matter of earning bread and butter but educational achievements, opportunities, choices and health outcomes are now various indicators of richness of life. Population trends and human security are the factors which are to be taken more seriously than ever before. Creating more and more opportunities and choices with stability, order and peace at the same time, are the challenges of our times which we have to face in the age of technological revolution.

The present book is a collection of various articles contributed by the scholars, professors, researchers and young students diving deep into different aspects, dialogic and serious debates on human rights issues, trying to find out of box solutions, if at all possible, to the problems of human rights violations.

Prof. Punjabi explores the concept of Human Rights Regime in the present context and the inter linkage and interdependence of the three aspects of human rights: civil and political, economic, social and cultural rights and solidarity rights like peace and environment which are well established. The essence of value of fundamental and basic human rights has expanded. The right to life is affected by right to clean environment and right to health and there is a need to redefine the human rights violations in terms of changing perspectives. There is also a need to redefine the city, citizenship and civilization which Prof. Aikant elaborates in his article where he identifies the existence of city and a move towards global city as a compulsive choice but the challenges to ensure human rights to the underprivileged in a modern global city are unique and would require more deliberation with the rise of more MNCs and spatial segregation of city space.

A case study of underprivileged in Mumbai slums presented by Dr. Rajlakshmi with various indicators which are really alarming and disturbing, draws attention to the miserable and vulnerable conditions under which human beings survive. A human rights approach to providing basic amenities of life is crucial to human dignity. Role of NGOs in protecting child right in Tripura also presents a case study which culminates into policy recommendations for better status of child right in Tripura.

Cultural diversity and pluralist society are the conditions in which human rights are severely threatened as the solidarity is often missing in societies. The ethnic groups and the concept of a superior religion pressurize the minorities to adopt their culture, religion and language. The Universal Declaration on cultural diversity has marked cultural identity as an inseparable part of human dignity which should be ensured by developing a multicultural approach in society.

Embedded journalism highlights the conflict between military and media. There has been a need of war to show the people a picture as they wished to project while the basic job of media is to project the truth. Therefore, the embedded journalism always suffered from excess, context, censorship and objectivity giving one sided view of warfare which has been questioned on ethical grounds.

Another problem is insurgency and sub-continental operations where the enemy is unidentified. A Brigadier in command deliberates on the issue of sub-continental operations which are undertaken against unidentified/invisible enemy within our population, that too without complete application of principles of war but the operation still falling within the purview of military action with due respect to the law of the land. Any violation of human right is as much as a cause as the consequence of armed conflict and poses a threat to human rights yet the extraordinary condition in which the armed forces work, need to be well understood while dealing with such cases. The question of safeguarding human rights during communal violence is also an important issue as it is unpredicted and may happen any time but can be dealt successfully only when political, legal and social systems in country start working in tandem that we know is very difficult. A young law student Abhijay Negi analyses here the cases of riots in 1984, 2002 and recent one in Muzaffarnagar and expresses his concern over human rights threats and communal issues weakening our cultural connect.

Spectral chains of oppression define the direct link between oppression and injustice as oppression draws its life from discrimination and domination inherent in structural prejudices. The paper on human rights issues and Israel occupied territory examines the implication of such settlements on political, social and economic rights of Palestinian people which Israel has been advocating for so long.

Different forms of violence in the form of molestation and patriarchal pressures, freedom, sexuality and reproductive health and cooptation, female infanticide, dowry system, forced virginity tests, honour killings and surrogate motherhood have been analysed in the different chapters of the book. A new form of violation in terms of cultural image of women projected by media and making of women body image and selling it thereby is a real threat to their human rights. A discussion on negotiating rights in Mahasweta Devi's novel *Mother of 1084* as a text where a female protagonist, the mother of corpse number 1084 finds no legitimacy for her son's unlawful killing and challenges the wider morality and its immediate unit—the family. Illegitimacy is another severe threat to a human rights which are brutally violated as a part of basic denial of the mother as subject.

As the human claim to the rights does not vanish with age, rights of aged people is also an area where the government and the society together need to focus on to ensure their human rights of decent living and a dignified life.

Notwithstanding the human rights issues are a matter of prime concern internationally and are dealt in the most comprehensive way, the subject of good governance is a prerequisite which emphasizes on and protects human rights by meeting the challenges of accountability, transparency and efficiency in a corruption free environment. This issue has also been taken up in the volume, along with the right to education of those poor children who face food insecurity and are pushed out of school for early employment to feed their families despite government efforts to provide MDM in primary schools.

Some international issues related with women and children's right have also been discussed in detail. The armed conflict has deprived the children from their childhood recruiting them as soldiers to let them die young in the battlefield of Congo or to take up arms in the mountains of Afganistan. Ensuring political and economic rights of women in Iraq and the unsafe environment of growing insecurity, violence, religious fundamentalism and economic rights, where hundreds of women have been abducted and killed depriving them a public life, are the concerns which need to be taken seriously.

All these deliberations from various perspectives collectively strengthen the human development approach to growth in an inclusive society which cares one and all and ensures equity and justice to all its people, rich or poor. The dialogical analysis of human rights issues and healthy debates are the steps towards a better human society to live in 'where the mind is without fear and the head is ever held high'.

If we look at human development, not only in terms of per capita income but also in terms of enhancing equity which includes gender dimension, enabling greater voice and participation with the inclusion of youth, confronting environmental pressures and demographic changes reducing vulnerality and building resilience, we are sure, that we would be able to change all the threats into opportunities for the sustainable world tomorrow.

I am thankful to Gyan Publishing House for their patience as this book has been pending with me for long, due to my new work assignment which deserved more focus and attention for a while. However, I hope that the book will extend the human rights regime further to the new innovative and creative spaces which have been unexplored so far.

Pratyush Vatsala

1

Human Rights: Expanding Universe

—Riyaz Punjabi

Introduction

Human rights regime has come a full circle encompassing a vast gamut of human existence and activities. The continuing process of debates and discussions on UN Declarations on human rights and the general discourses in different forums relating to human rights regime have considerably enlarged the universe of human rights. The mechanisms evolved by the UN bodies over a period of time to monitor the status of human rights and accountability procedures in this regard are prodding the states to be sensitive in protecting and upholding the human rights of not only their citizens but all the inhabitants of their land. The Annual Periodic Report of UN Human Rights Council which holds its sessions periodically in Geneva has emerged as an effective mechanism to monitor the human rights situations the world over. The states debate and discuss these reports rigorously, although in the closed-door sessions in which non-governmental organisations or the visiting public are not allowed.

The New Focus

The emergence of a new world order in the aftermath of the disintegration of Soviet Union in 1990 and the new phase of globalisation exhilarated the focus on human rights. This focus was reinforced in the Vienna Declaration and Program of Action, 1993. The Declaration was adopted in the concluding session of World Conference on Human Rights convened in Vienna. This Declaration brought a new focus in sensitizing states, institutions, groups and individuals underlining the universality, indivisibility and interdependence of all human rights. The guiding principles of the Declaration found global endorsement, recognition and approval.

The Equal Emphasis

It is well recognised that International Convention on Civil and Political Rights and International Convention on Economic, Social and Cultural Rights (1966) form the backbone of human rights regime. However, the fact remains that greater emphasis was accorded to the Civil and Political Rights aspect of human rights for a long time. In the context of prevailing political order of those times in some parts of the world, this emphasis might be well comprehended. The protection and promotion of individual freedoms and liberties did necessitate pressure and persuasion on totalitarian and authoritarian regimes to uphold these very human rights in their societies. Be that as it may, multiple factors contributed in keeping the other features of human rights, which deserved the similar attention and emphasis, in a low key.

Gradually, after persistent deliberations and discussions in different fora concerned with human rights issues, a consensus emerged that the three aspects of human rights deserved equal attention and emphasis. Thus, it is now well recognised that indivisibility and interdependence of all these rights is non negotiable. Therefore, the three aspects of human rights, viz; Civil and Political Rights, Economic, Social and Cultural Rights and Solidarity Rights like Peace, Environment and Habitat are to be placed on even keel. It may be mentioned here that the overall evaluation and estimation of all these rights during the last more than three decades, which have been significant from the perspective of developments in the field of human rights, is a gigantic task. That is beyond the scope of this brief study. However, fresh insights have come to the fore in this very area signaling growing concern and zeal towards the protection of human rights, apart from widening the scope of these very rights.

Creative Interpretations

The human rights mechanisms, over a period of time, have gradually but effectively evolved in order to ensure that the three aspects of human rights mentioned above are enforced and realised without according a preferential treatment to any particular right. This approach has considerably expanded the sphere of human rights regime. And it has equally brought many neglected human rights issues within the realm of enforcement through different mechanisms.It is a refreshing development that creative interpretations and a broader approach on the part of Human Rights Council experts and special rapporteurs made it possible to incorporate the larger existential issues within the framework of human rights regime. One of the innovative interpretations relate to right to life as a fundamental human right which forms the core of human rights.

The strengthening of democratic order has been a perennial concern of human rights defenders because it forms the base of the system of governance. The UN bodies have been monitoring the status of democracy in the states from time to time. It is quite well known that some states have been maintaining the façade of democracy. The authoritarian rulers of these very states have been manipulating the system astutely to garner and enjoy the power and privileges at the cost of common inhabitants of their land. In order to keep a track of these situations, the UN bodies have been, through diverse techniques, examining and monitoring different facets of such claims and making the global opinion makers aware about the situation on the ground.This effort is equally pressurizing these states to bring in transparency and transform their style of functioning. In the present day scenario in which human rights regime is asserting itself these states have to adhere to the benchmarks which have been set and recognised globally or face the international isolation.

Of late, the UN Council on Human Rights has been monitoring and estimating the status of right of 'Freedom of Speech and Expression'. It is well established that democracy is a nucleus to promote and protect the right of Freedom of Speech and Expression. In fact, this right provides strength and sustenance to a democratic order. The recent reports of the Human Rights Council have reiterated that the fundamental human right of freedom of Speech and Expression is very closely linked to the *right to democratic and transparent governance, freedom of faith and ideas, enjoyment of cultural, linguistic and other related rights.* The recent report of the Special Rapporteur on the Promotion and Protection of the Right to Freedom of Speech and Expression in the Electoral Process (Document A/HRC/26/30, May 2014) provides effective guidelines towards the protection of the freedom of opinion and expression in the electoral process. It has been emphasized that in order to sustain the claim of the prevalence of a democratic order on the part of a state, *the presence of a transparent, normative and legally oriented electoral process is a sine qua non (Emphasis Added).* It may be pointed out that this essential requirement is a major challenge in nascent democratic orders in some parts of the world. The reports by the human rights defenders and media on the transparency requirement have exposed the claims of some countries to democracy which were found to be hollow. It has been found that some states have perfected the techniques and devices to manipulate the electoral process resulting in enhancing the levels of public dissatisfaction and disenchantment regarding the system. It may be observed that in view of these aberrations, the fundamentalist religious theories are floated as an alternative to democratic system. The rise of non-state actors using violence to replace the existing order may be seen in this very context. The situation has come to a pass that in some parts of the world, the violent groups in their quest to establish the theocratic religious order are threatening the political parties and common people to keep them away from participating in the elections.The practices of manipulating the electoral process provide them a convenient rationale for their action. These groups are churning out literature on regular basis pointing out to the inadequacies of the democratic system. However, a close examination reveals, that these so called inadequacies are not inherent in the system but are the manipulation of the same.

The Special Rapporteur on Freedom of Speech and Expression visited some countries of her choice to report on the status of this right in the electoral processes. It is gratifying to note that the countries she chose to visit welcomed her. However, as noted in her report one country (Pakistan) did not respond to her request to visit that country. The report very ably deals with the sources, state as well as non-state actors, in dealing with the challenges to the freedom of speech and expression during the electoral processes. The report reinforces, as brought out in earlier reports, the responsibility of states to prohibit incitement of hatred, hostility, discrimination and violence during the electoral processes. The report underlines that the candidates should not make use of a language of hatred and hostility while campaigning, targeting, *inter alia,* women, racial, linguistic or religious minorities and others. The report maintains that it is very important to protect journalists from violence during elections. The report highlights the golden principle that *"free flow of ideas is core requirement for the promotion of democratic space" (Emphasis added).* In case these measures are effectively adopted and applied it would enhance the faith of the general public and strengthen the credibility in democratic governance of a state. It is not enough, and there are instances in that behalf, that these principles are merely drafted in laws and regulations of a state without their effective implementation in practice. It should be recognised that in the face of challenges of religious and militant fundamentalism, authoritarian trends and military dictatorships, it is highly desirable to adopt and apply these principles.

The creative interpretations on human rights is expanding the range of influence of these rights. As mentioned earlier that right to life has been recognised to form the nucleus of human rights. Now the Right to *Clean Environment and Right to Health* have been incorporated within the scope of Right to Life. It may be mentioned here that American and some African countries had already recognised the Right to Clean and Healthy Environment as a Human Right. However, it is now a universal human right.

Another creative interpretation relates to the *Right to Pure Drinking Water*. In fact, the human rights defenders and activists have been raising this issue in different forums of Human Rights from time to time. Ironically, in the year 2000, after lengthy deliberations during a conference of Second Water Forum in Hague it was concluded that ' *water was a commodity which was bought and sold and it could not be declared as a right (Emphasis Added).* However, the persistent efforts of human rights defenders triumphed and in July 2010 the UN declared that *access to soft and clean drinking water* was a human right. The declaration equally brought the *adequate sanitation* within the scope of human rights. The UN held that it was a step towards achieving Millennium Development Goals.

Corporate Responsibility

In the ongoing phase of Globalisation the role and influence of big corporations and business houses is considerably increasing. It appears that political governance is gradually being replaced by the corporate governance. It is interesting to note that this sphere of activity is expanding in the name of 'development'. Thus, the economic advancement and development is laying its impact on other aspects of human life including human rights.

There is an increasing concern about the role and responsibility of business corporations in ignoring and even violating human rights of the citizens. This state of affairs is prevailing particularly in the areas of agriculture, labour, forestry and mining. The UN Working Group on Business and Human Rights has been monitoring the situation for quite some time now. It is an irony that human rights activists and defenders feel helpless because the states generally are on the side of companies and big business on the plank of economic development.

The Bhopal gas tragedy in India where a poisonous gas leak from Union Carbide Corporation's fertilizer plant killed more than 200 people and disabled more than 20,000 persons received global attention. The tragedy brought the issue of corporate responsibility and human rights to the fore. The issue of acquiring the forest lands for the purposes of industrial development depriving the forest dwellers and those who depend on the resources of forests to earn their livelihood is a perennial issue of human rights violation. This issue is equally related to environmental degradation. In the same vein, the violation of human rights of migrant workers in foreign lands and use of child labor is yet serious concern of human rights regime. It is well documented that a persistent abuse of migrant workers is taking place particularly in the Gulf and other West Asian states. In a revealing report, 'The Case Against Qatar", a report produced by Sharan Burrow, Secretary General of the International Trade Union Confederation and her colleagues has held that 'Qatar's development model is based on enslaved labour'. In an interview (The Hindu, May 31,2015) Sharan Burrow said that 'what Qatar chose is a system where a worker is owned by his employer'. It may be mentioned that Qatar is hosting the Football World Cup in 2022 and is building stadiums. However, according to

Ms. Burrow the migrant labour is not used only to build stadiums but in fact they are building the whole city. She said that around 400 migrant workers from India and Nepal die every year in Qatar. She further said that the number of work-related deaths is much higher than the number of on-site deaths which are reported. The rationale of presenting these details here is to highlight the challenges to human rights which are being posed in diverse settings.

The health hazards being faced by the mining workers are generally being ignored. The unregulated mining activities are posing a danger to the environment and ecology of the concerned areas as well. The widespread media reports have been highlighting the sexual harassment cases at the workplace which is a gender based violation of human rights. These cases which take place in Corporate Houses are usually ignored unless the media highlights such cases. The office of the High Commissioner of Human Rights is constantly and seriously considering the issues of corporate responsibility.

A comprehensive Declaration on the part of UN Human Rights Council regarding the corporate responsibility is still awaited. However, in view of the global outcry on these issues, the UN Human Rights Council requested the UN Secretary General to appoint a Special Representative to address these issues in depth. In June 2011, the UN Council on Human Rights endorsed the Guiding Principles on Business and Human Rights presented to it by the Special Representative of UN Secretary General. These Principles provide Global standards of practice that is now expected of all States and businesses with regard to business and human rights. These Principles elaborate on the implications of existing standards and practices for States and businesses and include points covered in international and domestic law and are based on '*Protect, Respect and Remedy'* framework which cover the broader aspects of the corporate and business responsibility towards protection of human rights. The principles define 'Adverse Human Rights' impact as: "an adverse human rights impact" occurs when an action removes or reduces the ability of an individual to enjoy his or her human rights. Again, it is relevant to note that the definition of 'Business relationship' as provided by the principles runs as:' where a non-state or state entity is directly linked to its business operations, products or services and the consequent result should not result in violation of economic, social and cultural rights. These principles further provide that mitigation of adverse human rights impact refers to actions taken to reduce its extent with any residual impact then requiring re-mediation. The principles underline that the states have the legal obligation to respect, protect and fulfill the human rights set out in the international human rights conventions they ratify. These principles are the forerunners of a clear and definite Convention on Corporate and Business responsibility and Human Rights.

Conclusion

In view of the foregoing brief analysis of developments relating to human rights regime it becomes clear that the regime is providing an alterative paradigm to the fading world order. This paradigm is not necessarily tied to the international politics of pulls and pressures. Nonetheless, it is a new beginning to a peaceful and humane world order. It may be mentioned here that well defined and systematic responses to many an issue impinging on human rights are still awaited. The Guiding Principles on corporate responsibility as mentioned above have not assumed the form of a Declaration or Convention. It may take some more time for the same to happen. The same is the case with regard to corruption and graft. The response of the UN bodies to this phenomenon is lackadaisical, to say the least. The responses of Human Rights mechanisms to human rights challenges are some times tardy but, nonetheless, these issues are ultimately adequately addressed. The case of 'Terrorism' provides an illustration to the point. This issue was not addressed for a long time by the UN bodies. Curiously, when a Special Rapporteur was assigned the task to study and report on the issue she did not take up her assignment. The argument put forward was that the issue did not fall with in the framework of human rights regime. However, when this issue grew in magnitude posing a new challenge to human rights, the Human Rights Council responded and now we have Declarations in place to deal with it. However, care has been taken by providing guidelines to ensure the protection of human rights while dealing with 'terrorism'.

It may be underscored that younger generation has to be a torch bearer in bringing about a refreshing and meaningful change in the world order. In this regard the UNESCO has provided a roadmap by adopting a Declaration on the '*Responsibilities of the Present Generation Towards Future Generation*'. The Declaration covers a variety of issues including protection of the environment, the human genome, biodiversity, cultural heritage, peace, development and education. Several UN Declarations and UN General Assembly Resolutions have endorsed this declaration. It is the responsibility of our educational institutions to sensitize the younger generation about their responsibilities towards realizing these rights. It is well recognised that Education is the chief instrument of social change. All the concerns identified in the foregoing paras which relate to human rights fall within the scope of education in general and value education in particular. The educational planners have to devise strategies to bring these concerns within the sphere of curriculum and pedagogy. The revamping of educational system and redesigning it in tune with changing human rights concerns needs to be met to bring it in harmony with international standards on human rights.

2

Redefining the City: Citizenship, Globalisation and Human Rights

—Satish C. Aikant

All over the world the social pattern of human population is rapidly changing. With half of the world's population now residing in cities there is a phenomenal growth of urban population, especially, in developing countries. The statement, that India lives in her villages, is no longer as valid as it earlier was. The city in modern India has usually been defined in opposition to the village, which stands as the repository of tradition, religious faith and rituals. The village symbolizes a certain kind of piety and control over self whereas the city is characterized as an amoral space and a place of self-indulgence. The city has a seductive charm on account of its glitz and cultured ambience whereas village has an idyllic and utopian fascination. City is projected as an entity which is severed from the past, tradition and community. However, the village no longer retains its pre-eminence in the national imagination. The city is portrayed as an agent of change, but viewed with apprehension, as it proves to be detrimental to the stable, organic world order of the village. One of the reasons for the vilification of city is the predominance of the influence of Gandhi, and his insistence on building a nation on the basis of what he termed *gram swaraj*. The contrary perceptions held by Gandhi and Nehru about the role of the village in nation building further consolidated the divide between city and the country.

Analyzing the dialectical relationship between the village and the city, Ashis Nandy observes that over the years village has declined in the imagination of Indian mind, and for the new generation of Indians the village has merely become "a demographic or statistical datum."[1] Nandy believes that the move toward the urban could have been a compulsive choice: The anonymity and atomisation in a city are doubly seductive in a society scarred by socio-economic schisms and cultural hierarchies. A Dalit, landless, agricultural worker or a rural artisan seeking escape from the daily grind and violence of a caste society has reasons to value the impersonal melting pot of a metropolitan city.[2] Though, the rural population significantly contributes to the national economy, village is no longer a viable presence in the mainstream Indian economic planning and does not appeal to the intellectual mind. On the other hand, the Indian city has emerged stronger in the popular imagination, despite the fact that it has not stabilised itself as in the case of the village.

Though, the city appears as an interminable point of reference to human experience through different stages of history, the urban experience has not been received in unequivocal terms. The eternal distinctions between good and evil, civilised and primitive, colonised and the colonizer, collective and the individual, modern and pre-modern are outlined, in a large sense, around the configurations of the city. Several prominent sociologists have characterized the city in negative terms considering the urban world-view as impersonal, materialistic and antagonistic to social integration. The modernist movement of twentieth century has, in fact, painted city as draconian and dangerous and portrayed it as a place of anomie, alienation, and existentialist angst. In such imagination, the city often appears as dark, dysfunctional, mechanical, engulfed in ecological and social crises, seduced by capitalist consumption, paralyzed by crime, wars, class, gender, and racial conflicts, social inequality, moral depravity and subjected to excessive technological and technocratic control. Even popular culture does not provide salutary images of the city. Since, the industrial revolution the city, as a prevailing form of the organisation of space and of economic and social relations, has been a dominant feature of many novels, although the way in which cities were represented changed dramatically through changing social and economic relations. The writers have reflected in their writings the effects of these transformations, especially the technologically induced fallout on the overall environment. Nineteenth century European novelists felt revolted by the mixture of environmental and moral ugliness, symbolised by the image of poisonous smog. Their writings deplore the conditions of the workers and their families, the greed of the middle class, and the inhuman character of the city fabric. Theodore Drieser, the American novelist, depicts the big city as a kind of magnet that attracts the protagonists to chase the American Dream and nurture hopes of social emancipation which in the end prove illusory. Emerson believed that "cities give not the human senses room enough."[3] The prevailing image of the city, particularly the big city, is increasingly associated with that of the danger and fear of getting lost in an anonymous world. The city as a synonym of corruption and social disintegration, as a place where money governs every single activity, is a recurrent theme in modern fiction, drama and poetry. The domination of technology in corporate capitalist cities has given rise to disorientation, meaninglessness, fragmentation and violence. With social breakdown, the hold of the traditional community is weakened, which results in making the city a space of alienation, disorientation and disorder. The city becomes a site of corruption, ill health, immorality, chaos, pollution, congestion, and a threat to social order. There is, in fact, an embedded relationship between crime, disorder and the social, economic and political values and processes within the city. The construction of the city as a dangerous and unruly place of criminal activity, of threat, of licentiousness and of disorder is frequently reflected in popular literature and visual media. Bombay cinema in the fifties and sixties constituted the city as a particular kind of political space, that powerfully foregrounded the failures of the nationalist imaginary that was invested in the village. Even as the city became the site of modernisation and hope for the future the ideals propounded by the village offered a moral imperative for adaptation to a new mode of life. The village, in this sense, was the guiding star. The city had lost that direction. The experience of getting lost in the crowd produces feelings of estrangement and loss of identity, while the multitudes become part of the spectacle of mass society created by capitalism. In such a situation the rhythm of daily urban life, instead of suggesting a symphony, only brings the boredom of routinisation. As the historian Gyan Prakash observes, "Monstrous megacities do not promise the pleasures of urbanity but the misery and strife of the Hobbesian jungle."[4]

According to Georg Simmel, who has explored the sensory impact of the city on the urban residents' perception of space, time and sense of self, the metropolis[5] has always been the seat of money economy, developing materialistic attitude towards life. He remarks that an individual in metropolis is affected by what is called a blasé attitude.[6] The blasé attitude results first from the rapidly changing and closely compressed contrasting stimulations of the nerves. A life in boundless pursuit of pleasure makes one blasé because it agitates the nerves to their strongest reactivity for such a long time that they finally cease to react at all. The essence of blasé attitude consists in the blunting of discrimination...Money with all its colorlessness and indifference becomes the common denominator of all values; irreparably it hollows out the core of things, their individuality, their specific value and their incomparability. All things, float with equal specific gravity in the constantly moving stream of money...That is why cities are also the genuine locale of blasé attitude[7]

It must be said, however, that even though the modern western cities are known as the places of treachery, deceit and duplicity, in traditional sense of the term, the cities did have a venerable position in various societies. The archetypal city of Athens stood, and continues to stand, for notions of democracy, civic culture and urbanity. In ancient and medieval India a city was variously known as *puram* or *nagara*. The word *puram* actually meant an organised city, and accordingly, most of the cities across India developed as the hubs of power and religion. To achieve all the noble virtues of civilisation in Indian life one had to become a *nagarik*, a dweller of town. With the advent of colonial modernity, the ancient *nagara* was transformed into the stronghold of modern industrial capitalism. The forces of colonisation, modernity and urbanisation thoroughly revamped the basic features of the city and, with the steady accumulation of wealth and consolidation of power, they were transformed into the centers of imperial authority. Apart from being the sites of modernisation, urbanisation and colonialism the cities during the colonial period articulated the might of the colonial empire. The colonial culture projected in architecture shows how building a city with massive monuments, phallic towers, huge domes and buildings, became an act of underlining imperial authority. By building huge cities, the "colonial rulers sought to transform the mysterious and exotic sub-continent according to European image, and so claim a right to rule"[8] and carry on with their "civilizing mission."

India after independence, more or less, followed the colonial system of administration and governance. Gradually as the cities developed into centers of power, administration, industrial and economic activities, they attracted people belonging to different socio-cultural and economic backgrounds, eventually transforming the cities into the sites of heterogeneity, cosmopolitanism and multiculturalism. The current prominence of neo-liberalism in India, along with its several other impacts, has affected the material and ideological re-mapping of the modern city. One of the most important transformations witnessed by the modern Indian city is polarisation of spaces—the marking out of separate spaces for the rich and the poor; and a dispossession of the socio-economically marginal groups from the inner city to the urban fringes. A modern city such as Delhi embodies the spatial alienation of the elites and the marginalised, constructing the poor as criminal subjects and structuring the urban space in the neo-liberal model, which, very often, is built upon the conversion of rural lands into private property for elite consumption, resulting in the encroachment on agricultural lands[9] and a gradual displacement of the farmer by the urban elite. Even as public spaces are reclaimed for general use by proper citizens, there is a proliferation of segregated and protected spaces for elite consumption, elite lifestyle and elite culture.[10] The elites jealously secure their private space, with high walls guarding them from prying eyes and private security guards guarding its inhabitants and boundaries. The darker side of this urban reconstruction exposes how the poor and the marginal groups live a precarious life of dispossession, criminality and violence in complete contrast to the luxurious and sheltered lives of the urban middle and upper classes. As a matter of fact, the city restructures itself for the entrepreneurial elites, while the underdogs are pushed to farther margins into darker realms of violence and criminality. The beautification and modernisation of the urban space emphatically bears out the undeniable marks of a neoliberal urban restructuring that prioritizes the 'productive' class, but the preservation of the spaces of productivity and capital formation are essentially guaranteed by an exclusion of the 'nonproductive' class of the socio-economically marginalised, who are pushed off the city limits.

Segregation of the weaker and the marginalised population follows an invidious form of spatial regulation, ostensibly aimed at producing social order by creating zones for the privileged few, who have to be shielded from witnessing socially undesirable behavior of the multitude. As Henri Lefebvre remarks, the modern city is something akin to a vast and variegated whirlpool replete with all the ambivalence of a space full of opportunity, playfulness and liberating potential, while being entwined with spaces of oppression, exclusion and marginalisation.[11]

The spatial governmentality of the neoliberal city operates by not only cordoning off spaces, but also by monitoring the populations from specific social strata to prevent potential disorder. This regulation of the space, spells out a new mode of urban governance that seeks to maintain order, and render the city safe and attractive to the rich, by guarding the core urban spaces from contamination from the homeless and the so-called criminals. In this neo-urban imaginary, the masses need to be contained and controlled, for if they are left to their own devices the city will become a site of crime and disorder. Ironically, it is only the poor who have been seen as a potential threat to public health, political order and stability since the colonial period.[12]

It is quite obvious that the city is the primary site of globalisation, which is also related to the crucial issues of development and human rights. The phenomenon of globalisation and the large scale migration of people belonging to different nationalities to metropolis have diversified the social character of city spaces. The decline of colonial empires and communist economies has also contributed to the creation of single global market and the integration of cities into a global network. The global cities have emerged as centres of the various forms of power, in the new worldwide networks of economic, political and information activities, which transcend the borders of the nation-states, shaping new global hierarchical relationships. But, even as the global cities accumulate immense concentrations of economic power, the low income urban and metropolitan areas are starved for resources.

As we know, the chief objective of globalisation is to integrate the economies of the developing nations with that of the developed nations, in order to promote the formation of a new social and economic world order, through growth and spread of investment, trade and production and introduction of new technology. There are certain areas that the globalisation focuses more on. There is investment in terms of capital, including human capital. Then, money and financial services are getting globalised, as well as liberalised. Trade is getting liberalised by private, transnational corporations, policy makers of various governments of Western Europe, Japan and U.S.A., World Trade Organisation, and G-8 nations through reduction in tariffs, taxes, regulations and barriers. There is also an effort to import technology through invention and diffusion of new devices, particularly hi-tech electronics and biochemical tools, using techniques and services for increased growth and development. With all this happening, the globalisation of economy has weakened the national boundaries facilitating the free flow of information, products, labour, money and people.

The liberals claim that globalisation is likely to promote development, democracy, personal empowerment and global governance. One should therefore also hope that the new global regime will accommodate all sections of society in participatory democracy and entitlements respecting their human rights. But the empirical evidence shows that globalisation is posing many new challenges for human rights, especially in the context of developing nations.

Globalisation has caused environmental hazards such as spread of pollution and waste, global warming and destruction of natural habitat. It has not only created more opportunities for environmental pollution, but has also enabled the export of hazardous waste and contaminated materials to developing countries, including India. Globalisation has also resulted in increasing the drug trafficking, and has raised the drug abuse among the youth. The spread of tourist industry has brought in greater reliance on the female labour force and, consequently, there has been an increase in the trafficking of women across the globe.

With the decline of the state sovereignty there is a shift of power from state to global or institutional sponsors such as multinational corporations, the World Bank and the IMF. It is increasingly being felt that the quality of life has deteriorated in many ways over the last few years due to lack of good jobs, poor working conditions, unmanageable cost of health care and growing gaps between the rich and the poor. In fact, on one side, you have a world of incredible human and financial resources, technologies and know-how, while on the other, we have a world of unspeakable poverty, insecurity and injustice. Globalisation has created a flat world[13] only for those who are privileged to participate in its technocratic and consumerist agenda. In fact, it appears to be a double edged weapon; those who have used it effectively have achieved an elitist class status while the majority of the people, who failed to realize its opportunities, have regressed into poverty, a classic example of a gain for a few and pain for the many. Although, globalisation's economic imperatives have enabled certain sections of the population in India to gain upward mobility, its ideologies of prosperity have not benefited the vast majority of poor urban and rural Indian citizens who continue to struggle for their basic needs such as food, water, shelter, primary education, and medical care. It seems that globalisation's excursions to India have only exploited and exacerbated the legacies of colonialism.

The question is often posed whether globalisation is pro- or anti-human rights, or is it a neutral phenomenon?[14] Though, globalisation as a concept is not inherently anti- or pro-human rights, the same cannot be said about globalisation as a process. In view of the nature and motive of the actors involved, the process of globalisation is widely seen more as a foe than a friend of human rights. Globalisation has serious implications for the realisation of human rights everywhere, but more so in developing countries.[15] It presents the most potent challenges to human rights realisation in those states which do not have an optimal level of good governance. Moreover, it is a problematic concept that goes against the spirit of the traditional foundations of citizenship[16] which can be described as equal membership, participation and sovereignty of the self. In this new context of globalisation, the 'global citizen' is rendered 'deterritorialised' and becomes a dependent entity.

In India the process of globalisation which focused on market economy, privatisation and de-regulation of tariffs, initiated since early 1990's, appears to have generated a greater marginalisation of certain groups, as well as violation of human rights because of its negative effects. The supremacy of market economy to promote economic growth has benefitted a small minority of population. Such concerns are alarming in the context of human rights of individuals and groups especially, those of the marginalised groups. No doubt, the United Nations World Conference on Human Rights in Vienna (1993) was a milestone for the mankind in recognizing the universal validity of human rights and the commitment of all nations to respect them. But poverty cannot be overcome if individual citizens are denied fundamental human rights in a society, which is not egalitarian. The Vienna declaration on human rights has clearly mentioned in one of its recommendations, that right to development is an inalienable human right, and that it needs to be constantly monitored at the international, regional and national levels. For sustaining it on a long term basis there is a need to implement the effective development policies at the national level, so as to provide equitable and favourable economic environment at the international level while giving due regard to the rights of the people to control their national resources.

We do know that equal rights are the basic conditions of a civilised life in a modern society. These equal rights express the claims of an individual to liberty, security and dignity, based on the premise that there is a sanctity attached to every human being, who is an end in himself. Today, citizenship faces challenges at both the national and the international level. The idea of citizenship has been defined as the capacity of individuals to defend their rights in front of a hegemonic and oppositional authority. Citizenship is consolidated and enlarged when individuals acquire rights and participate actively in governing themselves. According to Gunstern "Citizenship has three aspects, namely, that citizens have a say in political decision making; access to courts of law that are manned by co-citizens who judge according to rules that equally apply to all citizens; and a guarantee of minimum socioeconomic conditions of existence. Citizenship is a matter of emancipation, of successively realizing these threes aspects of political, legal, and socioeconomic participation for all people who find themselves on the territory of the state."[17]

But, is it possible to guarantee human rights to the underprivileged in a modern globalised city? The answer is in the negative because of the spatial segregation of the city space. In the extreme cases, several sections of our society such as those belonging to adivasis or nomadic tribes, are not even allowed to live in their natural habitat. They are driven out to make way for Special Economic Zones. The encroachment of the city into the countryside through urban sprawl and the consequent loss of agricultural land is a rampant practice in India. This progressive urbanisation of society is perceived as a threat to rural cultures. In a way, a sort of transnational space is created for the capitalists and the MNCs making unwarranted claims on the space, that would rightly belong to others struggling for recognition and entitlement. Besides, of nearly half the population of women in our society, an overwhelming majority of them are marginalised, as they are denied basic rights to emancipate and empower themselves, because of illiteracy, ignorance and low social and ritualistic status in a male dominated society. There is also a small section of population in our society, especially the aged persons, delinquent children or otherwise challenged persons, who need special attention and must be provided basic rights of decent living, to overcome their marginal status. Facilities for them are almost non-existent in a city. There is an urgent need for equity and justice to be provided to them within the democratic governance of a developing nation like India.

Corresponding to the weakening of regulatory states, there is a steady rise in the number and influence of multinational corporations. Despite the fact that MNCs of today dwarf many modern states in terms of economic and also political might, their activities by and large are still not subject to concrete, legally binding human rights obligations, flowing from either national or international law. Not only this, MNCs are also able to influence policy and law making nation-wide, in key areas such as public health, child labour, workers' rights, consumer protection, foreign investment, environmental protection, women's rights, and the rights of indigenous peoples.[18]

Technology, too, has the potential to shape the nature of human rights. The internet, for example, enables the transmission of information to consumers swiftly and in a cost-effective manner. But the internet has also raised thorny issues related to, say, the cyber crime and the right to privacy. Similarly, other technologies, such as digitalisation, biotechnology and genetic engineering, do have serious implications for the realisation of various human rights. We still need to guard against monopolisation and manipulation of information, and also ensure that a wider population becomes part of the 'information society.'

Consumerism is another important facet of globalisation, increasingly used as a device for 'market-creation,' whereby the interests of consumers are the obvious casualties. Consumers' choices are manipulated, sometimes even in total disregard to their health and safety. The production, trafficking and use of illicit drugs are typically the problems of global ramification and pose grave challenges to criminal justice, health, public policy and social and political governance. The involvement of MNCs in human rights violations and generating environmental hazards is widely known, yet goes on unchecked. Corporations undoubtedly produce wealth, but they also produce risks, both to humans and to the ecosystem. Globalisation has facilitated the export of risks to those countries that are least capable to handle them.[19] Since the culture of consumerism, often incompatible with sustainable development, dictates life's priorities, not on the basis of rational and free decision making but on corporate interests, this poses a serious challenge to the realisation of human rights. Unfortunately, life in a modern city is not free from the baleful effects of globalisation which adversely impact human rights. It is neither possible nor desirable to reverse the process of modernisation and urbanisation. All we can do is to make efforts to redefine the city to make it look more human and more equal.

Notes

1. Ashis Nandy, *An Ambiguous journey to City*, New Delhi: Oxford University Press, 2001, p. 22.
2. Ibid, p.12
3. Ralph Waldo Emerson, 'Nature' Essays by Ralph Waldo Emerson, *The Complete Works by Ralph Waldo Emerson,* Vol. III, Boston & New York: Houghton Mifflin Company, 1903, p.171.
4. For a historical examination of the classic image of the modern city, see Gyan Prakash and Kevin Kruse, eds., *The Spaces of the Modern City:*

Imaginaries, Politics, and Everyday Life, Princeton: Princeton University Press, 2008, pp. 1–18.

5. The modernizing context of the metropolis is a Western and colonial form of material and social organisation. See Vyjayanthi Rao, "Embracing Urbanism: The City as Archive," *New Literary History*, 2009, 40: p. 272.
6. Malcolm Waters, ed., *Modernity: Critical Concepts*, London: Routledge, 1999, pp. 35-46.
7. Ibid.
8. Nirmala Rao, "Projections of Empire: India and the Imagined Metropolis," *Asian Affairs*, 251.2 (2010), p. 162.
9. Baleshwar Thakur et al, *City, Society and Planning*, New Delhi: Concept Publishing Company, 2007, p. 573.
10. Partha Chatterjee, "Are Indian cities becoming bourgeois at last?," in Indira Chandrasekhar and Peter C. Seel, *body.city: siting contemporary culture in India*, New Delhi: Tulika Books, 2003, p.171
11. See Lefebvre, Henri, *The Production of Space*, Oxford: Blackwell, 1989.
12. Nandini Gooptu, "Economic Liberalisation, Urban Politics and the Poor" in *Understanding India's New Political Economy*, eds. Sanjay Ruparelia, Sanjay Reddy, John Harris, London New York: Routledge, 2011, pp. 7-8.
13. See Thomas L. Friedman, *The World is Flat: A Brief History of the Twenty-first Century*, Gordonsville: Farrar, Straus and Giroux, 2005.
14. The neutrality of globalisation is deceptive. Similarly, as Murray Dobbin has argued, democracy has become little more than an illusion maintained by our governments on behalf of the transnational corporations that have taken control of civil society and really govern us. See *The Myth of the Good Corporate Citizen: The Democracy Under the Rule of Big Business*, Don Mills: Stoddart, 1998.
15. Anghie offers a critique of the impact of globalisation on people in third world countries. Antony Anghie, "Time Present and Time Past: Globalisation, International Financial Institutions and The Third World," *New York University Journal of International Law and Politics*, 243 (2000), p. 32.
16. It is difficult to provide a clear definition of citizenship. As Alisdair Rogers observes, "From a focus on the relationship between individuals, states and rights, it has broadened to include more sociological questions such as the access to resources, inequality, membership in a political community, and identity. Under the influence of new social movements,

citizenship has been extended from formal matters of belonging to some nation-state to more substantive ones of civil, political, social, economic and cultural rights and obligations." Citizenship, Multiculturalism, and the European City,' in Gary Bridge and Sophie Watson, eds., *A companion to the City*, Oxford: Blackwell Publishers, 2003, p.283.

17. Herman van Gunstern, *A Theory of Citizenship: Organizing Plurality in Contemporary Democracies*, Boulder Colorado: Westview Press, 1998, pp.13-14.

18. As W. Friedmann wrote more than three decades ago, that big corporations "have a direct and decisive impact on the social, economic and political life of the nation is no longer a matter of argument" W. Friedmann, *Law in a Changing Society*, Berkeley: University of California Press, 19759.33 (2d. ed.1972), p. 333.

19. Weir and Schapiro also note: "If one country bans your product, move to where sales are still legal. It's just good business." David Weir & Mark Schapiro, *Circle of Poison: Pesticides and People in a Hungry World*, Food First Books, 1981.

Works Cited

- Anghie, Antony. "Time Present and Time Past: Globalisation, International Financial Institutions and The Third World," *New York University Journal of International Law and Politics*, 243 (2000).
- Bridge, Gary. and Sophie Watson. eds., *A companion to the City*, Oxford: Blackwell Publishers, 2003, p.283.
- Chatterjee, Partha. "Are Indian cities becoming bourgeois at last?, in Indira Chandrasekhar and Peter C. Seel, *body.city: siting contemporary culture in India*, New Delhi: Tulika Books, 2003.
- Delanty, G. *Citizenship in a Global Age: Society, Culture, Politics*, Philadelphia, PA: Open, University Press, 2000.
- Dobbin, Murray. *The Myth of the Good Corporate Citizen: The Democracy Under the Rule of Big Business*, Don Mills: Stoddart, 1998.
- Emerson, Ralph Waldo, 'Nature' Essays by Ralph Waldo Emerson, *The Complete Works by Ralph Waldo Emerson*, Vol. III, Boston & New York: Houghton Mifflin Company, 1903.
- Faulks, K. *Citizenship,* New York: Routledge, 2000.
- Friedman, Thomas L. *The World is Flat: A Brief History of the Twenty-first Century*, Gordonsville: Farrar, Straus and Giroux, 2005.
- Friedmann, W. *Law in a Changing Society*, Berkeley: University of California Press,1972.

- Gooptu, Nandini. "Economic Liberalisation, Urban Politics and the Poor" in *Understanding India's New Political Economy*, eds. Sanjay Ruparelia, Sanjay Reddy, John Harris, London New York: Routledge, 2011.
- Gunstern, Herman van. *A Theory of Citizenship: Organizing Plurality in Contemporary Democracies*, Boulder Colorado: Westview Press, 1998.
- Holston, J. ed., *Cities and Citizenship,* Durham, NC: Duke University Press, 1998.
- Lefebvre, Henri. *The Production of Space*, Oxford: Blackwell, 1989.
- Marshall, T.H. *Citizenship and Social Class,* Cambridge: Cambridge University Press, 1950.
- Nandy, Asis. *An Ambiguous journey to City*, New Delhi: Oxford University Press, 2001.
- Prakash, Gyan. and Kevin Kruse, eds., *The Spaces of the Modern City: Imaginaries, Politics, and Everyday Life* (Princeton: Princeton University Press, 2008).
- Rao, Nirmala. "Projections of Empire: India and the Imagined Metropolis," *Asian Affairs*, 251.2 (2010).
- Rao, Vyjayanthi. "Embracing Urbanism: The City as Archive," *New Literary History*, 2009.
- Thakur, Baleshwar, et al, *City, Society and Planning*, New Delhi: Concept Publishing Company, 2007.
- Waters, Malcolm, ed., *Modernity: Critical Concepts*, London: Routledge, 1999.
- Weir, David & Mark Schapiro. *Circle of Poison: Pesticides and People in a Hungry World*, Food First Books, 1981.

3

Provision of Human Rights, Human Dignity and Human Development in the Slums: A Case of Mumbai

—Rajlakshmi Datta

The Context

Development and economic attainment are neither substitutable terms nor can be measured in the same scale. Development is basically a multidimensional concept whereas economic attainment is primarily focused on attaining financial and physical resources like land, property etc., Development without human dignity, development excluding minimum human rights does not convey a scenario where the State plays its absolute role to fulfill its obligations for its citizens. The primary focus of development should therefore be on expansion of opportunities for all its citizens and enhancement and enrichment of choices through building capacities. It is observed that development with more space for human dignity has emerged as an important policy tool throughout the globe which is expected to help mobilize and focus resources on certain critical areas for overall social development.

As a reflector of the level of human development attained by a community, a general sense of well being does serve the purpose. But the sense of well being is delicate, personal, subjective and difficult to quantify. However, certain methodologies have been successful in trying to quantify the well being and hence development to some extent. But since the methodology is not unique, there is huge space to explore the area to capture well being of the citizens under various development parameters and understand the level of attainment by the community and the role of the State in facilitating such attainment by providing its citizens the provision to enjoy life of human dignity with the fundamental human rights.

Millennium Development Goal declares "Ensure Environmental Sustainability" as one of the eight goals; by 2015 it targets to halve the proportion of the population without sustainable access to safe drinking water and basic sanitation and by 2020 to have achieved a significant improvement in the lives of at least 100 million slum dwellers [Report of State World Cities]. On 28th July 2010, through Resolution 64/292, the United Nations General Assembly explicitly recognised the human right to water and sanitation and acknowledged that clean drinking water and sanitation are essential to the realisation of all human rights. The Resolution calls upon States and international organisations to provide financial resources, help capacity building and technology transfer to help countries, in particular developing countries, to provide safe, clean, accessible and affordable drinking water and sanitation for all [United Nations]. Inspite of all such efforts there seems to be a wide gap between what 'ought to be' and 'what is' especially in the context of India and more specifically for a larger section of urban poor.

It is universally acknowledged that access to safe water is vital in prevention of diseases and ensuring a healthy life. However, the significance of an accompanying wastewater disposal or drainage system was very not often recognised in earlier studies or reports but gradually drawing attention of policy makers. In areas where the water is being delivered, there needs to be a mechanism of removing the wastewater to avoid stagnant water from gathering. In the absence of a proper drainage system, it is difficult to find a solution to this problem. Solid waste management system is also a critical area that needs attention because garbage is often deposited in open drains which leads to the blockage and has severe consequence on environment and health status of the community.

India still has the largest number of people in the world who defecate in the open-625 million – which represents 51 per cent of

India's population (67 per cent in rural areas and 14 per cent in urban areas) [Human Rights Council Resolution]. Quoting the 2011 census data, one of the Union Ministers for Rural Development, acknowledged that 60 per cent of rural households still do not have access to proper toilet facilities and called for urgent measures for what he named "another distressing national shame"[The Hindu]. According to UNICEF, the combined effects of inadequate sanitation, unsafe water supply and poor personal hygiene are responsible for 88 per cent of childhood deaths from diarrhea." 21 per cent of communicable diseases in India are related to unsafe water [World Bank]. It is very unlikely that the largest democracy in the world has not succeeded in providing access to safe drinking water, latrine and proper drainage facility to all its citizens ensuring them their fundamental human rights to live like a human being.

This paper is an attempt to draw attention of policy makers by focusing on the miserable and vulnerable conditions under which human beings survive in a financial capital city like Mumbai. This paper analyses slum dwellers access to certain basic amenities and the ways in which they gain access to such services. It raises question on the State's role to provide a life of minimum dignity to a section of population and raises grave concern on the issue of development i.e development for whom? Human right to water, sanitation and drainage are also so indispensible to live a life with minimum human dignity that its violation raises serious questions on the nature of development dynamics taking place in the economy even after more than six decades of India'a Independence and more than two decades of adoption of liberal economic policies.

Right to Water, Sanitation and Clean Drainage : Linkage with Development and Human Dignity

It perhaps cannot be denied that right to water, sanitation and clean drainage has a strong linkage with development as it has a direct bearing on the economy's health, education and environment. Reasonable access to a satisfactory quantity of safe water may be considered fundamental to the health and dignity of human beings. It is high time that the nations recognize that access to hygienic sanitation along with safe and affordable drinking water is equally important to ensure health and dignity. It is still unbelievable and shocking that over a billion of the world's population remains without access to safe drinking water and almost over twice that number are deprived of access to proper sanitation. As a result, millions of lives are at risk from diseases and the future of millions follow subsequent deprivations. Therefore, there is huge challenge before the nations to ensure its citizens, a life of minimum dignity through the minimum right to water and sanitation and also clean drainage so that its present generation of citizens can lead a healthy life and can also ensure a healthy life for the future.

A human rights approach to those basic necessities of life through right to water and sanitation, clean drainage with its stress on accountability, non discrimination etc. is a crucial aspect in achieving the goals of development. It therefore requires special attention on the most marginalised sections of society such as people living in informal settlements like slums.

The Indian Government in its UPR II National Report stated that the Total Sanitation Campaign- a flagship programme for providing sanitation facilities in rural areas "has been able to accelerate the sanitation coverage from a mere 22 per cent as per 2001 census to approximately 68 per cent in December 2010" [Human Rights Council Resolution]. This clearly reveals that still 32 per cent of India's population donot have a 'humane' sanitation coverage. As per NSSO 68th round, "a system , if any exists, for carrying off waste water and liquid wastes of the area, is called a drainage system. Drainage could involve natural or artificial removal of surface and sub surface water from a given area. However, if water flows down by its own weight under gravity, in an unregulated manner, then it is considered a case of 'no drainage'. "The report of the 69th round of NSSO says that at the All –India level 31 per cent of all slums had no drainage facility- the figure being considerably higher for non notified slums (45 per cent for non notified than for notified slums 11 per cent). It seems that drainage system which forms an integral part along with water and sanitation has not been addressed adequately in the National agenda and hence needs to draw attention of all stakeholders along with the other two indicators i.e. safe and clean water and sanitation.

Methodology

As per 2011 census, the total population of Mumbai was 12.48 millions. The city though has experienced significant growth rate during last five decades, most of which may be acknowledged to high level of industrial development and also growth in the suburban areas of greater Mumbai, but the picture is not as rosy as it seems. Data from the 2011 census shows that nearly 41.3 per cent of the city's population lives in slums. Dharavi the slum that became famous and drew attention worldwide due to the world of cinema is a part of G north ward and its population is 5.82 lakh. Now Dharavi is no longer considered Asia's largest slum. It has now to compete with four slum clusters in Mumbai itself. Major slum pockets in Mumbai and suburbs now are Kurla Ghatkopar belt (70 per cent -80 per cent slum population), Dindoshi belt (80 per cent slum population), Bhandup belt (70 per cent slum population), Mankhurd Govandi belt (95 per cent slum population). This paper focuses on the living environment in the context of some the basic indicators of the slums in Mumbai.The study is primarily based on data from secondary sources. However some primary evidences have been incorporated to make the study more lively where M East ward has been considered as a case. No such rigid methodology was followed for the primary data collection as mostly the data has been collected by focus group discussion and individual conversation with some residents in the area.

East Ward was chosen as a representative for case study because it has the lowest Human Development Index among all 24 municipal wards in Mumbai. According to Census 2011, 85 per cent of the ward's population lives in slums. The M –East ward which forms the Eastern boundary of Mumbai is also home for the city's biggest dumping ground, which receives huge amount of garbage every day.

The following are the main indicators based on which the discussion is carried out in the paper

- Access to water
- Access to Latrine facility
- Nature of drainage system
- Garbage disposal

The study tried to understand the defiance of human rights and human dignity if any in the light of those basic provisions to live with a minimum standard of health in the sample area.

Slum Population in India: An Overview

A Slum, for the purpose of Census of India, has been defined as residential areas, where dwellings are unfit for human habitation by reasons of dilapidation, overcrowding, faulty arrangements and design of such buildings, narrowness or faulty arrangement of street, lack of ventilation, light, or sanitation facilities or any combination of these factors which are detrimental to the safety and health. For the purpose of Census, slums have been categorized and defined as of the following three types:

- Notified Slums
- Recognised Slums
- Identified Slums

Notified Slums are all notified areas in a town or city notified as 'Slum' by State, UT Administration or Local Government under any Act including a 'Slum Act'. Recognised Slums are all areas recognised as 'Slum' by State, UT Administration or Local Government, Housing and Slum Boards, which may have not been formally notified as slum under any act. On the other hand, Identified Slums are a compact area of at least 300 population or about 60-70 households of poorly built congested tenements, in unhygienic environment usually with inadequate infrastructure and lacking in proper sanitary and drinking water facilities.

In Census 2001, information on Slums were released only on demographic characteristics based on the Population Enumeration. For this purpose, Slum Blocks were identified in Statutory Towns having a population of 20,000 by the local authorities at the time of Population Enumeration phase. In Census 2011, Slum Blocks have been delineated in all statutory towns irrespective of population size. Hence in 2011 Census, one obtains better statistics for slums at the national level as well as disintegrated units.

Slums manifest the worst form of deprivation that transcends income poverty. They are characterized by acute over-crowding,

Table 1: Estimated Slum Population in Indian States and Union Territories

State	*2011*	*2012*	*2013*	*2014*	*2015*	*2016*	*2017*
Andaman and Nicobar Island	33722	35294	69867	38265	39663	41060	42633
Andhra Pradesh	8188022	8273434	8357451	8440074	8521999	8602530	8681318
Arunachal Pradesh	98248	103459	108669	114127	119833	125788	131494
Assam	1070835	1100118	1129636	1159857	1190780	1222406	1253798
Bihar	1683954	1707378	1730148	1752590	1774376	1795671	1816639
Chandigarh	332473	348685	365154	381881	397321	411474	429744
Chhattisgarh	2111546	2169237	2228058	2287634	2347964	2409802	2470886
Dadra and Nagar Haveli	26083	28813	31542	34424	37305	40035	43219
Daman & Diu	9187	9316	9316	9445	9445	9575	9575
Delhi	3163430	3260984	3360874	3463999	3570716	3681745	3793313
Goa	154759	161494	168229	174815	180801	185741	192476
Gujarat	4662619	4759581	4856740	4954094	5051840	5149782	5245569
Haryana	3288292	3390907	3495059	3600364	3707207	3815202	3923582
Himachal Pradesh	87281	89143	91005	92983	94845	96707	98685
Jammu & Kashmir	494180	504243	514306	524369	534275	544180	553771
Jharkhand	931912	948949	966239	983530	1001202	1019382	1036673
Karnataka	3631147	3700490	3770161	3839998	3910162	3980656	4049341
Kerala	533278	536057	538776	541314	543671	545906	548021
Lakshad weep	1560	1560	1498	1435	1435	1435	1373
Madhya Pradesh	6393040	6523229	6654059	6785528	6917636	7050705	7181214
Maharashtra	18151071	15549628	18950624	19352665	19754009	20152914	20557046
Manipur	75197	75915	76514	76993	77592	78190	78789
Meghalaya	205176	208590	212003	215416	219209	222622	226415
Mizoram	105720	107700	109679	111659	113639	115619	117599
Nagaland	83200	84292	85365	86223	87295	88368	89226
Orissa	1736064	1770623	1805436	180503	1876078	1912161	1948244
Punducherry	136899	143316	149876	156435	162282	167131	174118
Punjab	2798236	2864014	2930296	2996316	3062598	3128094	3193590
Rajasthan	3826160	3894590	3962311	4029561	4095395	4160049	4224939
Sikkim	13321	13803	14124	14605	14926	15408	15729
Tamil Nadu	8644892	8862969	9081045	9298651	9515080	9729624	9940165
Tripura	131080	134137	137003	140061	143118	146175	149232
Uttar Pradesh	10878336	11127210	11378552	11631376	11885434	12139739	12394291
Uttarakhand	826257	846181	866105	886615	906832	927342	947559
West Bengal	8546755	8640642	8733188	8825399	8918616	9014179	9106055
India	93055983	94977993	96907923	98845215	100786594	102729415	104668340

Source: Report of the Committee on Slum Statistics/Census 2011, GOI.

insanitary, unhealthy and dehumanizing living conditions. They are subject to insecure land tenure, lack of access to basic minimum civic services such as safe drinking water, sanitation, storm drainage, solid waste management, internal and approach roads, street lighting, education and health care [GOI 2013]. Table 1 gives an estimation of slum population in Indian states and Union Territories. The figures clearly reveal the increasing trend of slum population in almost all the regions of the country. In the national scenario, Maharashtra shows the highest figure in slum population with 13.25 per cent growth by 2017 which is a huge area of concern.

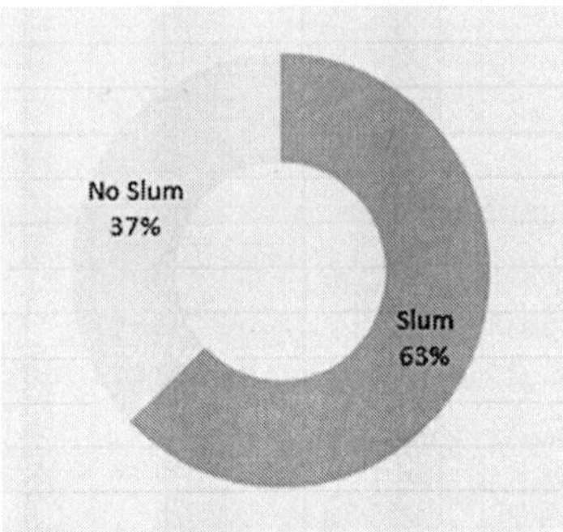

- Out of 4,041 Statutory Towns in Census 2011 Slums reported from 2,543 Towns (63%)
- Total Slum Enumeration Blocks (SEBs) in Census 2011 is about 1.08 lakh in the country
- Largest number of Slum EBs reported from Maharashtra (21,359)

Source: Census 2011

Figure 1 : Towns Reporting Slums in India

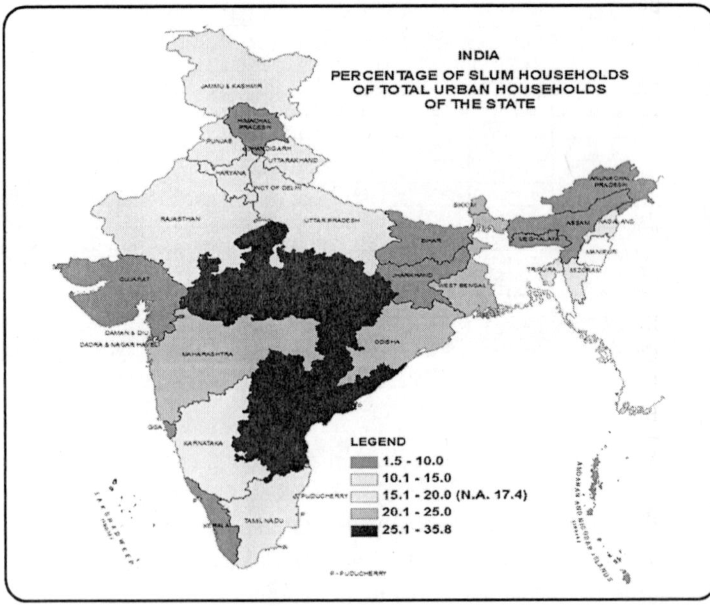

Source: Registrar General And Census Commissioner 2011 Census

Figure 2: Percentage of Slum Households of Total Urban Households

The census 2011 reveals that 63 per cent of the statutory towns have slums. Thus the major share of the towns in the country are reported to have slum settlements and the state of Maharashtra reported the largest slum enumeration blocks.

The National Commission on Urbanisation stressed that poverty cannot be characterised adequately in terms of income, expenditure or consumption patterns alone but should include environment, access to services and social and psychological supports. It recognised that the most visible forms of urban poverty are – (i) Proliferation of slums; (ii) Growth of the informal sector; (iii) Crushing pressure on civic amenities; (iv) High rates of educational and health contingencies and under utilisation of social services; (v) Growing sense of hopelessness (Government of India, 1988).Figure 2 gives a glimpse of slum households as a percentage of total urban households in the different states and union territories of India.Madhya Pradesh and Andhra Pradesh shows the largest concentration of slum households as a percentage of urban households.

The Report of the Committee on Slum Statistics, census 2011 clearly indicate that out of the concentration of slum population in the four metros, Mumbai has the largest concentration of slum population.

Table 2: Slum population in Metro cities

Million Plus Cities	*Proportion of Slum HHs to Total Urban HHs (per cent)*
Greater Mumbai (M Corp.)	41.3
Kolkata (M Corp.)	29.6
Chennai (M Corp.)	28.5
Delhi Municipal Corp (U)	14.6
BBMP (M Corp.)	8.5

Source: censusindia.gov.in

Mumbai :The Slum Capital of India

More than half of Mumbai's population now lives in its slums, according to latest statistics from the World Bank (WB), one of the world's largest financial institutions. While almost 54 per cent of the metro's inhabitants live in shanties, another 25-30 per cent live in '*chawls*' and on footpaths, with just 10-15 per cent living in apartment buildings, bungalows or high-rises. Projections are, that in 20 years, due to factors like a halt in the city's controversial unchecked migration into the city by people in search of jobs, antiquated housing laws and skyrocketing real estate prices, slums will overtake the Mumbai landscape. The World Bank estimates that 22.5 million people will be living in slums in Mumbai by 2025.

'*Zopadpattis*' are squatters in the local terminology. These are the most predominant low-income informal settlements falling under the category of slum. Squatting began in Mumbai even before independence in 1947and continued growing. The first official census of slums was carried out by the State Government in January 1976 (Government of Maharashtra, 1995) and 902,015 huts in 2,335 pockets were identified [Urban Slums Report, the case of Mumbai]. Hence it is quite evident that the unchecked informal settlements in the island city has drawn the situation into its present condition.

Figure 3 distinctly specifies the Slum and Non Slum Households in Mumbai from 1981 to 2011. It clearly indicates that there has been a steep growth of slum households from 1991 to 2001 which naturally

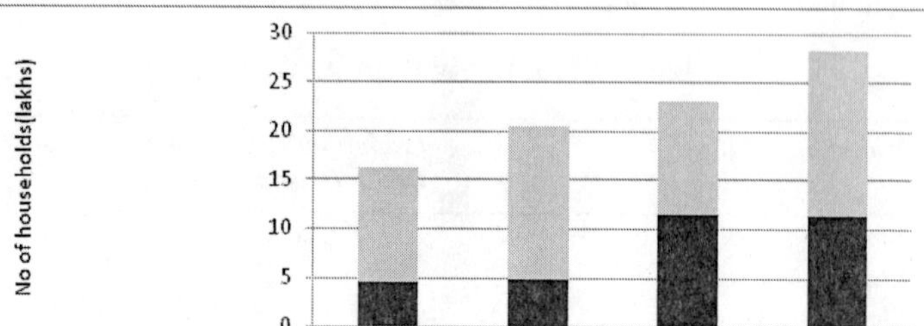

	1981	1991	2001	2011
Non Slum households(lakhs)	11.76	15.66	11.67	17.01
Slum households(lakhs)	4.49	4.85	11.49	11.36

■ Slum households(lakhs) ■ Non Slum households(lakhs)

Source: Data has been taken from Mumbai Human Development Report 2009. *Note*: Slum household separately was enumerated from Census 2001. Therefore the data for 1981 and 1991 are the data collected by Urban Local Bodies as obtained from MHDR 2009.

Figure 3 : Number of Slum and Non Slum Households in Mumbai

pushed down the number of Non Slum households. However it is observed that though total population has risen from 2001 to 2011 , the number of slum households did not show a significant change in 2011.One of the reasons for such a trend may be due to unavailability of land or space to grow slums in the island city which has land constraint and inability to expand geographically due to the oceans covering it.

Table 3: Human Development Index in the Municipal Wards of Mumbai

Sr. No	*Ward*	*HDI*	*Rank*
1.	A	0.58	13
2.	B	0.71	5
3.	C	0.89	2
4.	D	0.96	1
5.	E	0.54	14
6.	F/N	0.41	21
7.	F/S	0.67	8
8.	G/N	0.49	18
9.	G/S	0.66	11
10.	H/E	0.47	20
11.	H/W	0.68	7
12.	K/E	0.67	9
13.	K/W	0.66	10
14.	L	0.29	23
15.	M/E	0.05	24
16.	M/W	0.33	22
17.	N	0.52	16
18.	P/N	0.47	19
19.	P/S	0.59	12
20.	R/C	0.84	3
21.	R/N	0.69	6
22.	R/S	0.54	15
23.	S	0.51	17
24.	T	0.76	4
	Total	**0.56**	

Source: Data taken from MHDR 2009. A higher value in rank implies poor condition as far as the indicators of Human Development Index are concerned.

Table 3 indicates the HDI for all the 24 municipal wards of Mumbai. It is clear that the case study area i.e M/E Ward has the lowest

HDI of 0.05. It is therefore understandable that the indicators of human development are not favourable at the M East Ward.

Table 4 : Access to some basic amenities in major suburban wards in Mumbai

Indicators	*Percentage Households*	*Percentage Households*	*Percentage Households*
Source of Drinking Water	Common Connection 65	Other Sources 27	Individual Tap8
Solid Waste Management	BMC Garbage Bin55	Garbage on Road35	Other 10
Availability of Bathing Facility	Attached 10	Detached20	Not Available 70
Latrine Facility	Public84	Private02	Sulabh/ Open 10/04
Drainage	Closed05	Open85	No Drainage 10

Source: Survey data 2012, Deshmukh M.S.

Table 4 indicates the overall condition in some indicators of basic amenities in the slums of Mumbai. 65 per cent have common water connection, bathroom facility is not available in 70 per cent of the households. 84 per cent of the households use public toilets and 85 per cent have open drains. All those statistics reveal human living in slums of Mumbai with an anti human rights condition especially as far as the basic amenities of living with minimum rights and dignity is concerned.

M East Ward of Mumbai –A Case Study

The visit to the ward revealed that almost all the households in the slum were living in one room the size of which varied from 6 ft by 4 ft to the maximum of 10 ft by 10 ft. On an average each household had 5-6 adult members and 2-4 children.There were some households with members as large as 10-14. The community revealed that drinking water facility is through community water connection i.e municipal 'tap' which is not available regularly and in sufficient quantity. They have to buy water from outside sources, the rate of which varies from rupees 3 to rupees 5 per 'handi'. During summer the crowd in the community tap is so large that it becomes difficult to arrange 2-3 '*handis*' per day for the family by spending the whole day.

Majority of households were totally dependent on public latrines. There was no latrine facility in any of the houses in the locality. When it comes to public latrines, the municipal toilet situated there remains so unclean that no one prefers to go there. The privately owned public ones which are comparatively cleaner charges rupees 3-4 per person per visit but the demand is too large for the available number of such toilets. Therefore as a consequence, the children usually use the open drains and adults use the marshy land behind the area.

All drains observed in the area were open drains. The drains were situated between the rows of houses. The drains were broad and uncovered. They were filled with dirty water, garbage and human waste. The municipal gets it cleaned only once in 3-4 months as per the community people. The overflowing drainage is the invitation for many chronic diseases like malaria, typhoid, jaundice and dengue which are very common in the area. The community reported that there is a child death almost in a fortnight in the locality due to such diseases. The whole locality smells very badly during the rainy season and it becomes difficult to identify the drains separately.

Here are some special cases from the ward that portrays the conditions under which human beings have to survive in the slums of India's financial capital and raises huge concern on human rights of a section of population.

Sabnam is a student of standard IX in the local Madrasah. Her family comprising of 10 members privately buys water at the expense of rupees 650-rupees 1000 per month depending on the season which provides the family with water every alternative day. She also has an option to fill water for 10 minutes daily on an expense of Rs 2 per day. She often tries to collect water for her family before rushing to her school but the crowd is often too large. Sometimes she has to drop her school only to help her family acquire some water at low cost. She has never seen a washroom near the room where she stays since she was born. She complained of the problem of latrine facility for female members especially when they are in their menstrual cycle, are pregnant or are suffering from any disorders that requires the facility. It is also a challenge for the elderly persons.

Sahazad is a 18 year old young boy. He is studying at ITI. His struggle to live a life with minimum dignity has been immense. He complains of the lack of sanitation facility in the community. Moreover he informed about the local 'touts' who have started to charge money for providing early chance to use the community toilets. The charges vary from rupees 6-7 per person depending on the time, season etc. He understands the problem faced by the female members of his family but there cannot be any provision of latrine in their home as the size of the only room they have is 10 ft by 8 ft and they are 10 members in the family including children. He cannot study at home as hardly there is any space for study, so he prefers to go and study in the graveyard in the locality. He too sometimes collects water for the family. During monsoon the area becomes so filthy with garbage water flowing throughout the area that his only space to study, the graveyard cannot be used. He then tries for the local railway station during off peak hours.

Deepti is a 36 year old housewife with 6 members in the family at present which includes 3 children. She has lost her elder son at a tender age of 6 who suffered from dengue due to the unhygienic condition in the area owing to open drains. She is now expecting again and her health condition is very poor. She is in her advanced stage of pregnancy and has to walk half a kilometer to access the public toilet where she has to wait for 20-30 minutes on an average if she needs to use it in the morning. Her two children who are 3 years and 7 years old use the open drains as their toilet. She brings water from the community tap for which she spends 2-3 hours a day. She and her family members often skip bathing even in the scorching heat in order to save some water for the next day even if it is a peak summer time!

Concluding Remarks

The cases cited above and the data from secondary sources clearly reveals the nature of development dynamics taking place within a section of population of our country and the nature of exclusion from 'basic human rights'.The dichotomy in an urban city like Mumbai is clear and visible. The people in such slums are living in plight facing the worst conditions of human life. The minimum condition to live a life of minimum dignity was missing. The worst part was that people in the community have lost faith in the system, they were confident that their expectations will never be fulfilled. An elderly man from the community made a touchy comment '"*Har mahine ek do team a jate hai hame sawal puchne. Aj challis sal se yahi dekh raha hoon. Lekin hamara stiti to wahi ke wahi hai. Ab kisi pe hamara viswas nahi hai. Hamara pardada ne bhi aise hi zindegi gujara, hum bhi gujar rahe hai, hamare bachhe bhi gujarenge...Kuch marenge...kuch jiyenge... kisika isse koi lena dena nahi......*" [Every month one or two teams visit our locality and ask questions. For the last forty years I am witnessing this. But our condition remains the same. My forefathers have lived a life like this , I am living like this, my children will also live like this. Some will die...some will live...no one bothers for these...] He himself is a severe asthmatic patient but forced to stay in the condition which is acting as a boost to worsen his health status.

It naturally raises the question on State's role to provide a life of minimum dignity to a section of population and raises grave concern on the issue of development i.e. development for whom? Human's right to water, sanitation, drainage to live in a clean environment are so indispensible to live a life with minimum human dignity that its violation raises serious questions on the nature of development dynamics taking place in the economy even after more than six decades of the country's freedom from the British rule and more than two decades of adoption of liberal economic policies. It seems from the figures of our GDP growth often quoted by our politicians, that a huge section of the population have been bypassed by the process of growth and this raises grave concern on the issue of human development as well.

High levels of rural to urban migration, lack of focused public policy, or an aversion to high cost housing due to affordability may be the reason for such high level of slum population but such slum population are a great threat to the health status of Indian citizens. The health status of children, the future of the nation growing up in the slums is under severe risk. The child and maternal health needs to be addressed for the slum population separately otherwise it will lead to a population of more unhealthy Indian citizens in the future.

An analysis of the various reasons for the miserable conditions of essential services is just not enough; rather, solutions to develop the scenario needs to be looked into. There is an acute need to look outside the existing schemes centric intervention. A comprehensive agenda for the overall development of slums through a time focused mission perhaps needs to be formulated. Finally considering the nature of slums which varies from region to region, the policies needs to be more region specific and hence calls for decentralised planning and including various stakeholders of the society as implementing agencies for accelerating such programmes and schemes.

Works Cited

- Deshmukh M.S. (2013):Conditions of slum population of major sub-urban wards of Mumbai in Maharashtra,Voice of Research , Vol 2, Issue 2.
- Government of India: Various Census Reports of 2001 and 2011.
- Government of Delhi(2010): Urban Slums in Delhi, (NSS 65th Round Survey, 2008-09), (http://www.envi ronmentpor ta l . in/ files/UrbanSlum 65th Round.pdf).
- Government of India (1988) Urban Poverty, Report of Working Group for National Commission on Urbanisation, Ministry of Urban Development, New Delhi.
- Indian Express, Rural India will banish open defecation in 10 years:Ramesh, available at:www.indianexpress.com/news/rural-india-will-banish-open-defecation-in-1/934406/.
- Mitra, A. (1994):Urbanisation , Slums, Informal Sector Employment and Poverty: An Exploratory Study,Delhi:BR Publishing Corporation..
- Mumbai Human Development Report 2009, OUP.
- National Sample Survey Organisation .2003.Condition of Urban Slums 2002: Salient Features NSS 58th Round(July2002-December 2002). Report No. 486. New Delhi: Ministry of Statistics and Programme Implementation. Government of India. Resolution A/RES/64/292. United Nations General Assembly , July 2010.
- National Report submitted in accordance with paragraph 5 of the annex to Human Rights Council resolution 16/21: India, A/ HRC/ WG.6/13/IND/1, UN General Assembly, March 8, 2012, para 6.

- National Report submitted in accordance with paragraph 5 of the annex to Human Rights Council resolution 16/21: India , A/HRC/ WG. 6 /13/IND/1, UN General Assembly, March 8 , 2012, para 6.
- National report submitted in accordance with paragraph 5 of the annex to Human Rights Council resolution 16/21: India, A/HRC/WG.6/13/IND/1,UN General Assembly, March 8, 2012.
- NSSO 69th round Report on 'Key Indicators of Urban Slums in India', MOSPI, Government of India. (year)
- Primary census Abstract of Slums available at www.censusindia. gov.in/ 2011-Documents/Slum-26-09-13.pdf
- Report on The State of Affordable Housing in Mumbai November 2014 available at http://www.praja.org/praja_downloads/Report%20on%20 The%20State% 20of%20Affordable%20Housing% 20in%20Mumbai.pdf
- State of Slums in India-A Statistical Compendium 2013 Government of India, Ministry of Housing and Urban Poverty Alleviation.
- The Hindu, Jairam urges Manmohon to give highest priority to sanitation , January 17, 2012,available at :www.thehindu.com/todays-paper/tp-national/ article2806719.ece
- United Nations Human Settlement Programme(UN –HABITAT), Report of State World Cities 2006/07
- United Nations, The human right to water and sanitation , available at :http:/ /www.un.org/waterforlifedecade/human right to water.shtm
- Urban Slums Report, the case of Mumbai] , India available at http:// www.ucl.ac.uk/dpu-projects/Global_Report/pdfs/Mumbai.pdf.
- World Bank, India's Water Economy, Bracing for a Turbulent Future, 2005, available at . http://www.worldbank.org.in/WBSITE/EXTERNAL/ COUNTRIES/SOUTHASIAEXT/INDIAEXTN/o, contentMDK:20674796 pagePK:141137 piPK:141127theSitePK:295584,00.html.
- WHO/UNICEF Joint Monitoring Programme for Water Supply and Sanitation, 2010statistics, available at:www.wssinfo.org/data-estimates/table
- World Bank, India's Water Economy, Bracing for a Turbulent Future, 2005, available at : http://www.worldbank.org.in/WBSITE/EXTERNAL/ COUNTRIES/SOUTHASIAEXT/INDIAEXTN/0, contentMDK:20674796 pagePK:141137 pi141127 the Site PK: 295584,00.html.

4

Reconstructing Lost Future: Role of NGOs in Protecting Child Right in Tripura

—Jayanta Choudhury, Reshmi Ghosh

Human Right is considered universal to humanity, regardless of citizenship, residency status, ethnicity, gender, or other considerations. All human beings are born free and equal in dignity and rights. They are endowed with reason and conscience and should act towards one another in a spirit of brotherhood (International human Rights). Children's rights are the human rights of children with particular attention to the rights of special protection and care. The opportunity for children to participate in political and legal decisions that affect them is significant; in a broad sense, the rights of children to live free from hunger, abuse, neglect, and other inhumane conditions. In Tripura, Children are facing various problems like child labor, child trafficking, child abuse and kidnapping of the child in border area etc. The NGOs can play vital role for in every stages of Development. This paper is divided into three sections. The first section deals with the present state of children in Tripura in the context of Child Rights, while the second section documents the role of NGOs towards protecting child rights in Tripura. In Tripura, NGOs are working independently or in collaboration with Child Welfare Committee, Government of Tripura. The NGOs are facilitating the children by providing home, nutritional food & education etc. The main objective of the NGOs is to work with vulnerable children so as to bring them to the mainstream of the society where they can ensure their future as a proper human being in the next generation. The third section comes out with policy direction for strengthening GO-NGO collaboration towards protecting Child Rights in Tripura.

The concept of human rights though is central to political science (Vijapur, 2009). The term "human rights" refers to those rights that are considered universal to humanity, regardless of citizenship, residency status, ethnicity, gender, or other considerations (Tom Head). Human rights are rights inherent to all human beings, nationality, and place of residence, sex, national or ethnic origin, colour, religion, language. People are all equally entitled to human rights without discrimination. These rights are all interrelated, interdependent and indivisible. International human rights law lays down obligations of Governments to act in certain ways, in order to promote and protect human rights and fundamental freedoms of individuals or groups. (Bruce Thao, M.S.)

According to Article 1 of UNCRC, "A child means every human being below the age of 18 years unless, under the law applicable to the child, majority is attained earlier." (United Nation's Convention on the Rights of the Child). Child Rights are fundamental freedoms and the inherent rights of all human beings below the age of 18. These rights apply to every child, irrespective of the child's, parent's/legal guardian's race, colour, sex, creed or other status. All children should have the same rights and should be given the same opportunity to enjoy an adequate standard of living. (cry.org)

Importance of Child Rights

All children are innocent and full of hope. Their childhood should be happy and loving. But for many children, the reality of childhood is altogether different. These children have been abused and exploited. They suffer from hunger and homelessness; work in harmful conditions, high infant mortality, and deficient health care and limited opportunities for basic education. The Charter of Child Rights is built on the principle that "All children are born with fundamental freedoms and all human beings have some inherent rights". The Charter confers the following basic rights on all children across the world:

- **The right to survival** - To life, health, nutrition, name and nationality

- **The right to development** - To education, care, leisure, recreation
- **The right to protection** - From exploitation, abuse, neglect
- **The right to participation** - To expression, information, thought and religion.(Child rights and cry.org)

Different Types of Child Rights

Children's right is a wide spectrum of civil, cultural, economic, social and political rights. (Mangold, 2002). One Canadian organisation categorizes children's rights into three categories:

- **Provision:** Children have the right to an adequate standard of living, health care, education and services, and to play and recreation. These include a balanced diet, a warm bed to sleep in.
- **Protection:** Children have the right to protection from abuse, neglect, exploitation and discrimination. This includes the right to safe places for children to play; constructive child rearing behavior and acknowledgment of the evolving capacities of children.
- **Participation:** Children have the right to participate in communities and have programs and services for themselves. This includes children's involvement in libraries and community programs, youth voice activities, and involving children as decision-makers (Springer, 1997).

In a similar fashion, the Child Rights Information Network (CRIN) categorizes rights into two groups (Freeman, 2000):

- Economic, social and cultural rights, related to the conditions necessary to meet basic human needs such as food, shelter, education, health care, and gainful employment. Included are the right to work and rights at work, as well as the cultural rights of minorities and indigenous people.
- Environmental, cultural and developmental rights, which are sometimes called "third generation rights," and including the right to live in safe and healthy environments and that groups of people have the right to cultural, political, and economic development.

Section-I

Child Rights *vis-à-vis* Status of Children in Tripura

India is a party to the UN declaration on the Rights of the Child 1959. The policy reaffirmed the constitutional provisions for adequate services to children, both before and after birth and through the period of growth to ensure their full physical, mental and social development. It has also developed appropriate monitoring procedures to assess progress in implementing the Convention-involving various stake holders in the society. India is also a signatory to the World Declaration on the Survival, Protection and Development of Children. In pursuance of the commitment made at the World Summit, the Department of Women and Child Development under the Ministry of Human Resource Development has formulated a National Plan of Action for Children. Most of the recommendations of the World Summit Action Plan are reflected in India's National Plan of Action- keeping in mind the needs, rights and aspirations of 300 million children in the country. The priority areas in the Plan are health, nutrition, education, water, sanitation and environment. (Child Rights in India, Smile Foundation)

Status of Children in Tripura

The state of Tripura resides at the far north-eastern corner of India. It has spread over a small expanse of about 10,000 kilometer square, which makes it one of the smallest states in India. Tripura attained full statehood on January 21, 1972. According to 2011 Census, Tripura has population of 36.74 Lakhs. It has eight districts in all over Tripura. Total population of child is 444,055. In Tripura 12.48 per cent of male population and 12.45 per cent of female population are in age group of 0-6. State Government has decided Universalisation of ICDS by covering all Villages, 100 per cent enrollment of the Children in the AWCs and CDPOs are ensuring enrollment of 6+ Children into the nearby School. Providing non-formal Pre-School Education for the children (3-6 years) in overall development of the children, different study materials / play materials are being provided in each AWC every year. Percentage of Fully Immunised Children in Tripura State 50 (NFHS-III) where as all India average 44 (ICDS.2012-13). Malnutrition is the greatest single threat to the world's public health and accounts for 11 per cent of global diseases. It includes both under-nutrition and over-nutrition (Ray and Chandra, 2013). The crude birth rate (CBR) is 16.5, infant mortality rate (IMR) is 48 and the percentage of underweight children under the age 3 is 51.7 (Child Survival and Development Report Card of Tripura).

General Profile

Table 1: Child population and Child sex ratio as per 2011 census

Table 1 depicts a picture on child population and child sex ratio. According to 2011 census, the ratio of females to males is 914: 1000 –

Country/ State	*Child population*			*Percentage of child population (0-6 years)*			*Child sex ratio (0-6 years)*		
	Total	*Rural*	*Urban*	*Total*	*Rural*	*Urban*	*Total*	*Rural*	*Urban*
India	158,789,287 (100 per cent)	117,585,514 (74.051 per cent)	41,203,773 (25.948 per cent)	13.12	14.11	10.93	914	919	902
Tripura	444,055	354,459	89,596	12.10	13.08	9.32	953	955	945

Source: Census, Office of the Registrar General of India (ORGI) & Children in India-2012.

a disturbing indicator of gender discrimination. Sex ratio varies from as high as 919 in rural India and 955 in rural Tripura to low as 902 in urban India and 945 in urban area of Tripura. The percentage of child population is more in rural area (80 %.) in comparison to their urban counterpart of Tripura as similar to the national data. So, comparatively child sex ratio in rural area of India as well as in Tripura is better than urban areas.

Table 2: Sex ratio in the age group 0-6 years 2001 & 2011 and goals of 11th Plan

Country/State	*Sex ratio (0-6) 2001*	*Sex ratio (0-6) 2011*
India	927	914
Tripura	966	953

Source: ORGI & Children in India-2012.

According to 2011 census shows in Table 2 that the sex ratio among children 0-6 years has touched an all time low. It has declined to 953 female children for every 1000 male. It was 966 during the previous census but then, every census shows a reduction in the girl child compared with the previous one.

Health & Nutritional Status

Table 3: Infant Mortality Rate (IMR) (per 1000 live births)

Country/State	2007	2008	2009	2010	2011
India	55	53	50	47	44
Tripura	39	34	31	27	29

Source: Sample Registration System, ORGI & Children in India-2012.

Infant mortality is defined as the infant deaths (less than one year) per thousand live births. Reflects in Table 3 that in 2010, IMR is reported 47 at the national level and in Tripura it was 27 which declined. Though, IMR is showing a declining trend over the years but the progress is slow. It has been observed that, the per year decline in IMR was approximately 5 points. But in Tripura 2006 & 2007 respectively increased after that it slowly decreased which is a good sign of development of children.

Table 4: Early childhood and Perinatal mortality rates

Country /State	*Neonatal mortality*	*Post Neo-natal mortalit*	*Infant morta-lity*	*Child morta-lity*	*Under-five morta lity*	*Perinatal mortality rate*
India	39.0	18.0	57.0	18.4	74.3	48.5
Tripura	33.1	18.3	51.5	8.2	59.2	42.0

Source: National Family Health Survey, 2005-06

Table 4 discussed about the various mortality rates among the children. Neo- natal deaths refers to the deaths of infants less than 29 days of age. In 2005-06, the percentage of neo- natal deaths to total infant deaths is 39.0 per cent at national level and in Tripura it was 33.1 per cent. At national level, under –five mortality rates are estimated at 74.3 per cent which is declined in Tripura (59.2 per cent). The percentage of Post neonatal mortality and child mortality rate in India is almost same but in Tripura child mortality rate is less (8.2 per cent) than post neonatal (18.3 per cent). For India, perinatal mortality is estimated to be 49 per cent and 42 per cent in Tripura deaths per 1,000 pregnancies lasting seven or more months (including live births and stillbirths) during the period 2001-05.

An indicator of utilisation of different ICDS services was shown in Table 5. Nationally, one-third of children under six years of age served by an Anganwadi centre received ICDS services in the 12 months preceding the survey. The percentage is 27 per cent in Tripura. The proportion of children receiving supplementary food from an Anganwadi centre is 26 per cent in India and 20 per cent in Tripura.

Table 5: Indicators of utilisation of ICDS services, 2005-06

Country/ State	*Percentage of children age 0-71 months who received any services*	*Percentage of children under age six years who-*					*Percentage whose mothers received counseling from an AWC afterchild was weighed*
		Received food supplements	*Received immuni-Sations*	*Received health check-ups*	*Went for early childhood care/ preschool*	*Were weighed*	
India	32.9	26.3	20.0	15.8	22.8	18.2	48.9
Tripura	26.6	19.6	15.3	10.4	22.5	7.7	43.8

Source: National Family Health Survey, 2005-06

Overall, 20 per cent and 15 per cent in Tripura received immunisation. Only one in six children (16 per cent) has gone to an AWC for a health check-up. Both India and Tripura, nearly one-fourth of children went for early childhood care or preschool education to an AWC. Eighteen per cent of children have had their weight measured in an AWC while in Tripura it was only 7.7 per cent. Mothers of half of the children who were weighed received counseling services from an anganwadi centre after their child was weighed.

Table 6: Status of malnutrition of children under 5 years of age

Country/ State	*Per cent of under weight children< 5years*	*Per cent of stunted children< 5years*	*Per cent of wasted children<5years*
INDIA	42.5	48	19.8
Tripura	39.6	35.7	24.6

Source: National Family Health Survey 3 (2005-06), & Children in India-2012.

In India 48 per cent of children under age of five years are stunted (too short for their age) was shown in Table 6 which indicates that, half of the country's children are chronically malnourished. Acute malnutrition, as evidenced by wasting, results in a child being too thin for his or her height. 19.8 per cent of children under five years in the country are wasted which indicates that, one out of every five children in India and one out of every four children in Tripura is wasted. 43 per cent of children under age five years are underweight for their age. Underweight status is a composite index of chronic and acute malnutrition. In Tripura, percentage of children stunting and underweight is less than national level whereas percentage of children wasted in more than national level.

Table 7: Status of Vaccinations, 2005-06

Country/ State	*BCG*	*DPT*			*Polio*				*Measles*	*All basic vacci-nations*	*No vacci-nations*	*Percentage with avacci nationcard seen*
		1	*2*	*3*	*0*	*1*	*2*	*3*				
India	78.1	76.0	66.7	55.3	48.4	93.1	88.8	78.2	58.8	43.5	5.1	37.5
Tripura	81.1	80.2	76.0	60.2	56.0	84.7	77.8	65.3	59.9	49.7	14.7	67.7

Source: National Family Health Survey, 2005-06.

Table 7 discussed about the vaccination of children and the immunisation coverage rates for each type of vaccination, according to either immunisation card. At national level, 43.5 per cent and in Tripura 49.7 per cent of the children aged 12-23 months have received full immunisation that means one dose of BCG, three injections of DPT, three doses of polio and one injection of measles. The BCG rate is to be found 81.1 per cent and 78.1 per cent respectively in state level and national level .In this table one thing is observed that incase polio2 and polio3 the percentage was less compared to polio1. Total 5.1 per cent in India and 14.7 per cent children in Tripura did not receive any vaccination and suffer from several diseases. It means that till date people are not fully aware about the vaccination of children.

It may be observed from table 8 that percentage of children for whom advice or treatment was sought from a health facility or provider when sick with diarrhoea is considerably higher in Tripura (64.5 per cent) than in India. Use of ORS packets for treatment of diarrhoea in Tripura was also comparatively better (58.1 per cent) than all India level (26.0 per cent). Use of antibiotic and other unknown drugs is more or less same in both state level and national level.

Table 8: Diarrhoea treatment, 2005-06

Country/ State		India	Tripura
Percentage of children with diarrhoea taken to a health provider		59.8	64.5
Oral rehydration therapy (ORT)	ORS Packets	26.0	58.1
	Gruel	20.2	23.4
	Either ORS or Gruel	38.5	64.5
Increased fluids		10.2	19.1
Any ORT or increased fluids		43.0	66.6
Other treatments	Antibiotic drugs	15.5	12.8
	Antimotility drugs	1.5	2.1
	Zinc supplements	0.3	0.0
	Other drug	3.9	3.5
	Unknown drug	30.4	20.5
	Intravenous solution	0.5	0.0
	Home remedy/ herbal/ other	7.5	20.6
Missing		0.3	0.0
No treatment		26.1	10.7

Source: National Family Health Survey, 2005-06.

Table 9: Initial breastfeeding by state India, 2005-06

Country/ State	*Percentage Ever breastfed*	*Among last-born children born in the last 5 years who were ever breastfed*			
		Percentage who started breastfeeding-			*Percentage who received a prelacteal feed*
		Within half an hour of Birth	*Within one hour of birth*	*Within one day of birth*	
India	95.7	23.6	24.5	55.3	57.2
Tripura	97.1	33.7	34.6	77.1	36.4

Source: National Family Health Survey, 2005-06.

Table 9 presents data on feeding practices among children. After child birth within half an hour and one hour is a recommended practice which is encouraged for a number of reasons. But the data says that in Tripura, only 33.7 per cent children were fortunate to be breastfed within half an hour of child birth though it was slightly better than the national level (23.6 per cent). There was a little improvement in case of breastfed within one hour of birth. In case of prelacteal feed, Tripura (36.4 per cent) is well behind the national level (57.2 per cent).

Educational Status

Table 10: Drop Out Rates for Primary and Upper Primary Level

Dropout rates in classes I-V, I-VIII and I-X –All India		
	India	*Tripura*
Classes I-V	28.86	4.55
Classes I-VIII	42.39	9.19
Classes I-X	52.76	-

Source: Sarva Siksha Abhiyan, 2009-10.

Table 10 shows the dropout rates for primary and upper primary level. The percentage of dropout rate is more in upper primary level (42.39 per cent and 9.19 per cent respectively in India and Tripura) compared to primary section.

Table 11: Distribution of Working Children according to 1971, 1981, 1991 and 2001 Census in the age group 5-14 years

Country/State	*1971*	*1981*	*1991*	*2001*****
INDIA	10753985	13640870	11285349	12666377
Tripura	17490	24204	16478	21756

Source: Children in India-2012

**** includes marginal workers also

The census result was shown in Table 11 about child labour. A fluctuating trend in child labour over the years. The trend on the magnitude of child labour is not uniform across the country. On one hand, there is considerable increase in the absolute number of child labour between 1991 and 2001. In Tripura more than 21 thousand are working children in 2001 census. It reveals that various government and non-government organisations are working for development of children. This also proves that child labor is existing in a huge way.

Table 12: Incidence & Rate of Crimes Committed Against Children in States and country during 2012

Country/ State	*Incidence*	*Incidence Percentage Contribution To All–India Total*	*Children Population# (in lakhs)*	*Rate Of Total Cognizable Crimes*
India	38172	100.00	4294.04	8.89
Tripura	20	0.05	12.01	1.67

***Source**:* Crime in India 2012, NCRB.

It is alarming that from Table 12, in 2012, the Crimes against children incidence rate (0.05 per cent) which is decreased from the previous year with a total of 20 cases in the Tripura as compared to 102 cases during 2011. But incidence wise rate of total cognizable crimes is more in Tripura as compared to India.

Table 13.A: Incidence (I), Rate (R) and Percentage Contribution (P) To All India Total of Crimes Committed Against Children During.

Country/ State	*Infanticide (Sec. 315 IPC)*			*Murder (Sec. 302 IPC)*			*Rape (Sec. 376 IPC)*			*Kidnapping & Abduction (Sec.363-369, 371-373 IPC)*		
	I	R	P	I	R	P	I	R	P	I	R	P
Tripura	0	0.00	0.00	2	0.17	0.13	17	1.42	0.20	0	0.00	0.00
India	81	0.02	100.00	1597	0.37	100.00	8541	1.99	100.00	18266	4.25	100.00

Table 13.B: Incidence (I), Rate (R) and Percentage Contribution (P) To All India Total of Crimes Committed Against Children During 2012

Country/ State	*Foeticide (Sec.315,316 IPC)*			*Abetment to Suicide (Sec.305 IPC)*			*Exposure And Abandonment (Sec.317 IPC)*			*Procuration Of Minor Girl (Sec.366A IPC)*		
	I	*R*	*P*	*I*	*R*	*P*	*I*	*R*	*P*	*I*	*R*	*P*
Tripura	0	0.00	0.00	0	0.00	0.00	0	0.00	0.00	0	0.00	0.00
India	210	0.05	100.00	144	0.03	100.00	821	0.19	100.00	809	0.19	100.00

***Source**: Crime in India 2012, NCRB.*

In 2012, among the IPC crimes in case of Infanticide, Foeticide, and Kidnapping & Abduction, abetment to Suicide, exposure and abandonment, Procuration of minor Girl, buying of girls for prostitution, selling of girls for prostitution, Prohibition of child marriage, the children in Tripura is safer in comparison to all India level. But rate of murder cases and rape cases are quite worrying in Tripura.

Table 13.C: Incidence (I), Rate (R) and Percentage Contribution (P) To All India Total of Crimes Committed Against Children During 2012

Country/ State	*Buying Of Girls For Prostitution (Sec.373 IPC)*			*Selling Of Girls For Prostitution (Sec.372 IPC)*			*Prohibition of Child Marriage Act 2006*			*Other Crimes*		
	I	*R*	*P*	*I*	*R*	*P*	*I*	*R*	*P*	*I*	*R*	*P*
Tripura	0	0.00	0.00	0	0.00	0.00	0	0.00	0.00	1	0.08	0.01
India	15	0.00	100.00	108	0.03	100.00	169	0.04	100.00	7411	1.73	100.00

Source: *Crime in India 2012, National Crime Records Bureau*

Section: II

Role of Ngos in Child Right in Tripura

NGOs are playing a vital role for protection of child rights in our country. Following some notable NGOs are working for promoting and protecting the child rights in Tripura through a several issues. Their major activities are as follows:

a. **Voluntary Health Association of Tripura**

Voluntary Health Association of Tripura as a federation of Civil Society Organisations gained worth-while experiences in different parts of the state of Tripura. One of the main objectives of the organisation is child development through mainstreaming the orphan, street & disable children through different way. These are:

- **CHILDLINE Agartala**

VHAT as a collaborative organisation has been implementing CHILDLINE Agartala project. This is a national 24-hrs emergency free phone service (No 1098) for the children in crisis. The project is supported by the

Ministry of Women and Child Development, Government of India through the nodal organisation CHILDLINE India Foundation, Mumbai. Under this the activities are call received, outreach activities, open house done (through Puppet show, street drama, folk songs), IEC activities, Organisation meeting, creating awareness of the protection of child rights. To ensure participation of the children in CHILDLINE Project, to give their opinion in CHILDLINE activities, 12 open houses were organised by the project. The main message of wall writing and bill boards was "Dial 1098 when you see a child in distress conditions".

- **Ratanmani Vidayalaya - a Residential Primary School for Tribal Children in remote inaccessible area of Tripura**

  The total students of this school are 300. The services are education in the school, cultural Education, sports, capacity building of the teachers etc. At last yearly monitoring & evaluation was done by committee with executive director.

- **ANWESHA Child Protection Centre**

  Children of age group between 6-18 of the following category are the target group of the project: Orphaned Children, Street children, rag pickers, victims of addiction, Children rejected by the parents especially the father, Abandoned child, Victims of violence, Victim of insurgency, Missing child who will be sent to her/his family through a proper process. Every child is eligible for getting emergency services & the achievements are shelter & nutrition, Education, legal registration for children. Regular shelter for 50 children out of them 49 were attending school and short term shelter for 06 children is provided by VHAT. Recreation, medical support, water and sanitation facilities, life skill development facilities are provided. (Annual report of VHAT 2011-12)

b. **Sanghadeep**

Child welfare programme (Creche): Child will be the citizen of future and children are the greatest asset of the nation. With a view to protecting the rights of the children, government has initiated various schemes for the well-being of the children in need of care. In the light of ensuring the right including right to receive support for development and care during early childhood, Rajiv Gandhi Creche scheme has been introduced in this context. Aiming to associate in welfare activities towards underprivileged children, Sanghadip has successfully been implementing the scheme. The following objectives are focused to archive the desirable outcomes of RGNCS:

- Providing services towards underprivileged children who are in need
- Establishment of child rights in basic needs & protection of violence against children.(Annual report of Sanghadeep 2011-12)

c. **Tripura council for Child welfare**

Tripura council for Child welfare (TCCW), was established in May, 1965. It is having a 3 Sishu Grihas for providing in-country adoption. Total number of adoption from 1996-2009 is 308. The programme is funded by the Ministry of Social Justice and Empowerment, Government of India. TCCW is running a special school for CPMR which is to make mentally retarded children adoptable in the society to make them self-dependent in their day to day personal work by means of 'Learning by doing Method', to make the society aware of the fact that these children are also the integral part of the society.One short stay home for girls and women for providing various training and 106 creches are running in Tripura. TCCW work for child line in Agartala, for thousands of children out there who are often neglected, cheated, exploited and beaten. (Annual report of TCCW, 2011-12)

d. **Tripura Adibasi Mahila Samiti**

Tripura Adibasi Mahila Samiti was established in the year of 1953 with the objective of spreading the education and socio-economic development of rural people. TAM provides various types of support for children, working regarding the issue of human trafficking for children. TAMS has one Residential School for Tribal Girls and total students are 101. The Samiti has introduced Creche Programmes at Tea gardens. 3 nos. crèche centres are running in tea gardens of Mohanpur Block area. Nearly 75 nos. tribal children of below 6 years are being looked after in these Crèches by providing nutritional food, medicine etc. The centre houses in tea gardens require renovation immediately. CHILDLINE India Foundation, Mumbai has selected the Samiti as the Nodal organisation for Agartala City and work for oppressed, persecuted and missing children. A City Coordinator has been engaged to liason with Collab & Support Organisation under CHILDLINE India Foundation. (Annual report of TAMS, 2011-12)

e. Abhoy Mission

This organisation is running one residential special school for mentally retarded children with the name "SWAVBALAMBAN" in the state, capital "Agartala" since 1991 from the organisations own resources . This is the first and foremost school in the state of its kind to impart teaching in special methods and with latest modern techniques. Residential facility is also being provided to the deserving children / student of the school hailing from rural and remote areas of the state, whose parents belong to BPL category. Since 2006, this project is being run as SAMARTH project. 14 children of the institute have been

Name of Organisation	*Activities*				
	Awareness	*Research*	*Rescue*	*Rehabilitation*	*Networking*
Voluntary Health Association of Tripura	✓	✓	✓	✓	✓
Sanghadeep	✓	✓	✓	✓	
Tripura council for Child Welfare	✓	✓	✓		
Tripura Adibasi Mahila Samiti	✓	✓	✓	✓	
Abhoy Mission	✓	✓	✓	✓	

Source: Trafficking in Women & Children, 2012.

admitted to the normal school to favour integration and they are prosecuting their studies undisturbed and uninterrupted. (Annual report of Abhoy Mission, 2011-12)

Section: III

Policy Recommendation

- **Child population:** Government should implement a process for finding out the reason of low sex ratio through involvement of NGOs by spreading several IEC messages in favour of protection of girl children in the state particularly in urban areas.
- **Improved ICDS services and health status:** Improved Nutritional status of stunting and underweight children through NGOs like they can evaluate and monitor the ICDS services, providing supplementary feeding of the child with food rich in Vitamin 'A', several medicine to the anganwadi center, primary school etc. Intensive campaign to create awareness programme for mainstreaming the children with the help of NGOs and also increase the participation for polio2 and polio3 through several activities. NGOs should provide the training for ICDS workers, health workers, traditional dais for prevention of infant, Neonatal, Post neonatal, Child, Under-five mortality rate and perinatal mortality rate.
- **Reduction of Dropout Rate:** Reduction of dropout rates, especially among the upper primary stage. NGOs and different organisation together should implement a different skill development school for developing student's creativity and to utilize such income to meet the opportunity cost to families for sending their children to school.
- **Reduction of Child Labour:** NGOs and government together should conduct a survey of child labour engaged in hotels, shops, households, workshops, brick industries and agricultural activities and designing special measures for their welfare and rehabilitation through special child labour school, shelter, etc.
- **Prevent Child abuse and Trafficking:** In the fight against child trafficking and crimes against children, government organisations, non-governmental organisations, civil society,

pressure groups, all should be playing a role. Law cannot be the only instrument to take care of all problems. Child commission should implement a strict role for protection of child rights.

- NGOs should create more posters that would enable children to understand the meaning of the rights and the implications for them in their lives and experience of the setting they are in (for example, a day nursery or law court). More cultural activities related to children must be associated with the several programmes. More crèche center in state for children are required.

Conclusion

The study gives an idea about the present state of children in Tripura along with child rights. Government also implements several rules and regulation for protection of child rights. On the other hand, NGOs are playing a vital role for protection and promotion of child rights in Tripura in numerous ways. Therefore it is important to build a strong GO-NGO partnership in the special issue.

Notes

1. Abdulrahim P. Vijapur, (2009), "**The Concept of Human Rights: National and International Perspectives**" , Vol.2, No. IV, Available at url: http://www.intpolitics.com/Articles/No4/National%20and%20International%20 Perspectives.pdf, Accessed on date : 7.11.2013
2. Annual Report of Abhoy Mission Tripura, 2011-12.
3. Annual Report of Sanghadeep Tripura, 2011-12.
4. Annual Report of Tripura Adibasi Mahila Samiti, 2011-12.
5. Annual Report of Tripura council for Child welfare, 2011-12.
6. Annual Report of voluntary Health Association of Tripura, 2011-12.
7. Bruce Thao, M.S, "Human Rights", Available at url: http://cis.uchicago.edu/sites/cis.uchicago.edu/files/resources /101210-thao-human-rights-day-activity.pdf , Accessed on date : 12.11.2013.
8. Child rights and cry.org, Available at url: Available at url: http://uk.cry.org/knowus/importanceofchildrights. html, Accessed on date : 12.11.2013, Accessed on date : 7.9.2013.
9. Child rights and cry.org, Available at url: Available at url: http://uk.cry.org/knowus/importanceofchildrights. html, Accessed on date : 12.11.2013, Accessed on date : 7.9.2013.

10. Child Survival and Development Report Card of Tripura, Available at url: http://www.bpni.org/information _sheets/Tripura.pdf Accessed on date : 27.10.2013.
11. Children's rights in the Canadian context, Interchange. 8(1–2). Springer, 1997, Available at url: http://en.wikipedia.org/wiki/Children's_rights, Accessed on date : 22.10.2013.
12. Freeman, M. (2000), "The Future of Children's Rights," A-Z of Children's Rights, Children's Rights Information Network and Jump up Children & Society. 14(4) p 277-93, Available at url: http://en.wikipedia.org/wiki/ Children's_rights, Accessed on date: 22.10.2013.
13. ICDS.2012-13 , Available at url : https://www.google.co.in/url?sa=t& rct=j&q=&esrc= s&source=web&cd=1&cad=rja &ved=0CCUQFj AA&url=http%3A%2F%2Fwcd.nic. in%2Ficds%2Fapip%2FTripura% 2520(6%252 0Nov).ppt&ei=bBXmUvymFtHPrQe1sYCIDw&usg=AFQ jCNFaqMJTVu73BelIxKbczoXLRQ9p7w, Accessed on date : 27.10.2013.
14. Mangold, 2002, "Transgressing the Border Between Protection and Empowerment for Domestic Violence Victims and Older Children: Empowerment as Protection in the Foster Care System", Vol36\36-1\05, Available at url: http://www.nesl.edu /userfiles/file /lawreview/vol36/1/ mangold. pdf, Accessed on date : 19.10.2013.
15. Ray and Chandra, "An anthropometric study on the children of Tripura: Nutritional and health coverage and redefining WHO per centile cut-off points", Volume 3, Issue 5, May 2013 ISSN 2250-3153, Available at url: http://www.ijsrp.org/research-paper-0513/ijsrp-p1707.pdf, Accessed on date: 27.10.2013.
16. S. Jeyalakshmi et al , (2012), "Children in India 2012 –A Statistical Appraisal", Available at url : http://mospi.nic.in/mospi_new/upload/ Children_in_India_2012.pdf , Accessed on date :7.11.2013.
17. Singh A.P, Singh A.K, "Care and Protection of Girl Children In India", Bal Vikas Prakashan Pvt. Ltd., 2013.
18. Smile Foundation, "Child Rights In India", Available at url: http:// smilefoundationindia.org/child_rights.htm, Accessed on date : 19.10.2013.
19. Tom Head, Available at url:http://civilliberty.about.com/od/international-humanrights/g/Human-Rights-Definition.htm, Accessed on date : 7.11.2013.

5

Embedded Journalism: Is it Ethical?

—Manjula Srinivas

Introduction

"I shall proceed to describe, to the best of my power, what occurred under my own eyes and to state the facts which I have heard from men whose veracity is unimpeachable, reserving to myself the exercise of the right of private judgment in making public and in suppressing the details of what occurred on this memorable day."

These were the opening lines of an October 1854 article about The Charge of the Light Brigade by William Howard Russell. Although, the charge from the British army was foolish and stupid (attacking the Russian army in formation from the wrong direction), the article consistently glorified the courage of the army men. Though, this was a century and a half before the term 'embedded' was coined, yet it remains one of the most famous pieces of embedded military journalism in history.

It is imperative to talk at length about the American contribution to this phenomenon of embedded journalism. The Americans learnt a lesson during the Vietnam war. The government recognised the importance of the 'media' and their folly to ignore and underestimate its power. The media could not be allowed to become an obstacle in America's future war plans. Furthermore, the potential of the media to sell the war to the audience was also acknowledged. Thus, in the interim period between "Desert Storm" in 1991(first Iraq invasion) and "Perfect Storm" (second Iraq invasion) in 2003, began one of the most panoptic propaganda campaigns by the government to fool the media and by extension, its own people. Large scale "global conflict" was given the name of "war against terrorism". The gun was already loaded and then 9/11 provided the perfect trigger to launch the assault. The propaganda was escalated to another level, one which eventually led to the destruction of Afghanistan and then Iraq. The deception exposed gaping holes in the depth of the American media and has left doubts over its reliability and righteousness. Doubts inked by the blood of innocents and the decisions of few.

The American invasion of Iraq in 2003 owes its perfection to a concept that made its full fledged debut during this war. The concept is termed as "Embedded Journalism" which in crude terms is a convenient and often unethical alliance between the media and the military. It is convenient because the media has access to reporting war material it might not have had access to otherwise and under the protection of the army. It is unethical because it means relinquishing journalistic liberty to the military over 'where to go', 'when to go', 'what to report' and at times 'how to report'. According to Bryan Whitman, US Assist. Sec. of Defense, when American forces crossed the Iraq border, around 700 reporters were embedded with the army. The reason given was that while dealing with a master manipulator like Saddam, it was necessary to have the media on the American side. They reported under the watchful and often tutored eyes of the Ministry of Defense in London and the Pentagon in Washington.

One problem with this kind of reporting was that it gave a one dimensional view of events, which goes against the basic fundamentals of neutrality and ethics in reporting. David Ignatius, an "un-embedded" reporter during the Iraq war, mentions in one of his articles that the "un – embedded" status meant that it was too dangerous to cover modern warfare without protection. Yet, he also admits that it was possible for him to cover locations that embedded journalists could not. It was also difficult for the embedded journalists in Iraq to become critical of their sources even if they had reason to do so, as they risked losing the source and thus subsequent information. An embedded reporter describes compares his experience to that of the second dog in a sledge team. "You saw an awful lot of the dog in front of you, and a little to the left and right." In a panel discussion suggestively entitled

"The LA Times Goes to War," Marjorie Miller, the editor of The Los Angeles Times said, "The embeds were valuable as mosaic pieces. But they could only see as far as they could see and it was up to Tracy and Tyler (rewrites) to begin the process of putting some of those little pieces of the puzzle into perspective." Also, every war correspondent had an agenda which he/she fixes in order to give a comprehensive account of the action. The rules of embedding ensured that the military kept interfering with the agenda, thus affecting the news content. "Embedding" hinders location and movement. Iraq and Afghanistan were essentially guerrilla wars where the army tries to avoid the enemy main force and instead attack where his opponent is weak or has no troops at all. This means that the correspondent embedded with the American or British military units is liable to miss or misinterpret crucial stages in the conflict.

Observation

Embedded journalism highlights a basic point of conflict between the military and the news media. The solitary goal of the military is to fight and win a war. The goal of the news media on the other hand is to seek and report the truth – a mission that is at loggerheads with successful warfare today which depends on secrecy and deception to a great extent. Thus the popular axiom states, "Truth is the first casualty of war". During the Iraq invasion of 2003, the American military and government attempted to find a solution to this conflict by tilting the balance of power towards them. As Lt. Col. Rick Long of the US Marine Corps said, "Frankly, our job is to win the war. Part of that is information warfare. So we are going to attempt to dominate the information environment". The flaw on the part of the media was that they allowed this domination to happen without objections. Far from asking questions, they merely took what they have been told as a gospel and at face value. One excuse that the American media came up with afer the unveiling of this deception was that the information they reported had come from the top echelons of the government and that they had every reason to believe it. Yet, there was evidence from the other end of the spectrum which was conveniently neglected. In an interview Scott Ripper, UN arms inspector from 1991-98 stated that by 1998, all chemical, biological, nuclear and long range ballistic infrastructures in Iraq were destroyed. Yet, America went to war in 2003 with the claims of finding weapons of mass destruction that were actually nonexistent. In 2001, Colin Powell and Condoleezza Rice delivered speeches in February and July respectively. The relevant part of both speeches was the same – Iraq was no more a military threat to the world and their weapons production was under control. Both officials contradicted their statements in 2003, when they supported and justified each and every claim to go to war against Iraq. No journalist reported these glaring contradictions before the war. A number of unspeakable atrocities were committed in Iraq. A number of embedded journalists were privy to it. Yet, the media became partners of the military and government in "normalizing the unthinkable" for the public. It is a concept explained by Edward S. Herman whereby ugly, degrading, murderous, and unspeakable acts become routine and are accepted as "the way things are done." It is beyond the realms of belief to think that no mainstream American media connected the dots during the deception. As a result, what is disturbing is that they choose not to connect them.

The Department of Defense policy with regards to military operations post Desert Storm in 1991 was that the media will have "long term" yet "minimally" "restrictive" access to United States military forces through "embedding". The policy further stated that these embeds would live, travel and work with the military unites they were assigned to, in order to convenience maximum and detailed coverage of U.S. forces in the war zone. Every embedded journalist had to sign a contract which served as their loyalty evidence to a memo of rules as prescribed by the DoD. These rules made provisions for military journalists on one hand and amputated their journalistic freedom on the other. A section of these rules mentions a "blackout" phenomenon which stated that the commanding officer in charge of each unit had the right to impose a curfew on the information flow from the embedded reporter to the media agency without giving any justification. To put it in crude terms, it served as a license to put the reporters on leash whenever and wherever required. Journalists from UK, Germany, Japan, Norway, Saudi Arabia, France, Czechoslo-vakia, Canada, Israel, Russia, Australia, Canada, China, Korea, and even Al Jazeera became part of this manipulative masterstroke by the Pentagon.

CNN went one step ahead and allocated $25 million for covering the war solely from the home perspective.

There are four main issues which need to be analyzed with respect to embedded journalism namely - access, context, censorship and objectivity. Bob Franken of CNN mentioned, "If there was combat, I wasn't usually able to move out and go shoot the other side. In fact, one could argue that one of the inherent problems with the embeds is that we didn't have anybody embedded with the Iraqi side. But the fact is that we did not. Physically we couldn't cover that. So chances are there is a lot that we missed simply because we physically were unable to get to it." The mainstream US media was unanimous in reporting the battle of Fallujah in the months of November - December 2004 and the large number of American causalities as a result. The UK Independent had reported that America had used Napalm, a banned incendiary while laying siege to Fallujah, resulting in the death of more than 800 civilians. The Pentagon confirmed the claims. (*Mike Whitney. 2005*) Shockingly, not a single mainstream media house in America picked up the story and gave it the required coverage. Dahr Jamail, an umembedded reporter reports in his article how rules of engagement were modified to the brink of extinction during the invasion. Blowing up a woman carrying a bag of groceries, making civilian victims look like insurgents, using Iraqi kids as human shields, firing at anything that moved in the dark during curfew, emptying magazines at a town crowd, harassing prisoners are some of the horrific practices recounted by marines who were part of the inhumanity. Not one of these atrocities was reported by the mainstream US media, most of whom were part of the embedded team.

A common comment was that "embed" really meant "in bed," and that the program was a truly ingenious method of the Pentagon subtly imposing censorship on the media. The argument goes that the very act of being physically embedded within a military unit—sharing all their hardships, problems and dangers—would effectively eliminate journalistic objectivity, and provide de facto censorship on the news coming out from the battlefield. Also self censorship comes into the picture while reporting in a war zone because it exposes the public to the brutality and ruthlessness of war and also because the families of soldiers have a right to learn of their loved one's death in a respectful, tactful and formal manner. This layer of self censorship is notwithstanding, government and military pressures of embedded journalism further restrict the world of a journalist. This combination serves not just as a threat to objectivity but often contributes to fabrication of reality. Judith Miller, a reporter from the New York Times in one of her many fabricated stories clearly stood by the claim that Saddam's irreversible desire of building up an arsenal of nuclear, chemical and biological weapons had brought America on the brink of war with Iraq. According to a quote in Miller's report, Iraq was still storing some 12,500 gallons of anthrax, 2,500 gallons of gas gangrene, and 1,250 gallons of aflotoxin and 2,000 gallons of botulinum throughout the country. Condoleezza Rice, Colin Powell and Donald Rumsfeld all used Miller's stories as part of their justifications for going to war with Iraq. One of her most reliable sources was an Iraqi exile named 'Ahmed Chalabi'. Chalabi's statements were later proven to be baseless as no weapons of mass destruction were recovered from the carnage in Iraq despite further fabrications by Miller which included the capture of an Iraqi scientist who had supposedly worked first hand with the WMD. To cap it all, Chalabi was made one of the presidents of the Iraqi interim governing council after the war before he became the deputy prime minister and oil minister in due course. A Stanford research journal presented a comparative study of embedded and umembedded reports in print and broadcast media during the 2003 invasion. The crux of the findings suggested that embedded reporters had access to much better sources for quotes or verification of information than their umembedded counterparts. Quotes from unit commanders, lieutenants' from the embedded side was complemented by quotes from ex-Pentagon authorities, media professors etc. from the umembedded side. However, this access came at a cost of limited scope. The embedded reports were extremely one dimensional in nature. Although detailed in the subject matter of the report, it provided no holistic view of the war.

Due to ethnic competitions and differences between the Tutsi and Hutu communities, there was a mass killing of more than 800,000 people in less than 100 days in the east African nation of Rwanda. Shockingly, this genocide failed to qualify as a media mega event to warrant maximum coverage by media across the world. The negligible media coverage was unquestionably marginalised, non - contextualised and misrepresented. Western media reporters were exclusively airlifted from the country where thousands begged for a way of freedom. The desensitisation by the media ensured that the horrific images did not move the world in a way that it should have. Almost a year before the genocide in Rwanda began; an interesting article appeared in the New York Times asking the question: "Does the world still recognize a holocaust?". An old newsroom adage says, "One dead fireman is worth 500 Africans". The media coverage of the genocide or the lack of it proves that the standoff is far greater as the details of several hundred thousand Africans failed to make a sizeable impact on the agenda lists of the world media. The question arises again: Who sets the agenda of these media houses? Would genocide of even half the magnitude in some European country generate the same interest?

Due to a multitude of excuses, the embedded media were extremely slow to reveal the Abu Ghraib prison scandal that ultimately became cause for international embarrassment for the U.S. and darkened the shadow over the Iraq war. Prisoners being subjected to sexual humiliation, snarling dogs by American soldiers were just the pinnacle some of the myriad ways in which Arabs were tortured. Yet, the media remained passive despite indications. In November, the Associated Press was among the first to raise alarms about abuse at Abu Ghraib – but few of the AP's clients showcased the story, if they ran it at all. On January 16 2004, the U.S. issued a one-paragraph press release which stated that an investigation has been initiated into reported incidents of detainee abuse at a Coalition Forces facility. This press release did not initiate a media storm with respect to further probing and questioning as it should have. The New York Times and the Philadelphia Inquirer had page seven stories which merely mentioned the government report in inverted pyramid style. Television largely ignored the announcement. CNN and Fox News Channel mentioned it briefly on January 16, NBC had a 41-word item the following morning, and that was about it. After more than three months, Abu Ghraib finally came into the elusive media limelight after CBS's 60 minute expose on the 28th of April as they aired pictured of U.S. military police posing and grinning next to naked, hooded Iraqi prisoners. What was the reason for such a delay? In the words of

Philip Taubman, the New York Times' Washington bureau chief, "Journalists were not aggressive enough and were slow to grasp the significance of the military's announcement. It was a failure of newsgathering." The strange part here is that the media which was so proactive in reporting, justifying and often glorifying every move of the American army in Iraq was so ignorant in picking up on a press release which obviously demanded introspection. Perhaps it was yet another side effect of being embedded with the perpetrators of torture.

Conclusion

Ron Harris, an embedded reporter of the St. Louis Post – Dispatch launched a smear campaign against Sergeant Jimmy Massey who publicly admitted to have killed innocent civilians in Iraq. Massey said on one of his articles, "We were like a bunch of cowboys who rode into town shooting up the place. I saw charred bodies in vehicles that were clearly not military vehicles. I saw people dead on the side of the road in civilian clothes." Harris launched a front page attack on Massey, questioning his motives and the veracity of his story with respect to civilian casualties. Massey however had three eyewitnesses to back up his accounts. The controversy questions Harris's trustworthiness as a reporter and the integrity of embedded journalists as a whole. Harris used metaphors like blasphemy to describe the war which according to him ended with Iraqis celebrating their independence from the Saddam government. The reality was starkly different. The Ron Harris case study is perhaps one of the worst examples of embedded journalism and its manipulative and deceptive effects.

In the Indian scenario, Kashmir has been the hub as far as embedded journalism is concerned. It is only state where media emergencies are frequently imposed and reporters from New Delhi belonging to different media houses accompany the government to help in framing a report. India has always been portrayed as the saint and Pakistan the evil as far the Kashmir saga goes. Few media houses have ever reported the failure of the Indian government to carry out a plebiscite in the region as decided during the ceasefire in 1948. Human rights violations in Kashmir have been on the rise consistently and yet the media agenda never shifts from the Pakistan atrocities in the state.

The phenomenon underlines a very important concept true to all conflict zone reporters. It is extremely difficult to remain objective to one's ethics as a reporter when one of the sides involved is the reporter's homeland. In addition to this, the various restrictions of embedded journalism to ensure the death of press freedom or what little of it existed.

A "glass half full" way of looking at the phenomenon of looking at embedded journalism is that it is a result of primitive human instinct. As humans, mutual benefit often becomes the order of the day and the process of embedding does provide a seemingly agreeable solution to the media and the military in what is an undeniably complicated situation. However, the third party on this whole transaction i.e. the public suffers in every way as a result. If the upper echelons of the government, military and the media team up to paint a picture for the public, even the most discerning critic or artist would perhaps will not be able to differentiate between the real and the fake. The fact remains that in a post-September 11th world, the media and military have reached an unprecedented level of cooperation through the use of embedded reporters, calling into question the separation and exclusivity of the government and press which lies at the heart of the principles of journalism.

Works Cited

- Michael R Gordon & Judith Miller. 2002. *THREATS AND RESPONSES: THE IRAQIS; U.S. SAYS HUSSEIN INTENSIFIES QUEST FOR A-BOMB PARTS.* [ONLINE] Available at: http://www.nytimes.com/2002/09/08/world/threats-responses-iraqis-us-says-hussein-intensifies-quest-for-bomb-parts.html? src=pm.
- David E Sanger with John F. Burns. 2003. *THREATS AND RESPONSES: THE WHITE HOUSE; BUSH ORDERS START OF WAR ON IRAQ; MISSILES APPARENTLY MISS HUSSEIN.* [ONLINE] Available at: http://www.nytimes.com/2003/03/20/world/threats-responses-white-house-bush-orders-start-war-iraq-missiles-apparently.html? scp=17&sq=&st=nyt&pagewanted=1.
- Transcript. 2003. *Full text of Colin Powell's speech.* [ONLINE] Available at: http://www.guardian.co.uk/world/2003/feb/05/iraq.usa.
- Washington Post online. 2003. *'All Nations of Goodwill Should Step Forward'.* [ONLINE] Available at: http://pqasb.pqarchiver. com/washingtonpost/access/410627931.html?FMT=ABS& FMTS=ABS:FT

&date=Sep+24%2C+20 03&author=&pub=The+ Washington+Post& edition=&startpage=A.25&desc=%2 7All+Nations+of+Goodwill+Should+Step+Forward%27.

- George P. Shultz. 2002. *Act now; the danger is immediate. Saddam Hussein must be removed...*[ONLINE] Available at: http://pqasb. pqarchiver.com/ washingtonpost/access/161940031. html? FMT=ABS&FMTS=ABS: FT&date=Sep+6%2C+2002& author=George+P.+Shultz&pub= The+Washington+Post&e dition=&startpage=A.25&desc=Act+Now% 3B+The+danger+is+imm ediate.+Saddam+Hussein+must+be+removed.
- Colum Lynch. 2003. *Powell Asks Countries for More Money, Troops in Iraq*. [ONLINE] Available at: http://pqasb.pqarchiver. com/washingtonpost/ access/387182721.html?FMT=ABS& FMTS=ABS:FT&date=Aug+22% 2C+ 2003&author=Colum+ Lynch&pub=The+Wa shington+ Post&edition= &startpage= A.14&desc=P owell+Asks+ Countries+for+More+Money% 2C+Troops+in+Iraq.
- Patrick Cockburn. 2010. *Embedded journalism: A distorted view of war*. [ONLINE] Available at: http://www.independent.co. uk/news/media/ opinion/embedded-journalism-a-distorted-view-of-war-2141072.html.
- David Ignatius. 2010. *The dangers of embedded journalism, in war and politics*. [ONLINE] Available at: http://www.washington-post.com/wp-dyn/ content/article/2010/04/30/AR2010043001100.html.
- Interview with Dahr Jamail. 2004. *Red Cross Estimates 800 Iraqi Civilians Killed in Fallujah*. [ONLINE] Available at: http://www.democracynow.org/ 2004/11/17/red_cross_estimates_ 800_iraqi_civilians.
- Mike Whitney. 2005. *Incinerating Iraqis; the napalm cover up*. [ONLINE] Available at: http://www.informationclearing house.info/article9307.htm.
- Dahr Jamail. 2010. *Iraq War Vet: "We Were Told to Just Shoot People, and the Officers Would Take Care of Us"*. [ONLINE] Available at: http:// dahrjamail.net/iraq-war-vet-we-were-told-to-just-shoot-people-and-the-officers-would-take-care-of-us#more-1763.
- Dahr Jamail. 2010. *The New 'Forgotten' War*. [ONLINE] Available at: http:/ /dahrjamail.net/the-new-%E2%80%98 forgotten-war#more-1753.
- Des Freedman, edited by Daya Kishan Thussu, 2003. *War and the Media - Reporting conflict 24/7*. 1st ed. London: Sage Publications Ltd.
- Media Lens. 2003. *Media Lens Alert: Vindication - A Statue Falls*. [ONLINE] Available at: http://www.medialens.org/alerts/03/030411_Vindication.html.
- James C. Moore. 2004. *Not fit to print*. [ONLINE] Available at: http:// dir.salon.com/news/feature/2004/05/27/times.

6

Human Rights: Challenges for Security Forces in Sub Conventional Operations

—*Sanjay Ahuja*

In recent years there has been a decline in classical armed conflicts between States and it has been noticed that the very threat of conventional conflicts has significantly diminished. At the same time, there has been a dramatic increase in the number of armed conflicts within the States, where there are no defined boundaries, no clearly recognizable enemy, and no accepted means of fighting. It is important to acknowledge that such conflicts are not simply the consequence of the threat or use of force. Their causes are complex and contributing factors include poverty, illiteracy, unemployment, discrimination, ethnic tension, religious intolerance, exploitation and the progressive depletion of natural resources. As each of these factors is also associated with human rights issues, it is only logical to conclude that violations of human rights are as much a cause as they are a consequence of these sub unconventional armed conflict.

Moreover, today's battles are no longer fought by soldiers alone. Irregular armed groups, isolated individuals and members of police and security forces also take part in the battle. An important outcome of the involvement of these forces for the common task is the blurring of previously absolute task distinctions between police and security forces on the one hand, and armed forces on the other, with one readily taking on the apparent responsibilities of the other. Thus we see examples of police and security forces involved in the conduct of hostilities, as well as of armed forces involved in the maintenance of public order and law enforcement. As for the battlefield, it is increasingly shifting to urban areas; and civilian populations are no longer spared. The enemy happens to be citizen of the state and has equal right to be protected by the state, as much as the state expects security forces to safeguard him. The issue of human rights concerns therefore, becomes more relevant and complex.

Armed Forces Status during Law Enforcement

The term "police, security forces and armed forces" often gives rise to confusion when employed in law enforcement duties collectively. The type of forces which are involved is not very significant and at times is irrelevant in such scenario. What is important to know is that the role they play in conflict situations may not be visible but it obviously exists. This can be broadly termed as law enforcement functions which typically involve in some form of maintenance of public order and security, detection and prevention of crime and provision of help and assistance to those in need of it.

In order to perform the law enforcement functions, forces in question have been empowered with authority to arrest, detain, search and seize and use of force and firearms. If members of armed forces engage in the maintenance of public order, they are performing a law enforcement function. Consequently, they must themselves observe the existing domestic legal framework, as well as relevant and applicable international obligations. From the standpoint of their legal obligations alone, it is not really of any substance that they are members of armed forces.

The UN Code of Conduct for Law Enforcement Officials also confirms the above mentioned view. According to the Code, the term "law enforcement officials include all officers of the law, whether appointed or elected, who exercises police powers, especially the powers of arrest or detention". The Code further provides that "in countries where police powers are exercised by military authorities, whether in uniform or civilian, or by the security forces of the State, the definition of law enforcement officials will be understood to include the agents of these services". It follows that civilian police services, armed forces and/or State security services may be entrusted with law enforcement responsibilities and resort to the use of law enforcement powers.

Sub Conventional Operations: Indian Context

Indian Army "Doctrine for Sub Conventional Operations" defines it as, "Sub conventional operation is a generic term encompassing all armed conflicts which are above the level of peaceful co-existence amongst States and below the threshold of war. It includes all actions taken by the nation to counter the asymmetric threats posed by irregular forces, terrorists, insurgents and such other non State actors, irrespective of their national identity, which may be supported or unsupported by external forces". Thus the tasks performed by the Indian armed forces in pursuance of assisting the State in preservation of law and order fall within the scope of Sub Conventional Operations. These operations are undertaken against the invisible/undefined enemy, within our own population, usually within own or friendly territory with enemy having no such territorial restrictions, with full respect for the law of the land and without full application of principles of war; but still operations falling within the purview of military action.

Violence and insurgency movements confronted India almost immediately after its independence in 1947 and the partition of British India into Pakistan with later as a homeland for the Muslims of the subcontinent. India's experience in sub conventional operations extends to North-Eastern States since 1956, Naxal movement since 1967 (now considered to be the gravest internal security threats to the country), Punjab State from 1981-1992, Sri Lanka from 1987-1990 and J & K since 1947 against Pakistan irregulars supported by the regular Army, which has acquired a distinct Islamist flavor of a proxy war. The legacy of fault lines drawn during the British era continued to have its negative effects in northeastern parts of the country.

Except Sri Lanka, Indian security forces were mostly expected to operate within own population and thus these operations were only to be directed against those who threatened the lives and properties of the people of India. These ensuing ethno-religious violence resulted into loss of many lives and property from all the communities and sowed the seeds of future conflict. However, the dimension of threats gradually and steadily became more complex for the State.

Few of these characteristics of sub conventional situation which are peculiar and more relevant to the Indian security forces are listed below:-

(a) Initial popular support is in favor of perpetrators of violence and induction of security forces is considered as occupational force. As operations are conducted amidst own population, the need is of an approach characterized by "minimum use of force".

(b) As causes resulting into unrest could range from social, economic, political, influence of neighbouring countries, thus need is for application of full National Powers rather than application of security forces alone in law enforcement tasks. Therefore, security forces are not the only respondent. The success of sub conventional operation lies in collective and well focused response from state administrative/executive and Judiciary.

(c) There is existing decentralised system of governance. State is responsible for law and order with generally weak police force at their disposal and employment of major responders (Armed forces, PMF) which are governed through federal system (Central government).

(d) Alignment of state boundaries is based on administrative conveniences, thus ethnic problem in one state directly affects the population of neighboring states, resulting into the need for coordinated and collective response from all states. Obviously lack of coordination between two States and Central/ State agencies and parochial political interests by few to garner popular support, at times take the form of direct or indirect support to the perpetrators of crimes.

(e) Invariably operations are conducted in full media glare. Thus operations are susceptible to wide positive as well as negative debate on real time basis, thereby affecting the psyche of the operational commanders at various levels.

India claims to be the frontrunner for respect for national and international laws on War and Human Rights. UNHRC as well as Human Rights organisations in India have been critical about Armed

Forces Special Power Acts and employment of security forces in various sub conventional operations within the country.

The Human Rights

It would be pertinent to dwell on Human Rights which the forces involved in law enforcement and sub conventional operations has to collectively respect, because as brought out earlier "any violations of human rights are as much a cause as they are a consequence of armed conflict".

The United Nations describes: Human Rights could be generally defined as those rights which are inherent in our nature and without which we cannot live as human beings. Thus, Human Rights are Universal and apply to all persons without discrimination. Respect for individual rights needs to be upheld at all times, irrespective of circumstances or political systems. Human rights are therefore called 'fundamental rights' or 'basic rights' or 'natural rights'. *As fundamental or basic rights, these are those rights which must not be taken away normally by any act of legislature or Government and which often are set out in the fundamental law of the land i.e. the Constitution.*

In addition to the above interpretation of the human rights, most relevant Article of Universal Declaration of Human Rights are mentioned below:-

Article 1 & 2. All Human beings are born free and equal in dignity and rights. They are endowed with reason and conscience and should act towards one another in a spirit of brotherhood. Everyone is entitled to all the rights and freedoms set forth in this declaration, without distinction of any kind, such as race, colour, sex, language, religion, political or other opinion, national or social origin, property, birth or other status.

Article 3, 5 & 6. Everyone has the right to life, liberty and security of person. No one shall be subjected to torture or to cruel, inhuman or degrading treatment or punishment. Everyone has the right to recognition, everywhere as a person before the law.

Article 7, 9 & 10. All are equal before the law and are entitled without any discrimination to equal protection of the law. All are entitled to equal protection against any discrimination in violation of this declaration and against any incitement to such discrimination. No one shall be subjected to arbitrary arrest, detention or exile. Every one is entitled in full equality to a fair and public hearing by an independent and impartial tribunal, in the determination of his rights and obligations and of any criminal charge against him.

Article 11 to 14. Everyone charged with a penal offence has the right to be presumed innocent until proved guilty according to law in a public trial at which he has all the guarantees necessary for his defense. No one shall be subjected to arbitrary interference with his privacy, family, home or correspondence, or to attack upon his honor and reputation. Everyone has the right to the protection of the law against such interference or attacks. Everyone has the right to freedom of movement and residence within the borders of each state.

Article 19, 20 & 22 Everyone has the right of freedom of opinion and expression; this right includes freedom to hold opinions without interference and to seek, receive and impart information and ideas through any media and regardless of frontiers. Everyone has the right to freedom of peaceful assembly and association. Everyone, as a member of society, has the right to social security and is entitled to realisation, through national effort and international co-operation and in accordance with the organisation and resources of each state, of the economic, social and cultural rights indispensable for his dignity and the free development of his personality.

Article 30. Nothing in this declaration may be interpreted as implying for any state, group or person, any right to engage in any activity or to perform any act aimed at the destruction of any of the rights and freedoms set forth herein.

Human Rights in India. India is a party to the Universal Declaration of Human Rights, proclaimed by the United Nations General Assembly. As such India is honour bound to comply with it and further the noble cause adopted therein. In India, the essential Human Rights have been embodied in the constitution, especially Article 3, 12, 14 19, 20, 21 & 22 without which all rights dwindle into insignificance. The important Fundamental Rights are, Right to life, Liberty, Security[1] . Equality before law and equal protection of law, No discrimination against any citizen on ground of religion, race, casts, sex, place of birth or any of them, Rights to assemble peacefully and without arms, Right to form associations or unions, right to move freely throughout the country, Protection of life and personal liberty and Protection against arrest and detention. Three things stand out. One, these fundamental rights are similar if not same in intent if not words as human rights promoted by UN. Secondly, all laws are not equally applicable in light of sub convention operations; some get more value than others. Thirdly, there may be difficult situation to adhere to all such human rights in the same manner if the situation where security forces are operating, does not permit it.

These above mentioned articles no doubt have been very thoughtfully drafted and enacted but as far as violations of Human Rights are concerned, it will strike to anyone's mind that by laying down constitutions and law and orders by the countries, certain basic fundamental rights are taken away or violated in pursuance of achieving national interest of the state. Thus, Human Rights violations get initiated at this stage itself. Therefore, there is also a case to review/debate these issues as far as human rights violations are concerned.

Justice J. Bhagwati speaking about the importance of Human Rights and fundamental rights, observed that *"The fundamental rights represent the basic values cherished by the people of this country since the Vedic times and they are calculated to protect the dignity of the individual and create conditions in which every human being can develop his personality to the fullest extent."*[2] In addition, there is also a case to review the violations carried out by the various militant organisations in the pursuit of whatever their goals may be, which violates the human rights of the normal citizens of that state or country. It also shows that no agency has yet been created/cannot be created to check on these violations and this has been just left as a food for thought. But, this case, by no imagination gives right or justification to security forces to fail human right demands.

Operational Environment and Challenges

To understand the Human Rights issue in the correct perspective in relation to armed forces, it is essential to study the operational environment and challenges as obtained in the trouble torn areas of our country where armed forces were/are employed for sub conventional tasks. It can be seen that often the armed forces are brought into these states as a last resort when the normal civil administration has completely collapsed. This was the case in the North Eastern States of Nagaland, Mizoram, Assam as also in Kashmir where the country had seen a total collapse of all state machineries. Certain clear characteristics of the operational environment and challenges involved in generic terms in these states are as follows: -

(a) **Public**. The armed forces invariably get into action when things have gone out of hand for the state administration and police/ para military forces to handle thereby making the initial sub conventional operations tough, harsh for the population and generate anti Armed Force sentiments. At a later stage, even if the rapport has been established, there is a sense of insecurity among the general public. They are reluctant to willingly cooperate with forces engaged in combating the situation. Hence, chances of false accusation of human right violation increase.

(b) **Militants**. There exists an overpowering cult of gun and defiance of authority. Sophisticated weapons and equipments are acquired from powers inimical to the State. The process of peaceful negotiations is shunned, unless there is outright acceptance of their demands. Human right violation accusation is used as weapon by them.

(c) **Administration**. The administration comes under tremendous pressure because of constant threat of retribution. The general prevailing conditions amount to the civil administration being ineffective and the authority of government gets eroded and they fail to induce any confidence amongst people.

(d) **Police/Para Military Forces**. It is the endeavor of militants to induce fear in them through intimidation which has adverse affect on morale of these forces. This leads to fall in their credibility and added sense of insecurity amongst populace. An example of this is the state of police in Jammu and Kashmir from 1990 to 1996 and that of in Punjab from 1983 to 1986, where the police were made irrelevant with respect to law and order situation, resulting in loss of credibility amidst local population. This led to believe that the insurgents can take on the might of the State administration and they are benefiting the local population by projecting demands of local population.

(e) **Media**. The official media and some national dailies are painted and viewed as the mouthpiece of the government and its credibility amongst masses is low. Inexperienced reporters employed for reporting related events lead to sensationalizing of events, which erode the image of administration and the security forces. Likewise local media comes under influence of anti-national organisations for various reasons and favors anti national news over unbiased reporting.

(f) **Hostile Neighbours**. They exploit the unstable situation to the full extent and resort to waging a proxy war. Insurgents tend to establish a nexus with identical anti-government forces and religious fundamental.

(g) **Political Directive & State Agencies** It has been seen in the past that the armed forces have been brought in to contain insurgency without clear political directive from the local government. Lacking a clear-cut political directive, the various state organisations work in cross-purposes. In addition, interference by the local politicians for short-term gains also adversely affects the operations on ground.

(h) **Intelligence Void**. Actionable/timely intelligence is the vital necessity for the success of any operation, which is woefully lacking in almost all cases. The local population seldom comes forward to give hard intelligence, as they are afraid of reprisals by the insurgents. The civil intelligence set-up is either defunct or non-forthcoming with any assistance. The consequence of this 'intelligence void' is that operations led by the armed forces are based on scanty and at times incorrect intelligence which has the counterproductive effect of further alienating the local populace and greater chance of human right violations.

(j) **Invisible Enemy.** During sub conventional operations, real enemy generally remains invisible and hard to identify. Those who are visible, are part of the society and do not have trail of evidence behind them to be sustainable in the court of law. Any military action against such individuals can easily be brought under the ambit of human rights violations.

Sub conventional operations tend to be long drawn thus resulting in armed forces getting involved over protracted periods. This leads to longer exposure of armed forces with the population and consequent growing grievances, which is exploited by the anti national elements. More so the resources required are out of proportion. In addition, where the inimical neighbor provides active support to the militants, a great deal of effort is also required to check infiltration across national boundaries. As the operations continue over protracted period, the fatigue and frustration sets in leading to some avoidable mistakes.

Armed forces are primarily trained and equipped to fight against external aggression. They are trained to concentrate maximum firepower at a point of decision to effect victory. However, during sub conventional operations, this basic principle of war is compromised to avoid collateral damage to public property and innocent civilians. Thus, there is likelihood of armed forces suffering higher casualties than they would otherwise avoid. The caution exercised by the members of the armed forces in ensuring that there is no loss of innocent civilian life and damage to public property and places of worship etc. directly tells on the efficiency of the force and prolongs the duration of operations which also has a negative effect on the troops. These are operations conducted mostly by small team, and it may not be possible that all operations are led by officers or an officer is present where things are going wrong in light of human rights.

When Allegations/Human Rights Violations Cannot Be Avoided

It would be worthwhile to analyze some of the instances where allegations /Human Rights violations cannot be avoided due to the reasons discussed above and the inherent nature of operations. These are appended below:-

(a) As per the Human Rights convention, All Human beings are born free and equal in dignity and rights; No one shall be subjected to arbitrary arrest, detention or exile; Forces cannot arrest / apprehend any person unless ordered by a Magistrate or is acting under Armed Forces (Special Powers) Act. Now, during cordon and search operations for suspected terrorists/ insurgents or while dealing with mob indulging in looting, arson, and destruction of Government property etc., few people have to be detained for questioning, obtaining further lead for the operations or as a witness. This action of the Armed Forces can be misinterpreted as illegal Arrest of innocent persons, and may be treated as violation of Human Rights[3].

(b) Human Rights provide everyone the right to life, liberty and security of person. However, in a situation like cross fire between Armed Forces and terrorist/insurgents, maintenance of law and order especially while involved in crowd control, situation may lead to loss of life of innocent person. Under these circumstances it may be ill perceived as causing death/ injury due to negligence or inhuman and degrading behavior.

(c) Human Rights give everyone a right to freedom of movement and residence within the borders of each state. In order to impose population control measures during curfew, cordon and search operation or any other search operations against suspect and terrorists, limited or temporary restriction become necessary from overall security point of view. This operational compulsion can also be misinterpreted as interference with right to work and earn a living, harassment, inhuman treatment or illegal detention.

(d) Under operational constriction, Armed forces at times have to break open the houses for search, impose censorship/ monitoring against the suspects or stop anybody during the patrolling for questioning. Under these circumstances, Armed Forces are susceptible to allegations of Human Rights violation under the conventions which says 'No one shall be subjected to arbitrary interference with his privacy, family, home or correspondence, or to attack upon his honor and reputation' and thus they may be accused of breaking into a house without a legal authority, violation of human dignity, illegal / unauthorized censorship or illegal / unauthorised search.

(e) There may be an occasion wherein Armed Forces have to get exposed to religious issues especially while flushing out terrorist / insurgents from a religious place, while trying to apprehend a terrorist / insurgents attending a religious function or if these elements are trying to melt away in crowd and while controlling communal flare ups between two or more religious communities. During such tasks, Armed Forces may be accused of Interference in social / religious customs, discrimination against a particular community, Desecration of a religious place thereby violating Right to freedom of thoughts, conscience and religion.

Recommendations

The debate can continue whether certain Human Rights violations committed by the Armed Forces be neglected or be left to the Commander on spot to decide as to whether it was a violation or necessity of his duty or it be called Human Rights violation and the individual be punished. However, notwithstanding the arguments in favour or against the human rights violations by armed forces, the clear message is Sub Conventional Operations are largely undertaken amidst own population and thus human rights has to be upheld under all circumstances. In view of the foregoing, following recommendations are made to further improve the human rights record and be the "armed forces of the nation-for the nation":-

(a) More extensive and specialised training for the Armed Forces personnel on Human Rights aspects and how to protect them (as also how not to violate Human Rights).

(b) Human Rights Cell (HRC) created at Army Headquarters has been a good establishment and should continue to perform its charter of duties to keep a check on Human Rights violations as also keep check on adverse publicity.

(c) The outside world, media, various Human Rights watch dogs like Asia Watch, Amnesty International, Human Rights Commissions should understand the constraints under which a soldier operates in an environment and then report or take actions accordingly, instead of acting in haste. For this, armed forces need to enhance their interaction with these organisations and improve their and own awareness.

(d) We should accept that certain violations to Human Rights as given below would continue to take place despite training given to the Armed Forces personnel:-

(i) Perceived illegal arrest while operating under Armed Forces Special Power Act (however they would be released/handed over to police within 24 hours).

(ii) Arrest of innocent persons, but only till operational requirements are met and safety and other human rights of the detainee is respected.

(iii) Causing death/injury due to uncertain environment (during cross fire between Armed Forces and Militants especially in crowded area).

(e) Interaction with media should be increased and an awareness campaign should be launched along with media personnel to sensitize them about the environmental realities under which armed forces are operating.

Conclusion. There can not be any justification for the violation of human rights but, the extra ordinary situations need to be well understood and appreciated by all stakeholders. There are no easy answers. For a country like ours, protection of human rights is an inescapable responsibility of security forces in order to keep the dignity of largest democracy as also to maintain sanctity of professional character of the armed forces. So far, except for few avoidable accidents there have been mostly unavoidable human right violations, and the security forces have been quick to learn its lessons. Upholding the human rights of its citizens is an ultimate responsibility of the State and thus all actions taken during the sub conventional operations should be in good faith and capable of delivering the sense of security, safety and dignity to fellow countrymen. To a great sense, intent of actions needs to be right and just.

Notes

1. Armed Forces (Special Powers) Act, 1958 for North East.
2. Armed Forces (J&K) Special Powers Act, 1990.
3. Asima Sahu, *Human Rights Violations and the Law Chapter 4* "Human Right and Law in India", Pointer Publishers, Jaipur, *India, Page 91.*
4. Armed Forces (Special Powers) (Punjab & Chandigarh) Act, 1983.
5. BP Singh Sehgal (Ed.) *Human Rights in India: Problems and Perspectives Section Sub Section II* "Arrest: Meaning and Necessity", Deep & Deep Publications, New Delhi, India, Page 250 .
6. Maneka Gandhi versus Union of India*: AIR.1978.5C.597.*
7. UNO *"Human Rights: Status of International Instruments" United Nations,* New York, 1987.

7

Cultural Diversity Pluralism and Human Rights

—Ritu Sharma

Introduction

Human rights are inherent to all human beings, whatever our nationality, place of residence, sex, national or ethnic origin, colour, religion, language, or any other status may be. We are all equally entitled to our human rights without discrimination. These rights are all interrelated, interdependent and indivisible. The uniformity of human nature; that is, all human beings, however much they are divided by time and space, share a common nature consisting of certain unique capacities, dispositions and desires. No culture is inherently superior or inferior, culture means the aggregate of social religious or behavioural norms, independently of political forces, developed by a community for survival as well as for prosperity at a time or place. Culture promotes cultures. Cultural diversity identifies and singles out a society cultural diversity and pluralism in a way represents the developed intelligence of a society. These both are abstraction of society identity and can be perceived as an integrated whole. A nation without culture evolution and pluralist society is like a boat in the ocean that may take some time before it sinks, these two give stability to a nation. The plurality of socio cultural groups is regarded as desirable and the identity of socio cultural groups are protected. In India, special treatment is given to them, which is constitutional.

Human rights are regarded as the most desirable virtue of a civilised society. Liberalism which developed during the period of

European colonial expansion, in that era great thinkers such as John Locke and J. S. Mill always supported the fact that every single society and culture are free to follow their own methods and way of belief and living. As liberalism gained intellectual and political ascendancy, it gave the state its modern character. It emphasized and institutionalised such idea like rule of law, equality of citizens, etc. We can see that Human beings are culturally embedded and a culture not only gives a distinct tone and structure to shared human capacities but also develop new ones of its own. Since cultures mediate and reconstitute human nature in their own different ways, no vision of the good life can be based on an abstract conception of human nature alone. Moral life is necessarily embedded in and cannot be isolated from the wider culture. A way of life cannot therefore be judged good or bad without taking full account of the system of meaning, tradition, temperament and the moral and emotional resources of the people involved.

Universalism and Cultural Relativism

Human rights as fundamental norms of freedom justice and peace, are no longer just a lawyers preserve. However the very nature of human rights is not free from controversy and debate, typically between the two opposing views : that which regards human rights as a single universal concept as opposed to that which supports cultural relativism. The latter recognizes that the world has a rich variety of people, cultures, traditions and religions, and that traditional culture values have a huge impact on a nations political, social and economic attitudes and aspirations.

From the very inception of the Universal Declaration of Human Rights, the international human rights discourse has revolved around one important issue : Can the declarations value be truly universal? In the cold war era, the debate was predominantly between the communist world, which championed economic and social rights, and the western democracies, which concentrated more on civil and political rights. That debate collapsed with the demise of Soviet Union, but some of its themes survive still in a different form. Now debate takes place primarily in an economic context between developed and less developed countries.

Today many scholars see human rights as a universal phenomenon, and they regard them as the means to a greater social end: they are, they believe, fundamental and common to all societies. They also believe that Human rights are part of the inherent dignity of every human being: they belong to all in equal measure because all are human, be they male or female, young or old, rich or poor, atheist or believer. Universalists thus base their understanding of human rights on the liberal tradition that right accord to the individual, a set of minimum standards by virtue of his or her being human – a universal concept in that they reach out to every person alive.

For cultural relativists, however, human rights represent values that attach to communities : it is the latter and not the individual that is their intended beneficiary, Relativists hold that because values are culturally oriented. They further contest the universality of human rights on the ground that such rights are 'western derived' and are designed to serve western interests. Those in the west who promote personal and political freedoms elsewhere in the world often claim merely to be bringing the admirable and traditional values of the west to continents and countries deprived of them. professor **Ruhard Falk** remarks that from the early days of the human rights movement, thinking in some leading western states even favoured the application of external pressure on other states to apply human rights standard. Admittedly, at the time of establishment of the united nations in 1945, the power alliances of the west were dominant, and a majority of countries were voiceless and powerless under colonial rule. Today the relativists argue that the imperial authority of the past may have declined, but the west can still exert its dominance by disguising its ulterior moves some questionably legal – while promising the fruits of human rights, e.g. democracy.

Human rights may be regarded as an absolute universal tool of measurement, but they result from a fusion of historical antecedents where "**universality**" and "**specificity**" co-existed without mutual exclusivity. We may describe human rights as universal, but in no way can they ignore cultural, social, gender and other considerations. The very quality of human rights lies in their flexibility in the sense that there is no country of society where their norms cannot apply and there is no subject or social issue that cannot be integrated into them.

Thus human rights are capable of breaking down cultural barriers and of becoming fully accepted as global norms while at the same time showing respect for different political, social and cultural values. In an age of globalisation, technological advancement and rapid information flow, cultural differences will tend gradually to lose their significance. Human rights can emerge as a replacement culture that is vital to the struggle for social justice and for the furtherance of human dignity. The world is changing on daily basis and will continue to be changing : there are more important issues to be solved than mere cultural differences.

Identity of Social Cultural Value

Culture are normal subject of sociology and of anthropology. It is a basic fact of human evolution that society came first and polity came next. One can imagine that societies get broken as migration of its members to other lands for better pastures and prospects enlarges them or when overtaken by natural calamities. Each breakaway part of society in time and space develops its own social and cultural identity. Irrespective of present day technological innovations, all the societies of the past have had same common problems, viz., finding food, shelter, instruments of defence against wild creatures or hostile men or societies, ideas about unseen and unpredictable supra-natural disturbing forces, means of travel or language for communication. In this process, religion represented how people interpreted natural forces and developed their social way of life and culture the distinctive pattern of societies distanced from each other. Culture and religion ultimately represent the behavior pattern between the members of a society, leading to an identity different from that of others. Then there have been patterns of social behavior, which evolved, differently in different social groups. Culture is a way of life of a group of peoples, consisting of learned patterns of behavior and thoughts passed on from generation to another and the next. The notion includes the group's belief, values, language, political organisation and economic activity as well as its equipment, techniques and art forms referred to as material culture. Culture is a term adopted by modern intelligentsia to accept that it is an abstraction of social identity, and the culture is to be perceived as an integrated whole, composed of the technology for dealing with necessities of life and survival, economic organisation, social relationships, political or group unity form, spiritual or cosmic or unknown forces feared by the community, political power adjustment methodology, the arts, music and dances, folk life, and lastly but not the least, the language and the literature. In Asia or East, the oriental cultures of India, China, Mongolia, Japan, Tibet or Nepal have much in common, yet these are distinguishable from each other because of their different cultural evolution. On European mainland, the English, French, Spanish, German, Czech, Polish, Italian, Serbian or Greek are different for their cultural variations. In the middle East, the Turks, Arabs, Persians, Baluchi, Pathan, Uzbek or Kazakh are different culture forms. On African land, the Khoisan, Bantu, Berger, Bedouin or Kabyle cultures have made their homes.

On one side of socio-cultural identity is 'national' identity when the culture or a composite culture has spread into a defined vast land area or islands. A culture is to be identified, "first by its essential spirit, then by its best accomplishment, and lastly by its power of survival, renovation and adaptation to new phases of the permanent needs of the race". Most of the states which have withstood centuries, like, England, France, Switzerland, Japan or China among others have had a uniform socio-cultural form. Pakistan, which was a composite of two distinct languages and culture of East Pakistan and West Pakistan, could not exist for long notwithstanding a common religion, and eventually broke into two states. Similarly, the composite state Soviet Russia could not be kept united by communist political philosophy and withered into several states in 1990s, on the basis of different cultures.

Social culture of a community are considered to be the material needs of man. The Flexibility of human rights is closely related to diverse human cultures, as otherwise also the promotion of human rights is facilitated by the establishment of minimum standards of living along with the incorporation of cultural rights in international system.

In place of imposing one culture on other, all cultures should be allowed to grow and develop under the principle of self-determination. Looking to the contemporary scenario of economic competition and free global economy, the future perhaps holds that culture will have better chances of survival that has a global outlook. Of course, in this process as cautioned by Sri Aurobindo "the culture which gives-up its living separateness (identity), the civilisation that neglects it (the culture) as an active self-Defence will be swallowed up and the nation which did not live by it will lose its soul and perish. Each nation (or separate society) is a Shakti or power of the evolving spirit in humanity and lives by the principle (cultural) which it embodies". Again, with the perspective of increase in culture related conflicts in the twentieth century, Nobel Laureate thinker Amaratya Sen has with sagacity observed that the "harmony in the contemporary world lies not in any imagined uniformity, but in the plurality of our identities, which cut across each other and work against sharp divisions around uniquely hardened line of impenetrable division (based on civilisational, national or religious lines)....The robbing of our plural identities not only reduces us (humans), but also impoverishes the world.

Further, from the point of view of social realities, culture is a social condition removed, away from raw, wild and animal behaviour. Culture is anti-thesis of barbarism. Culture determines the sustained socio-economic pattern for a society. Its strength provides those elements, which bring satisfaction and happiness to community life. Materialism on the other hand has individualised joy and happiness as its objective. All cultures recognize that some latitude to materialist happiness of individual who toils for the society is also necessary.

On the other elementary side of socio-cultural identity is the ethnic group or the tribe. These are clusters of small family unions that are living in villages, localised areas or are nomadic. These tribes were distinguished by their dress, language accent, family traditions and collective folk activities. In the course of centuries some of the tribes have numerically evolved and many of them have gradually become important constituent of States, like, Afghanistan, Namibia, Sierra Leone, Angola and in other State. However, from the national and international perspective, plurality of socio-culture groups is regarded as desirable and the identity of these socio-cultural groups are protected. In India, special treatment is given to them which is constitutional minority rights extends to guarantee, to maintain their own culture, religion or language alongwith the majority people in a state. This is ensured directly and also by ensuring the human rights included in freedom of expression, of press and publication, of religion, or worship, and freedom of group activities.

Right to Social Equality: Protection of Minorities

The denial of social equality within States may be a political act sponsored by State or it may be a class struggle within society: property, profession, language, tradition or religion based. But this evil is present in all States in one form or other. The USA abolished slavery but the attitude of white towards Negro has left a social or racial discrimination mark for the present generations to bear. In Europe, the frequent changes in the political map of the continent by creation of new States or conquests of the territories with people living there on after wars led to the problem not only of accommodation but also of social toleration and acceptance of such people, generally called minorities. Most of such resulting minorities, though Christian were based either on language, nationality or on difference in living traditions. Once the Turkish Ottoman Empire was liquidated after that First World War, Muslims as minorities appeared in Eastern Europe. After the German Empire was dissolved (1919), Germans became minority community in Poland and Czechoslovakia. Italians became a minority community in Albania (1919). When British India was partitioned (1947), problem of religion based accommodation and absorption of minorities arose both in Pakistan and in India. It happened when Palestine was divided into several States (1947-48). All such political events have led to longtime persisting sociocultural recriminations or internecine conflicts.

The problems of racial, ethnic or social discrimination arise since every state has unquestioned or unlimited sovereign rights in international law of dealing with or determining the status of its citizens as well as aliens living on the territories. But, at the same time, extermination, expulsion or political suppression of minorities that evokes international hostility become matters of concern to the United Nations since 1945. Since the end of first world war, the league of nations was by the treaty of Versailles of 1919, entrusted with the task of protecting the political, religious, educational and linguistic rights of national minorities in all those new states that were created by the Peace Treaties.

Religious Freedom of Ethnic or Socio-cultural Groups

It has been observed that religion from the beginning of human civilisation has been part of the fundamentals of human organisation, which has proceeded through the ethnic, tribal or modern socio-cultural groups. Anthropologists and sociologists regard that religion binds the people into a culture. The society & culture in turn are the reservoir of the inner strength of a particular community. Fidelity of the individual to his community and of the community or tribe to its culture has historically proved to be basic for the identity of individual as well as for continued or sustained survival of the particular community. It is now advised even by the UNO, that a cultural history and background are necessary part of a state; and maintenance of cultural background is part of the good governance, of that country. However, in the globalisation process, the plurality and co-existence of several socio-cultures in every state is also an accepted phenomenon, for example, England, USA and India have their cultural identities but at the same time, culture of majority of people should not suppress other cultures present in the State. In legal terms, the right to equality and equal protection of laws should govern different races and religions within the State. Racial discrimination shall be antithesis of the situation.

All human societies in fact have to cope with religious and secular dimension of daily life, any foundation for the universality of human rights must in-corporate religious and secular perspectives in the same process. Our challenge today is to prevent the purported moral superiority of one religious community from diminishing the human dignity and rights of those who do not subscribe to that faith. Secularism is critical for maintaining the equal human and dignity and rights of believers and non-believers. Secularism has evolved as the means for ensuring the possibility of pluralistic community among different religious communities. The key feature of secularism is its ability to safeguard the pluralism of diverse cultures. Secularism needs human rights for practical normal guidance in the daily protection of people against the abuse of the powers of the state. On the other hand, human rights need secularism for the stability and peace among communities. Secularism plays an important role in mediating relations between communities within the same political space.

Conclusion

In a diverse, plural society minority groups participate fully in the dominant society, yet maintaining their cultural differences. Any society benefits from such a condition. This gives growth to multiculturalism. Human rights ensure that every citizen has the right to choose and alternatives should be allowed to offer individual choices. A cultural pluralist diverse society preserve the opportunities for different expressions of identity that are granted in the sphere of human rights. 'Bhikhu Parekh' says that multicultural societies are the most important aspect of any society. He says that cultural diversity covers a much larger area of human existence than before and deeper because it is grounded in profound differences about the conceptions of good life. A good life which is preserved by basic human rights. Bhiku Parekh says that diversity is an inescapable fact of life in a multicultural society, and attempt to dismantle it provoke resistance, creates insecurity, deepen intercultural suspicions. When a cultural community feels threatened, it panics and tends to become self-obsessed, suppress internal differences, voids all but minimal contacts with other cultures and spwan a fundamentalist orthodoxy which fragments the wider society and undermines its cohesion and unity.

Cultural diversity enriches and vitalizes collective life and is desirable not only for minority communities but also for the society as a whole. Every culture fosters specific traits of temperament, psychological and moral dispositions, a particular kind of imagination, and needs constructive interactions with others to revitalize regenerate and enrich itself. A pluralist society should ensure that its cultural communities are able to preserve and transmit their cultural heritage including their languages, histories and religions. This gives them a sense of security, generates good will and gratitude, gives them the confidence to interact with others in a relaxed manner, and helps create a plural collective culture. Multicultural societies will be a great achievement for the human civilisation.

The link between cultural diversity pluralism and human rights was clearly established by the universal declaration on cultural diversity, adopted by the member states of UNESCO in 2001, which holds that "the defence of cultural diversity is... Inseparable from respect for human dignity" and that it implies a commitment to human rights and fundamental freedoms". The UNESCO convention on the protection and promotion of the diversity of cultural expressions, adopted in 2005, states that "cultural diversity can be protected and promoted only if human rights and fundamental freedoms are guaranteed" (Article 2[1]). Cultural diversity and pluralist society is the common heritage of humanity. In our increasingly diverse societies, it is essential to ensure harmonious interaction among people and groups with plural, varied and dynamic cultural identities as well as their willingness to live together. Cultural pluralism gives policy expression to the reality of cultural diversity. Indissociable from a democratic framework, cultural pluralism is conducive to cultural exchange and to the flourishing of creative capacities that sustain public life. Human rights are guarantee of cultural diversity. No one may invoke cultural diversity to infringe upon human rights guaranteed by laws, nor to limit their scope. Universal human rights do not impose one cultural standard, but they always protect necessary human dignity. Human rights represent the consensus of the international community not the cultural imperialism of any particular region or set of traditions. Human rights facilitate respect for and protection of cultural diversity and pluralism. We can be sure that our future will be guided above all by human rights, non discrimination, tolerance and cultural pluralism.

Notes

1. Runzo Joseph & Martin M., Human Rights & Responsibilities, Oneword Oxford Publication, 2003.
2. Reichert Elisabeth, Challenges in Human Rights, A Social Work Perspective, Rawat Publication, 2008.
3. Leiser M. Burton & Campbell D. Tom, Human Rights in Philosophy & Pratice British Library Cataloging Publication, 2001.
4. Freeman Michael, Key Concepts Human Rights, Blackwell Pub. Ltd, 2003.
5. Shivananda J., Human Rights, Concept and Issues, Alfa Publication, New Delhi, 2006.
6. Evans Tony, The Politics of Human Rights, Pluto Press, London, 2001.
7. Goodale Mark, Human Rights An Anthropological Leader, Wiley- Blackwell Publication 2009.
8. Shanishi Nayar, Human Rights in New World Order, Anmol Publication, 2004.

8

Child Rights and Out-of-School Children

—Rekha Kaul

There has been a great deal of emphasis on child rights through the UN Convention and obligations of states manifested through various constitutional provisions; amongst these the right to food and nutrition, healthcare and education (unicef.org) are basic and critical to the development of each child. In the case of India, while we may agree with the fact that a large number of children who gain access to government schooling are also able to partake of the food security provisioned for them in the form of the Mid-Day Meal Scheme (MDMS) by the state; yet there is another huge segment being largely neglected – the out-of-school and partially enrolled children most likely to drop out due their erratic and infrequent presence in schools. The paper argues that for such unenrolled children steeped in poverty and hunger, child rights of food security and education remain a far cry. The state needs to focus with greater seriousness on the poorest of the poor to tackle hunger and malnutrition amongst the most disadvantaged children, enable them to access schools, and save them from the scourge of child labour.

From Survival to Education: Healthcare and Nutrition

The foremost right of the child is the right to survival linked with provision for healthcare and food. Undernourishment, poor healthcare-delivery system, and poor maternal and healthcare services in India are largely responsible for high infant and child mortality. The Special Advisor to the UN Secretary-General Jeffery Sachs had rightly observed that the health of the population, including child survival and maternal health, is both a fundamental end in itself and also a crucial input for economic development. The Millennium Development Goals really embody this dual importance of health (*Seminar*, 2009). However, the country could not achieve this goal which aimed to reduce under-five mortality by two-thirds by 1990-2015. The report release by the UNICEF and the Indian Council of Medical Research pointed out the related socio-economic, maternal demographic and environmental determinants were not adequately addressed (UNICEF 2015). As a result India has seen the highest number of child deaths in the world with an estimated 1.2 million deaths in 2015; these constitute 20 per cent of the 5.9 million local deaths (*The Indian Express*, 2015).

The challenges of mother and child health care require investments of several kinds, some within the household and many at the national level, particularly in the public health system. In the Indian context, the government is spending only around 1 per cent of the GNP on health in the public sector, a level so abysmally low in public finance support. Other than investments in a proper health system, the need for provisioning for related systems of safe drinking water and sanitation, food storage and nutrition need to be underscored for all citizens including children. Nutrition plays a fundamental role in the development of the brain and therefore in enabling children to reach their potential. A few years of undernourishment and poor health can permanently impair the lifetime potential of a child – it stunts growth, negatively impacts intelligence quotient, undermines the immune system and generally has a 'viciously cascading effect on the lives of the poor' (Panda, *Seminar*, 2009).

Undernutrition

Studies have proven that amongst the socio-economic determinants, a strong predictor of child nutrition in India is the household standard of living (Mishra, et al. 1999). Children from low-income families face many barriers to healthy eating due to economic constraints and the limited purchasing power of parents to provide the essential nutrients in food. What is less understandable is the slower reduction of undernutrition than that of poverty. The World Bank at one time called this the 'South Asian Enigma'. While poverty is often the underlying cause of child malnutrition, the superior economic growth experience by South Asian countries just half a decade ago compared to those in Sub-Saharan Africa did not translate into superior nutritional status for the South Asian child.

Undernutrition is the result of food intake that is continuously insufficient to meet dietary energy requirements leading to poor absorption and poor biological use of nutrients consumed. This usually results in stunted growth and loss of body weight (livestrong.com 2011). Brain development gets impaired leading to cognitive defect. According to the UNICEF India Report, there are 46 per cent children at the age of three who are underweight and 16 per cent are wasted (Torpy 2004). One malnourished child in every three in the world lives in India amounting to a total of 23 million malnourished children. Lack of iron leads to anaemia affecting 74 per cent of children under three, iodine deficiency reduces learning capacity by up to 13 per cent and deficiency of Vitamin A suffered by 75 per cent is a major cause of blindness and increases mortality among pre-scholars (Grognolate, 2006).

Reaching School and Mid-Day Meal Scheme (MDMS)

Bracing themselves against all odds that work in opposition to their right to nutrition, health and survival, children are still able access primary education; there has been an expansion of schools to nearly 1.3 million since Independence which have seen an increased enrolment of 229 million students in recent years (ASER 2013). However, as Amartya Sen has remarked, 'there is no barrier to learning as big as coming to school on an empty stomach' (*TOI* 2015). This results in poor learning outcomes in India's classrooms as has been revealed in the Annual Status of Education Reportby Pratham(ASER 2015).

To address the problem of classroom hunger, the Government of India, since 2001, has initiated the MDMS for all primary school children to encourage the poor and disadvantaged segments to attend school more regularly. The scheme also aims at food security providing school children at least one meal a day and is reaching to about 120 million children in over 1.265 million schools (Gracias 2013), providing 450 calories at the lower primary stage and 700 calories at the upper primary stage per child.

The MDMS as highlighted in many studies (Dreze and Goyal 2013, Afridi 2011, Singh et al. 2012) has resulted in increased enrolments, attendance and retention, especially in areas where hunger is endemic like tribal and drought-prone regions. However, others like Khera (2006) have stated that inadequate budgetary allocations and inefficient spending could seriously hamper the quality of MDMS. The laid out stipulation for each child at the lower primary stage is 450 calories, but requirements of children aged five differ from those aged ten years. Quality safeguards and hygienic conditions of cooking are not necessarily ensured and therefore Afridi underlines the need to fill in the gaps in areas like classroom learning and productivity and nutritional intake of children.

Supplementing State Efforts

Even though it is primarily the onus of the state to implement the MDMS, in view of the scales the state initiative has to address, there is room for some intervention through corporate social responsibility (CSR) activities of the industry offering healthcare choices to balance the nutritional deficiencies. For instance, if the Tatas could attempt to raise the levels of iodine in deficient cases through regularsupply of salt in a cluster of schools, or if Reliance Fresh could add a banana to the cooked meals, or if Amul Cooperative or Mother Dairy could provide butter-milk for additional protein or if Dabur or Patanjali could supply amla candies for additional Vitamin C, these would add to the variety and nutrition to the food being distributed through the MDMS. Also efforts by industry such as availability of clean drinking water supply and clean toilets with safe handwash facility could contribute towards better hygiene and reduce the level of risk exposure to illness and disease.

Of the 290 children interviewed in urban slum Delhi schools, 80 stated that the meal provided was hardly a motivation to attend school. Fifty of them said that the school management committees did not oversee the distribution of food. But the majority of 170 children responded that this meal was important and was a help to their families; they also wanted the scheme to be continued at the senior level as well, though the quantity of the food served was not always adequate. Food that was 'leftover' or 'saved' deliberately was sometimes siphoned off by the 'aunty' incharge of distribution. 'She carries it home in large polythene bags to feed her children and family,' remarked one of them. In the East Vinod Nagar Schools for Girls, meal distribution was effective and supervised by the Home Science teacher, while in the Joshi Colony School for Boys the Principal did not permit the distribution of spare food amongst other senior students.

Teacher's trainer and Group Leader of the Teach for India group, Anusiya Menon, observed that 'meals are very basic but for the poorest lot of parents in government schools, two children studying here means two less mouths to feed.' She also added that it is important to view the income differentials in the same schools. For example, 'a taxi driver's child will stroll in to eat a meal only if it is interesting and appetizing like puri-aaloo or rajma-chawal perhaps twice a week, while a rickshawpuller's child really needs food everyday and there is no question of displaying preferences or exercising choice for a particular kind of meal combination (Menon, 2016).

The story of MDMS differs in various regions of the country. In a shocking incident in Ariara's Gokhalapur Rajkiye Prathmik Vidyalaya in Bihar in February 2016, when a class five girl student, much likein Dicken's classic, *Oliver Twist* 'asked for more' khichri, she was allegedly hit, and when her father protested, he too was beaten and died a few hours later (*The Indian Express* 2016). The school has around 300 students up to class five student very poor parents send the siblings of their children along to have the mid-day meal, reflecting the hunger that pervades many parts of rural India.

As regards the right to food, the MDMS, although a flagship programme of the government, is able to take care of only one meal of the enrolled students. Every child needs three square meals; MDMS is certainly subsidizing food but not providing for adequate nutrition. Other meals of the child have to be taken care of the family, however, disadvantaged.

Out-of-School Children: A Low Priority

Since the programme of the MDMS deals with school-going children, the important question that arises is: what has been the response of the state towards the unenrolled and partially enrolled children who are much worse off than the school-going ones? And how has it been dealing with issues of endemic poverty and hunger of such children?

The goal of sending all children to school has not been achieved and low priority is accorded to basic education across developing countries. According to the 2014 UNESCO report, 124 million children and adolescents world-wide are out of school, 17.7 million, or 14 per cent of whom are Indians (UNESCO, 2014). The report attributes India's woeful performance to, among other things, the largest cuts in aid to basic education effected by any country. Public education is slowly but steadily falling off the policy map of the government. The share of GDP to education in India has remained at a low, hovering below 4 per cent for a decade. Public spending on health and education, as has been observed by Dreze, is only 4.7 per cent of the GDP in India, compared with 7 per cent in sub-Saharan Africa. While the right to food, education and health have been so vociferously advocated, the emphasis on building physical capital is huge as opposed to building human capital.

According to the 2014 Human Development Report (UNDP 2014), the human development index (HDI), a measure derived from life expectancy, education levels and incomes, barely grew from 0.700 in 2012 to 0.702 in 2013. Amongst the 187 countries across the world ranked in terms of HDI, India was ranked at 135. As per the 2014 data, Indians aged 25 years or more have received 4.5 years of schooling on an average, compared to the global average of 7.7 years. Not only do a fewer number of children in India access schools, low finances are also a significant part of the narrative behind the increasing number of out-of-school children (thewire.in 2015).

As has been observed in an earlier study by the author (Kaul 2001), the school system within India unravels disparities within the rural-urban, gender, caste and class structures in our society. These differentials have restricted the growth of education, especially amongst the poorest and have reinforced the prevailing inequities. The brunt of such gross inequality is also borne by children who are denied access to schools. A total of 1.7 million children at the primary level and 16 million at the upper primary level are out of school – a large number indeed who have been denied their basic right to education.

Estimating Out-of-School Children: A Problem

Compounding the problem is the fact that there is no standard definition of out-of-school children. This is of special relevance to the estimation of children who not only drop out but are also partially enrolled. Even as absence for extended periods of time is considered in the understanding of the out-of-school child, irregular absence is not included as a reason or cause for considering a child 'out of school'. The reality is that many children, particularly in the large rural landscape of the country, are in a position to attend school only intermittently – it could be a few days in the week or could be even a few hours a day – often leaving when the mid-day is served. It is worth asking if such children should be considered 'in-school'. And if the answer is 'no', the numbers would increase by a significant margin.

It is even more difficult to get near exact estimates of out-of-school children; this is also because reporting on attendance is highly unreliable. Teachers are under pressure to show high attendance to justify mid-day meal funds; additionally they are pressured by their parents, often working as migratory labour, to mark attendance even when children leave for long periods under seasonal migration. Thus, they may be absent for many months qualifying under the dropped-out category of out-of-school children. However, when the new academic year begins, the child is quite likely to be on the rolls. Hence even while the actual estimation of out-of-school children may be problematic, for the purpose of this paper, out-school-school children would include unenrolled/drop-outs as well as partially enrolled. In the context of child rights, an attempt is made here to put the spotlight on this most vulnerable segment. For the purpose of this study, a random sample of 150 students of Government Boys Senior Secondary School, Joshi Colony, and an another 140 girls at the Kendriya Sarvodya Girls School in East Vinod Nagar, of whom 15 had dropped out, provide some insights into their plight of their deprivation.

Why do Children Remain Out of School?

Despite claims to the contrary by the state, primary education is not really free, even in government schools. As has been made evident by some earlier studies (Panchmukhi 1990, Tilak 1996), households and parents have to incur miscellaneous expenditures at the elementary level of education. Forty of the parents in the sample stated that they were compelled to spend on transport, especially when the child is not able to walk alone to school, as well on items like stationery, water bottles, and on private coaching. Money for books and uniform under the government scheme arrives in schools to be disbursed to parents, but this comes in much after the academic session begins. As a result, parents are compelled to make advance expenses to cater the needs of children in schools.

The other charges for school education work out to be much more when we make a distinction between government and government-aided schools. In government-aided schools like the Kerala Senior Secondary School or the Gange Girls Senior Secondary School in Delhi, there are no charges levied as tuition fee. But the fee charged for computer facilities, laboratory usage, aerobics and some other activities are high; additional private publishers' books are also prescribed besides NCERT, and this adds to the cost.

Private tuitions have become a big business in the country and 74 per cent of the parents interviewed stated that they spent additional amounts to the tune of Rs 500 to 800 per month on private coaching. Children need these tuitions, more so at the upper primary stage as several parents do not have the time and are also not educated enough to help them with their studies. But the extra expenses involved in primary education meant to be otherwise free are such that it becomes difficult for parents with very low incomes like rickshawpullers, street hawkers, vendors, or petty shop assistants to fund and support their children's education.

Hunger and Poverty

Of the 150 student respondents in the evening shift of the Government Boys Senior Secondary School, Joshi Colony, 110 stated that they came from families where the income levels were between Rs 3000-6000 per month. Owing to the economic constraints of their families, boys felt uncertain about the ability of their parents to see them through school. Salman, one of the student stated, 'even though we are studying here, we cannot afford tuitions. Most parents will allow us in schools till we pass. If we fail more than once, they ask us to drop out and start working. This usually happens in class nine where only 30-35 per cent of the students pass. This year (2015), of the 195 students in class nine, only 60 have passed'. The failures drop out and get pushed into work. The markets near the slums absorb most children – they are car-cleaners, rickshaw pullers, scrap sellers, helpers at shops, delivery boys or work with mechanics and welders.

Almost 80 percent of the parents wanted their children in school, but 20 percent felt that the children would be able to manage life without education as they were hardly being taught in school and would not fetch them a decent employment anywhere. They themselves were daily wage labourers, working in shops, small restaurants, factories and workshops and did not nurture any great ambitions for their children. On account of the uncertainty they faced regarding completing their schooling, the aspirations for life of such students were also low. Further, if demotivated by any teacher, they begin to absent themselves and gradually drop out.

Salman reported that in his class, of the 75 per cent who failed, 60 percent dropped out due to low family earnings and poverty and a large number got engaged in some work to help sustain themselves; about 10 percent were drifting due to lack of work and absence of schooling; only two children had thought of trying out the option of entering an open school.

At the Rajkiye Sarvodya Kanya Vidyalaya, East Vinod Nagar, 40 percent of the girls failed in class nine. However, due to some subsidies available, a majority of them were repeating the class. Of the 10 percent who had dropped out, some were staying on at home for domestic chores like sibling care, cooking and cleaning. A few of them had joined their mothers as domestic household helpers in the neighbourhood. They also stated that school became uninteresting for them because they could not follow the curriculum and their parents could not afford extra coaching for them. A daughter's presence at home became more crucial to the running of the household where parents were engaged in daily wage labour. Through these respondents it became clear that below a certain threshold level, eking out an existence became critical and hence the number of drop outs increased.

Children in schools like above were largely slum dwellers where parents did not have sufficient employment; they faced insecurity and also uncertainty vis-à-vis housing. Rentals were high even in slums and those living there felt rootless and lacked a sense of belonging as a large number were also migrant workers. So, children were made to fend for themselves and they would often absent themselves due to illness, inability to complete homework and parental neglect after which they gradually stopped attending school. Rinky aged 12 and Rani aged 14, two sisters who were enrolled in a village school, dropped after classes five and six when they moved to a Delhi slum. Parental indifference and lack of their own interest were cited as reasons by them. They were now working as domestic household workers in a group housing society in Patparganj in East Delhi and were actually trying to help their parents save some money for their weddings; however, working out an immediate living was a priority after moving from the village. Not surprisingly though, the parents of Rinky and Rani were supportive of the idea of their younger sons going to school and were seeking admission for them. Gender disparities in such situations were seen to be getting reinforced when parents tend to prioritize the education of their sons.

Bottlenecks Compounded

The above is the case with urban slums, but the rural picture is more stark in many other ways. For example, a poor girl from a Muslim or tribal family in a village may face barriers that would combine being located in a rural area, limited access to resources, socio-cultural gender norms antagonistic to schooling of girls; for a girl from a Dalit family, social discrimination may be more acute. Language is an is an issue for tribal children living in remote areas as the teacher imparting classroom instruction may be unfamiliar with the language spoken by children at home.

Thus, we see that out-of-school children are concentrated in population groups who are disadvantaged due to their location, to social factors related also to caste, tribe, religion or gender. Multiple disadvantages are faced by these children (UNICEF 2014). Therefore, access becomes a problem and out-of-school children are more likely to be found among migrant families, tribal communities who live in isolated and hilly terrains, street children and children in slums facing various forms of violence where the pressure to earn a young age is even more. These factors impact negatively on school participation.

On the supply side barriers, adolescent girls in rural areas may also drop out of school due to reasons like lack of an upper primary school in the neighbourhood, or inadequate female teachers or even lack of toilets. Poor infrastructure and quality issues are however relevant for all groups insofar as low retention of children in schools is concerned.

Out of School and Child Labour: Further Erosion of Rights

Being out of school signifies a measure of deprivation among children and hence they are at the largest risk of entering the labour force – highly neglected and unorganised. From the earlier analysis, we may even accept the view that every child who does not attend school is a potential working child. India is sadly home to the largest number of child labourers with poverty and lack of social security being the main causes of child labour. The neo-liberal economic policies, with growing emphasis on privatisation of basic services, minimize the welfare role of the state (Gurumurthy and Batlivala 2012). Large segments of the population remain unemployed or a seasonally employed and are unable to meet the basic requirements. The view that in a liberal market economy, with changes in technology, employers will need a more educated, more skilled labour force and will no longer employ children has not been proven (Weiner 1991).

Various factors push children out of school into employment such as forced displacement due to development projects, special economic zones, loss of jobs of parents in a slow-down, drought conditions leading to farmers' suicides affecting families and children, and high costs of health care. There is also the prevalence of bonded labour which means employment of a person against a loan or debt by the family of the child or the entire family. Such children are found in the agricultural sector or helping their families in stone quarries or brick kilns (childlineindia.org.2016).

It would also be pertinent to add that the rate of economic growth cannot increase independently of the demands for equity (Kumar 2000). While the need for education is being consistently articulated in all fora and the civil society discourse as an instrument for freedom and equality, the resource allocation and public funding in this domain has been on the decline. The meagre outlays have resulted in blocking the opportunities for the poor. Besides inadequate funding, the persistence of child labour may be attributed to the inefficiencies of the legal and administrative systems and also because it is beneficial to employers who can reduce general wage levels. There also seems a lack of genuine political will to actually see the complete ban on child labour. Legislation like the Right of Children to Free and Compulsory Education Act, 2009, enjoins the state to ensure education to all children in the age group 6-14 years. A corollary of this would be that if a child is working then he or she is bound to miss school. The earlier Child Labour Prevention Act was not aligned to the Right to Education Act as it permitted employment of children below 14 years in occupations and processes not prohibited. The government in May 2015 gave its nod to a proposal allowing children below 14 years of age to work in family enterprises while banning their employment elsewhere; the rationale being that they need to acquire traditional arts and skills early on in life. However, child right activists have argued against this maintaining that such a "dilution" of the act is likely to promote child labour further (*The Indian Express* 2015).

Moving Forward

It cannot be denied that various governments have attempted to address some of the barriers in the way of educating children; the outreach of elementary education has expanded and enrolments have also increased. The MDMS has tried to deal with hunger that poor children face at home. Recruitment of more teachers and some improvements of infrastructure has provisioned for blackboards, a few more pucca buildings and toilets, but universalizing such provisions is still an unfinished agenda.

As has been argued earlier, the denial of the right to food and education gets intermeshed with children remaining unenrolled or dropping out of school and the likelihood of their entering child labour. Better governance with multiplicity of players in the education sector is required with better connect between officials of state education departments, local bodies, teachers and parents who play a critical role. School management committees can monitor and support schooling more effectively.

Resources for health and education require higher funding since the mismatch between need and allocation creates obstacles. Equally significant are the partnerships at various levels like with NGOs and engaging with the civil society as well as collaborating with private initiatives and activities related to corporate social responsibility. Improving the quality of teaching and learning outcomes, through in-service teacher training programmes and raising awareness and sensitivity amongst them to curb violence, abuse and discrimination would also help children stay in schools.

To boost access for the most vulnerable groups like tribals, dalits, girls, slum-dwellers, street children and children of displaced and migrant labour, identification may be made possible through school-mapping exercise. Providing one mid-day meal is not the only answer for such children, their right to three square meals could be better ensured through focus on more residential schools and other related facilities. Overcoming hunger will be a big step towards accessing education.

The costs of formal schooling for the above mentioned groups are high for most parents and alternative schooling could actually provide children in marginalised situations with a possibility to opt for the open school system at a pace more suitable for them. With the spread of television, mobile phones and internet increasingly children are becoming visual learners; this can be taken advantage of through digital technology to supplement teaching and learning (worldbank.org/edutech 2015).

Another area of concern has been the weak implementation of laws – laws pertaining to marriage and employment during childhood are often gender blind and contradictory (Kumar 2015). Community mobilisation could positively impact some of the prevalent socio-cultural norms like those related to female foeticide and the age of marriage with emphasis on the conviction that girls and boys are equal. However, legislation on paper is not adequate and the problem gets compounded by the fact that laws related to child rights are not covered by one single department or ministry. Therefore, coordination between different departments underscoring the need for an integrated approach would go a long way in making a difference towards concerns like child rights, whether for in-school, partially enrolled or out-of-school.

But to lend real meaning to the rights of the child in terms of provisioning for food, nutrition, good health and education, the need is to look beyond the formal classroom for inclusiveness of the most impoverished. The standardized education in schools with promise of one meal will not necessarily equip all children with robust health or the negotiating ability to deal with problems they face as part of the disadvantaged and deprived communities. Engaging seriously with some of the measures proposed could pave the way towards providing minimal guarantees for protection of child rights.

References

Afridi, F., 'Impact of School Meals on School Participation: Evidence from Rural India,' *Journal of Development Studies*, vol. 46, No. 11, (2011), pp. 1636-1656.

Annual Status of Education Report (ACER 2015), ACER Centre, All India Documents.

Dreze, J. and A. Goyal, 'Future of Mid-day Meals,' *Economic and Political Weekly*, vol. 38, No. 44, (2003), pp 4673-4683.

Grognolate, Michael, *India's Undernourished Child: A Call for Reformative Action*, World Bank Publication, November 2006.

Gurumurthy, A. and Batlivala S., 'Revisiting an Idea Called Empower-ment,' in Ramachandran, Vimala and K. Jandhyala, Eds, *Cartographies of Empowerment: The MahilaSamakhya Story*, Zubaan, New Delhi, (2012), pp. 438-474, .

Interview with Anusuiya Menon, Teachers' Trainer and Group Leader, Teach for India Programme, 5 February 2016.

James, Gracias, 'Fighting Classroom Hunger: Achievements of MDMS,' *Yojana*, September 2013.

Kaul, Rekha, 'Accessing Primary Education: Going Beyond the Classroom,' *Economic and Political Weekly*, vol. 36, No. 2, (2001), pp. 155-162.

Khera, R., 'Mid-day Meals in Primary School: Achievements and Challenges,' *Economic and Political Weekly*, vol. 41, No. 46, 2006, pp. 4742-4750.

Kumar, Krishna, 'Slow and Almost Steady,' in RomilaThapar (ed.), *India: Another Millenimum*, Penguin, New Delhi, (2000).

Kumar, Krishna, *Hindustan Times*, New Delhi, 25 July, (2014).

Mishra, Vinod K. SubrataLahiri and Norman Y. Luther, 'Child Nutrition in India,' National Family Health Survey Subject Reports, No. 14, June 1999.

Panchmukhi, P.R., *Private Expenditure on Education in India: An Empirical Study*, Indian Institute of Education, Pune, (1990).

Panda, Baijayant, 'Breaking the Malnutrition Impasse,' *Seminar* 604, December 2009, p. 18.

Sachs, Jeffery, in interview with Rashmi Rajan and Ashok Malik, 10 August 2009 in *Seminar* 604, December 2009.

Singh, A. A., Park and Dercon, 'School Meals as a Safety Net: An Evaluation of the Mid-day Meal Scheme in India,' Working Paper No. 75, *Young Lives*, OUP, Oxford, (2012).

The Indian Express, New Delhi, 30 May 2015.

The Indian Express, New Delhi, 9 September 2015.

The Indian Express, New Delhi, 18 February, 2016.

The Times of India, New Delhi, 6 January 2015.

Tilak, J.B.G., 'How Free is Free Primary Education in India,' *Economic and Political Weekly*, vol. 31, no. 5 and 6, 3 February and 10 February 1996, pp 275-282 and pp 355-366.

Torpy, M. James et al., 2004, 'Malnutrition,' www.unicef.org, last accessed 20 January 2015.

'UN Convention on the Rights of the Child,' www.unicef.org, last accessed February 2016.

UNDP, *Human Development Report* (2014).

UNESCO Report, 2014.

Weiner, Myron, *The Child and the State in India*, Princeton University Press, New Jersey, (1991).

'UN Convention on the Rights of the Child,' www.unicef.org, last accessed on 12 February 2016.

worldbank.org/edutech(2015), last accessed on 20 February 2016.

www.childlineindia.org.in, last accessed on 4 February 2016.

www.livestrong.com, last accessed on 2 Febraury 2016.

www.thewire.in/the-un-report, 7 July 2015, last accessed on 6 February 2016.

9

Spectral Chains of Oppression

— *Tahira Khatoon*

I

Oppression has plagued human society since time immemorial. With the evolution of human society, oppression as a concept has also evolved and taken so many shapes that it defies an easily acceptable definition. Young draws a historical map of its changing nature:

> In its traditional usage, oppression means the exercise of tyranny by a ruling group. [...] Oppression also traditionally carries a strong connotation of conquest and colonial domination. [...] New left social movements of the 1960s and 1970s, however, shifted the meaning of the concept of oppression. In its new usage, oppression designates the disadvantage and injustice some people suffer not because a tyrannical power coerces them, but because of the everyday practices of a well-intentioned liberal society.[1]

Thus, oppression cannot be understood as a uni-dimensional blanket term. It has a multi-faceted character, which the feminists have, and the following paper (as well) intends to understand in the particular context of patriarchy. In order to grasp the subtleties of the pervading presence of oppression under patriarchy, I use the insights of social constructivism to argue that oppression is a defining feature of the social construction of gender relations and allocation of constructed gender roles thereafter.

The nature of oppression is inherently negative in terms of its effect. Hence, any analysis of oppression inevitably brings in its ambit disturbing questions regarding equality and justice. As Young explains: 'Oppression names in fact a family of concepts and conditions, which I divide into five categories: *exploitation, marginalisation, powerlessness, cultural imperialism,* and *violence*[2].'[3] She goes on to draw a direct link between oppression and injustice:

> Justice should refer not only to distribution, but also to the institutional conditions necessary for the development and exercise of individual capacities and collective communication and cooperation. Under this conception of justice, injustice refers primarily to two forms of disabling constraints, oppression and domination.[4]

Following the above link, it can be extrapolated that oppression is injustice in so far as it is a form of domination. However that would still fail to capture the insidious manner, in which oppression establishes an overarching hegemony our lives. Bailey tries to capture this monumentality of oppression through what she calls "complex systems of domination"[5]. This monumentality is due to the fact that relations of oppression get reproduced in economic, political and cultural relations, thereby affecting each and every aspect of human life.

The complexity of this system of domination (as I would like to argue) lies in its all-encompassing nature. As a result, it often gets difficult to clearly categorize people into classes of oppressed and oppressors. For the purposes of this paper, I draw this distinction between the oppressed and the oppressor following Frye's distinction between oppression and harm[6] and a closely analogous distinction between privileges and advantages by Bailey[7]. The intent (as espoused by these theorists as well) is to adopt macroscopic rather than microscopic approach to oppression. A macroscopic perspective is also necessitated by the fact that oppression is a structural symptom[8] and therefore, makes it imperative to use a holistic approach which looks at both sides of the coin– the oppressed as well as the oppressor. To miss out on any of the two is to miss out the entire point of the false consciousness created by, what I refer to as the spectral chains of oppression (title of the paper).

The chains of oppression are spectral because oppression as a phenomenon is not rooted in the random choices made by a few individuals rather the causes of oppression are based in the larger societal norms, habits and cultural symbols; which then come to define the institutional rules and practices. Over a period of time, these norms and practices attain a level of non-questionability and get embedded in the unconscious assumptions and reactions driving the normal interactions among individuals in daily lives. The blame for oppression goes to the entire structure as a whole rather than to conscious intentions of particular individuals.

II

Oppressed: Losing Autonomy

Oppression can be seen variously as getting restricted, limited or denied. Etymologically, oppression resonates with the idea of getting pressed, becoming immobilised. To homogenize all such experiences of oppression, it would not be wrong to say that oppression results in a loss of autonomy[9]. If autonomy indeed is about choice-making, as I would like to argue (to keep it simple), oppression does a frontal attack on this capacity, thereby chaining[10] the individuals. As Frye explains: 'The experience of oppressed people is that the living of one's life is confined and shaped by forces and barriers which are not accidental or occasional, and hence avoidable, but are systematically related to each other in such a way as to catch one between and among them and restrict or penalize motion in any direction'.[11] Bailey explicates the nature of these restrictionsby taking Frye's argument further:

> In her careful analysis of oppression, Marilyn Frye argues that one of the reasons people fail to see oppression is that they focus on particular events, attitudes, and actions that strike them as harmful, but they do not place these incidents in the context of historical, social, and political *systems* (emphasis original). According to Frye, members of oppressed groups commonly experience "double-binds," that is, they are faced daily with situations in which their options are reduced to a very few, all of which expose them to penalty, censure, or deprivation.These binds are created and shaped by forces and barriers which are neither accidental nor avoidable, but are systematically related to each other in ways that confine individuals to the extent that movement

in any direction is penalised. To make visible the systemic character of the barriers shaping the double-bind Frye uses the metaphor of a birdcage.[12]

The analogy of a birdcage as expounded by Frye is perhaps the best way to capture the ambiguity of the pervasion of oppression:

> Consider a birdcage. If you look very closely at just one wire in the cage, you cannot see the other wires. If your conception of what is before you is determined by this myopic focus, you could look at that one wire, up and down the length of it, and be unable to see why a bird would not just fly around the wire any time it wanted to go somewhere. [...] There is no physical property of any one wire, *nothing* (emphasis original) that the closest scrutiny could discover, that will reveal how a bird could be inhibited or harmed by it except in the most accidental way. It is only when you step back, stop looking at the wires one by one, microscopically, and take a macroscopic view of the whole cage, that you can see why the bird does not go anywhere; and then you will see it in a moment. [...] It is perfectly obvious that the bird is surrounded by a network of systematically related barriers, no one of which would be the least hindrance to its flight, but which, by their relations to each other, are as confining as the solid walls of a dungeon.[13]

The larger point being made is that the various acts of discrimination and domination should not be seen as isolated occurrences of random events, rather they must be placed as connected episodes within one story of structural prejudice. This prejudice is also not directed against just any individual accidently, but there is an underlying pattern here as well, as pointed out by Frye:

> When you question why you are being blocked, why this barrier is in your path, the answer has not to do with individual talent or merit, handicap or failure; it has to do with your membership in some category understood as a "natural" or "physical" category. The "inhabitant" of the "cage" is not an individual but a group, all those of a certain category. If an individual is oppressed, it is in virtue of being a member of a group or category of people that is systematically reduced, molded, immobilised. Thus, to

> recognize a person as oppressed, one has to see that individual as belonging to a group, of a certain sort.[14]

This idea of seeing an individual as a member of a group requires an enlargementof the paradigm of liberalism which fails to think beyond the atomistic threshold of individual being the core ontological unit of analysis. One must take into account the social ontology of individuals. Group meanings partially constitute people's identities in terms of the cultural forms, social situation, and history that group members know as theirs, because these meanings have been either forced upon them or forged by them or both.[15] A social group is defined not primarily by a set of shared identity, but by a sense of identity.[16] Thus it is important to see individuals, not as unencumbered selves[17] but primarily as relationally embedded beings.

> As Stephen Epstein describes it, identity is "a socialised sense of individuality, an internal organisation of self-perception concerning one's relationship to social categories, that also incorporates views of the self perceived to be held by others. Identity is constituted relationally, through involvement with – and incorporation of – significant others and integration into communities". Group categorisation and norms are major constituents of individual identity.[18]

Thus, social relativity of individuals with respect to other individuals is a very crucial factor in the act of self-definition as well as in the creation of one's identity. This is where social construction comes to play a major role. Ore characterizes social construction as follows:

> Social construction theory suggests that what we see as "real" (in this case, cultural categories of difference and systems of inequality) is the result of human interaction. Through such interaction, we create aspects of our culture, objectify them, internalize them, and then take these cultural products for granted.[19]

Frye further argues 'that the social construction of difference is initiated with the purpose of discrimination and oppression– a relationship in which the dominant group benefits from the *systematic* (emphasis original) abuse, exploitation, and injustice directed at a subordinate group. Thus, the construction of difference is not arbitrary but systematically created and transformed into systems of inequality in an effort to advantage some at the expense of others'.[20] There is an unrelenting social construction of reality which sustains any structure of oppression. The process of social construction consists of three stages, which have been explained differently by different theorists. I present below two descriptions of social construction. Ore describes one such understanding of social construction:

> According to Berger and Luckmann, reality is socially constructed in three stages. In the first stage, externalisation, we create cultural products through social interaction. These cultural products may be material artifacts, social institutions, or values or beliefs concerning a particular group. [...] The second stage, objectivation, occurs when the products created in the first stage appear to take on a reality of their own, becoming independent of those who created them. People lose awareness that they themselves are the authors of their social and cultural environment and of their interpretations of reality. [...] In the final stage, internalisation, we learn the supposedly "objective facts" about the cultural products that have been created. This occurs primarily through socialisation, the process of social interaction, in which one learns the ways of the society and one's specific roles – the sets of rules and expectations attached to a social position (or status) in that society. In this stage, we make these "facts" part of our subjective consciousness.[21]

Hirschmann also provides a detailed account of the process of social construction, comprising of three levels[22]: micro, meso and macro – the ideological misrepresentation of reality, materialisation and the discursive construction of social meaning.[23] The first level aims at the distortion of reality at the ideological level. The second level works towards the materialisation of the ideological distortion.[24] In the third level, the materialisation of the ideological distortion validates itself through the medium of language, thereby seeping into the very daily lives of individuals leaving them with no option of escape. Thus social construction involves the ideological, materialistic and discursive creation of subjectivity itself. These three levels are interdependent and work together as a deepening process.[25]

Both the above descriptions of the stages of social construction portray a similar trajectory of creation of misrepresentation, objectifying or materializing the misrepresented reality and finally its internalisation in our ideologies. Social construction of an oppressive reality has detrimental effects on the very constitution of choice and actions of autonomy. If our choices are, in effect, the result of the social construction of reality we are a part of, it is important to understand how oppressive realities harm individual autonomy. The oppressed, therefore, comes to experience a loss of autonomy. As Hirschmann very rightly explains, the process of choice formation comes to be defined by the nature of socialisation one had:

> But choice is constituted by a complex relationship between "internal" factors of will and desire – impacting on the preferences and desires one has and how one makes choices – and factors "outside" the self that may inhibit or enhance one's ability to pursue one's preferences, including the kind and number of choices available, the obstacles to making the preferred choice, and the variable power that different people have to make choices [...] if chocolate and vanilla are the only flavors available, I am not free to choose strawberry, but that does not alter the fact that I would have preferred strawberry if it were available. What is not addressed by most freedom theories, however, is the deeper, more important issue of how the choosing subject is herself constructed by such contexts: could the repeated absence of strawberry eventually change my tastes so that I lose my desire for it? This question, as I conceive it, involves more than the "adaptive preferences" problem of rational-choice theory, or even the possibility of "oppressive socialisation". [...] Rather it involves the more complex and subtle process of social construction.[26]

III

Oppressor: Gaining Privilege

The vantage point of a social constructivist helps in understanding the dialectical relationship between individual and society. Frye explains the undeniable and inescapable role of societal structure in the constitution of individuals:

> Since we are a social species, almost all of our behavior and activities are structured by more than individual inclination and the condition of the planet and its atmosphere. No human is free of social structures, nor (perhaps) would happiness consist in such freedom. Structure consists of boundaries, limits and barriers; in a structured whole, some motions and changes are possible, and others are not.[27]

This leads us towards questions regarding the multiplicity of identities and corollarily, social roles. As Bailey points out, there is a plurality in terms of group memberships[28] which Collins tries to capture in what she calls "matrix of domination."[29] Such questions relating to multiple identities make it imperative to study oppression not in an aggregative or additive manner, but in a qualitative manner. Qualitatively, one needs to look into the systems of advantages and privileges, as developed by Bailey to understand how systems of domination are maintained. It is privileges which endow the oppressor class its designation. She explains the function of advantages and privileges as follows:

> [...] all privilege is advantageous, but that not all advantages count as privilege. Like the difference between harms and oppression, the difference between advantages and privilege has to do with the systematically conferred nature of these unearned assets. If we want to determine whether a particular harm qualifies as oppression, Frye argues that we have to look at that harm in context (macroscopically) to see what role, if any, it plays in maintaining a structure that is oppressive. Likewise, if we want to determine whether a particular advantage qualifies as a privilege, The need to look at that advantage macroscopically in order to observe whether it plays a role in keeping complex systems of domination in place. We need to know if the advantage enables members of privileged groups to avoid the structured system of forces and barriers which serve to immobilize members of marginalised groups.[30]

A set of social and economic barriers and forces separating two groups may be felt, even painfully, by members of both groups and yet may mean confinement to one and liberty and enlargement of opportunity to the other.[31] This is precisely how women indiscriminately remain within the class of the oppressed and men in the class of oppressors. So while men might 'feel' harmed in pursuing some of their interests in the short run and blame the structure of oppression for restraining their autonomy, the structure invariably works in their favour alone in the long run. Frye elucidates this very well:

> Acceptable behavior for both groups, men and women, involves a required restraint that seems in itself silly and perhaps damaging. But the social effect is drastically different. The women's restraint is part of a structure oppressive to women; the man's restraint is part of a structure oppressive to women. [...] Being male is something he has going *for* (emphasis original) him, even if race or class or age or disability is going against him. Women are oppressed, *as women* (emphasis original). Members of certain racial and/or economic groups and classes, both the males and the females, are oppressed *as* members of those races and/or classes. But men are not oppressed *as men* (emphasis original).[32]

Thus, there is differential impact of oppression which allows men to reign with a socio-cultural legitimacy through the privileges it bestows upon them. The distinction between privileges and earned advantages show how men and women are victimized differently in matters of both frequency and intensity. Frye elucidates how gender helps in gaining privileges under a system of patriarchy; whereas women may enjoy certain advantages here and there, they invariably remain in the class of the oppressed.

> [...] some advantages are more easily earned if they are accompanied by gender, heterosexual, race, or class privilege. Privilege and earned advantages are connected in the sense that privilege places one in a better position to earn more advantages. The link between earned advantages and unearned privilege generates a situation in which privileged groups can earn assets (e.g., control of resources, skills, a quality education, the attention of the mayor, a good reputation, a prestigious well paying job,

> political power, or a safe place to live) more easily and more frequently than those who don't have white, male, heterosexual, or economic privilege.[33]

Viewing constructions of difference and the resulting systems of inequality as interconnected also helps us to see how all groups experience both privilege and oppression in one socially constructed system.[34] This makes the label of oppression difficult to put down on any one group, especially when the issues of intersectionality make the question of oppression more problematic. Young believes her five-fold characterisation of oppression helps solve this problem to some extent:

> I have arrived at the five faces of oppression– exploitation, marginalisation, powerlessness, cultural imperialism, and violence– as the best way to avoid such exclusions and reductions. They function as criteria for determining whether individuals and groups are oppressed, rather than as a full theory of oppression. [...] these criteria are objective. [...] Each criterion can be operationalised; each can be applied through the assessment of observable behavior, status relationships, distributions, texts and other cultural artifacts. [...] Applying these five criteria to the situation of groups makes it possible to compare oppressions without reducing them to a common essence or claiming that one is more fundamental than another.[35]

The chameleonic nature of oppression demands a regular and intensive scrutiny of the social relations and the manner and form in which they are reproduced and represented. Social construction provides a good analytical tool to assess the functioning and the effect of oppression in the present and predict the possibilities of social change in the future.Taking from Ore to end on a positive note:

> [...] by understanding the process of social construction we can be more optimistic in working toward positive social change. If we recognize the processes by which systems of inequality are constructed as interlocking systems of oppression, we can gain a greater under-standing of how to deconstruct these systems while constructing systems of equality.[36]

Notes

1. Young, Iris Marion. *Justice and the Politics of Difference.* United States of America: Princeton University Press, (1990), pp. 40-41.
2. Italics are added by me to emphasis on the multiplicity of the forms in which oppression manifests itself.
3. Young, Iris Marion. *Justice and the Politics of Difference.* United States of America: Princeton University Press, (1990), p. 40.
4. Ibid., p. 39.
5. *Ignoring the systemic and interlocking nature of what I call complex systems of domination (e.g., racism, ableism, sexism, anti-Semitism, or homophobia) has misleading consequences. When the effects of sexism, for example, are not understood macroscopically as the products of systemic injustices, they are understood microscopically as the exclusive problems of particular women who have made bad choices, have poor attitudes, are too sensitive, or who are overreacting to a random incident. Failure to examine sexism, homophobia, racism, and anti-Semitism as harms produced by systematically related forces and barriers blurs the distinction between harm and oppression.* Bailey, Alison. "Privilege: Expanding on Marilyn Frye's "Oppression"." *Journal of Social Philosophy*, Vol. 29, No. 3, Winter (1998): 104-119, p. 105.
6. Frye, Marilyn. "Oppression." In *Gender Basics:Feminist Perspectives on Women and Men*, by Anne Minas, 10-16. United States of America: Wadsworth Publishing, (2000).
7. Bailey, Alison. "Privilege: Expanding on Marilyn Frye's "Oppression"." *Journal of Social Philosophy*, Vol. 29, No. 3, Winter (1998): 104-119.
8. I am using *symptom* in the strict Marxist sense as expounded by Karl Marx.
9. For the purposes of this paper, I am defining autonomy solely in the decision making power of making choices.
10. Hence the title of the paper- the spectral chains of oppression.
11. Frye, Marilyn. "Oppression." In *Gender Basics:Feminist Perspectives on Women and Men*, by Anne Minas, 10-16. United States of America: Wadsworth Publishing, (2000), p. 12.
12. Bailey, Alison. "Privilege: Expanding on Marilyn Frye's "Oppression"." *Journal of Social Philosophy*, Vol. 29, No. 3, Winter (1998): 104-119, p. 105.
13. Frye, Marilyn. "Oppression." In *Gender Basics:Feminist Perspectives on Women and Men*, by Anne Minas, 10-16. United States of America: Wadsworth Publishing, (2000), p. 12.
14. Ibid.
15. Young, Iris Marion. *Justice and the Politics of Difference.* United States of America: Princeton University Press, (1990), p. 44.

16. Ibid.
17. Michael Sandel criticizes liberal individualism for their theorisation of individuality as an unencumbered self.
18. Young, Iris Marion. *Justice and the Politics of Difference.* United States of America: Princeton University Press, (1990), p. 45.
19. Ore, Tracy E. *The Social Construction of Difference and Inequality: Race, Class, Gender, and Sexuality.* California: Mayfield Publishing Company, (2000), p. 5.
20. *Ibid.*, p. 15.
21. Ore, Tracy E. *The Social Construction of Difference and Inequality: Race, Class, Gender, and Sexuality.* California: Mayfield Publishing Company, (2000), pp. 6-7.
22. Hirschmann explains the three levels of its functioning: *Moreover, all of these happen in "levels" in another sense: at the micro level of individual practice, the meso level of institutional practice, and the macro level of conceptual categories. These levels cut across the three layers of ideology, materialisation, and discourse.* Hirschmann, Nancy J. "Response to Friedman and Brison." *Hypatia,* Vol. 21, No. 4, Autumn (2006): 201-211, p. 203
23. Hirschmann, Nancy J. *The Subject of Liberty: Toward a Feminist Theory of Freedom.* New Jersey: Princeton University Press, (2003), pp. 77-81
24. Hirschmann explains this second level: *Guided by concerns such as pornography, domestic violence, prostitution, sexual discrimination, rape and abortion, feminists argue that such social expressions of male domination have produced and codified customs and rules that restrict women's opportunities and choices; women cannot be doctors, for example, if they are denied access to medical schools.* Hirschmann, Nancy J. *The Subject of Liberty: Toward a Feminist Theory of Freedom.* New Jersey: Princeton University Press, (2003), p. 80
25. Hirschmann explains this interplay of the levels: *What I like about "levels" is that it communicates the idea of a "deepening": Ideology is closer to the surface, coming from a loosely identifiable source and having a more or less specific target; materialisation goes more deeply into lived experience, but is still somewhat identifiable in terms of source and outcome, even if less than ideology; discourse goes more deeply, to the macro-structures that are incredibly difficult to identify, both in source and outcome, because they come from and end up everywhere at once.* Hirschmann, Nancy J. "Response to Friedman and Brison." *Hypatia,* Vol. 21, No. 4, Autumn (2006): 201-211, p. 202
26. Hirschmann, Nancy J. *The Subject of Liberty: Toward a Feminist Theory of Freedom.* New Jersey: Princeton University Press, (2003), Preface-p. ix.

27. Frye, Marilyn. "Oppression." In *Gender Basics: Feminist Perspectives on Women and Men*, by Anne Minas, 10-16. United States of America: Wadsworth Publishing, (2000), p. 13.
28. [...] *two important comments regarding Frye's observations about group membership and its role in systems of oppression. First, because individuals are rarely members of one community, oppression is not a unified phenomenon. Group differences in race/ethnicity, sexual orientation, gender, or class cut across individual lives to the point that privilege and oppression are often experienced simultane-ously.* Bailey, Alison. "Privilege: Expanding on Marilyn Frye's "Oppression"." *Journal of Social Philosophy*, Vol. 29, No. 3, Winter (1998): 104-119, p. 106.
29. *Patricia Hill Collins refers to this interlocking system as a matrix of domination. This model provides the framework for our efforts [...] in seeking to understand how categories of difference are transformed into systems of inequality and maintained as systems of oppression. Such a framework will allow us to move beyond simply describing the similarities and differences between various systems of oppression and will help us to focus on how they interconnect. [...] The matrix of domination also provides a framework that permits us to avoid additive analyses of systems of oppression (e.g., a black woman being viewed as twice as oppressed as a white woman). Such analyses are problematic in that they suggest that oppression can be quantified.* Ore, Tracy E. *The Social Construction of Difference and Inequality: Race, Class, Gender, and Sexuality.* California: Mayfield Publishing Company, (2000), p. 16.
30. *Ibid.*, p. 108.
31. Frye, Marilyn. "Oppression." In *Gender Basics:Feminist Perspectives on Women and Men*, by Anne Minas, 10-16. United States of America. Wadsworth Publishing, (2000), p. 14.
32. *Ibid.*, p. 16.
33. *Ibid.*, p. 110.
34. Ore, Tracy E. *The Social Construction of Difference and Inequality: Race, Class, Gender, and Sexuality.* California: Mayfield Publishing Company, (2000), p. 16.
35. Young, Iris Marion. *Justice and the Politics of Difference.* United States of America: Princeton University Press, (1990), p. 64.
36. Ore, Tracy E. *The Social Construction of Difference and Inequality: Race, Class, Gender, and Sexuality.* California: Mayfield Publishing Company, (2000), pp. 16-17.

Works Cited

- Bailey, Alison. "Privilege: Expanding on Marilyn Frye's "Oppression"." *Journal of Social Philosophy*, Vol. 29, No. 3, Winter (1998): 104-119.

- Frye, Marilyn. "Oppression." In *Gender Basics:Feminist Perspectives on Women and Men*, by Anne Minas, 10-16. United States of America: Wadsworth Publishing, (2000).
- Hirschmann, Nancy J. "Response to Friedman and Brison." *Hypatia,* Vol. 21, No. 4, Autumn (2006): 201-211.
- —. *The Subject of Liberty: Toward a Feminist Theory of Freedom.* New Jersey: Princeton University Press, (2003).
- Ore, Tracy E. *The Social Construction of Difference and Inequality: Race, Class, Gender, and Sexuality.* California: Mayfield Publishing Company, (2000).
- Young, Iris Marion. *Justice and the Politics of Difference.* United States of America: Princeton University Press, (1990).

10

Human Rights Issues in Israel's Occupied Territories

—Sunil Kumar

Introduction

Israel is the only Jewish state in the world. That is located in just east of the Mediterranean Sea. Palestinians, the Arab population that hails from the land Israel now controls, refer to the territory as Palestine. They want to establish a state by that name on all or part of the same land. However, both Jews and Arab Muslims claim to the land, back a couple thousand years. The current political conflict commenced in the early 20th century. Jews fleeing persecution in Europe wanted to establish a national homeland in what was then an Arab- and Muslim-majority territory in the British Empire. The Arabs resisted seeing the land as rightfully theirs. Early United Nations plan to give each group part of the land failed. Israel and the surrounding Arab nations fought several wars over the territory.

Today's lines largely reflect the outcomes of two of these wars, one waged in 1948 and another in 1967. The 1967 war also called June War, took place on June 5-10, 1967, and was third of the Arab-Israeli Wars. It was particularly important for today's conflict as well as the issue of Human Rights in occupied territories. It left Israel in control of most of the territories such as West Bank and Gaza Strip as well as other part of land from Syria and Jordan. That is two territories home to large Palestinian populations. The status of these territories subsequently became a major point of contention in the Arab-Israeli conflict. Arguably, no other conflict on earth has combined such a complex mixture of religious, historical, economic and geopolitical elements. The existence and on-going expansion of the Israeli settlements in the region have serious implications on the civil, political, economical, social and cultural rights of the Palestinian people.

The Israeli government has been condemned and continues to be condemned by the United Nations for widespread human rights violations that take place in the territories under its jurisdiction (UN Doc. A/C.2/68/L.27, 2013). Arab Israeli live under a regime of discrimination, while Palestinians' right to life and to freedom of the person are constantly under attack by means of retaliation actions and counter-terrorism incursions. That often led to targeted assassinations and administrative detentions (Amnesty International 'Administrative Detention in Israel/ Occupied Territories, 1978). These violations contravene both Israel's international legal obligations, and the fundamental right enshrined in Israel domestic legislation to freedom from arbitrary searches of the property and the person. Israeli occupation's barricades and check points prevent the Palestinian population from the enjoyment of the very same rights. Israel jealously protects for its Jewish population: right to an education, the right to health, the right to water and sanitation, the right to freedom of profession, the right to dignity and, most importantly, the right to the security of the person.

The applicability of humanitarian law to the territories under its occupation, Israel denies the applicability of the Fourth Geneva Convention on the protection of the civilian population. Importantly, Israel denies its responsibility under international human rights instruments (such as the 1966 International Covenants and the 1989 UN Convention on the Rights of the Child) in the Occupied Palestinian Territories (OPTs). It was advocating for a separation of applicable legislation, after delving into the issue of human rights protected under Israeli domestic legislation.

Application of Domestic Legislation to the Territory of the State of Israel

1. Human Rights in Israel and the Basic Law on Human Dignity and Liberty

Israeli national law recognizes the value of man, the sanctity of his life and individual freedom (Jewish Virtual Library, 1992). The Basic Law on Human Dignity and Liberty is Israel's domestic provision that protects human rights at the highest level of legislation. The Knesset (the legislative branch of the Israeli government) gave it 'super-legal status', giving Israeli courts the authority to disqualify any law contradicting it at any lower level. Among the rights protected there are right to life, right to property, right to privacy, intimacy and the freedom to leave, to enter the country and the freedom from arbitrary searches of the person and private premises. Despite several cardinal human rights are missing from the document (such as the right to equality, the freedom of speech, freedom of religion, freedom of protest and others), the Basic Law's protection is interpreted as extending beyond its text. Some jurists, such as former President of The Supreme Court of Israel Aharon Barak, see these rights as directly derived from the 'right to dignity' protected in the Basic Law under Sections 2 and 4 (respectively, 'preservation' and 'protection of life, body, and dignity') (Basic Law: Human Dignity, sec. 2, 4.).

In this sense, it has been said that the missing rights were given to the residents of Israel by general principles of law pre-existing the Basic Law. If short-handed in enumerating protections, the law seemed farsighted in regulating its curtailing and suspension. Especially, Section 8 -which became known as the 'limiting paragraph on the violation of rights'- bans all violations of the rights protected except for the ones authorised by laws 'befitting the values of State of Israel, enacted for a proper purpose, moreover to an extent no greater than is required. While asserting the government's prohibition to change or suspend the Basic Law by enacting an emergency regulation. Another paragraph is Section 12-allows restrictions or denial of individual rights on the same grounds of 'proper purpose' and 'extent' when a state of emergency is in place. In other words, the protection from emergency regulations is not *in toto*, and it is up to the government and the Supreme Court to decide on the legitimacy of the restriction measures (Barak, 2006).

It is in line with this flexibility that the Supreme Court, generally rather liberal in recognizing rights for the Israelis, ruled as legitimate. The existence of check points and the carrying out of house searches and administrative detention. The rationale is that Islamist organisations such as Hamas, Hezbollah and even Lebanese Fatah al-basically leaves it up to the government to decide *how* and *for how* long rights can be restricted as long as a state of emergency is in place (Basic Law: Human Dignity, sec. 12.). In a country which has been in state of emergency since day one of independence (Human Rights Report, 2013). This has become a controversial provision. It appears clear that the logic underlying the Basic Law's limiting paragraph is circular. That provision is open to abuse. It should come as no surprise then that the provision is used on a regular basis to restrict and violate the rights of Arab Israeli citizens or other Palestinian residents.

Arab Deprivation and Discrimination

Israel national territory is home to 16,82,000 Arab Israelis (meaning that 20.6 per cent of Israel overall population has Arab descendants) (Jewish Virtual Library, 2013). In addition, there are about 2,78,000 Arab residents of occupied East Jerusalem and the Golan Heights. The majority has refused citizenship, but maintains Israeli residency (Nusseibeh , 2011). About 80 per cent of Israeli Arabs are Muslim; the rest is divided, roughly equally, between Christians and Druze. The majority of them identifies very closely with the Palestinians in Gaza and the West Bank. They often describe themselves as 'Palestinian citizens of Israel' (or '1948 Palestinians') (Peleg, and Waxman, 2011). Arab Israelis are citizens of the State of Israel as such; they are entitled to the same rights protected under domestic legislation. This precept was sanctioned in all Israeli Independence Declaration's 'equality for all' claims Declaration of Establishment of State of Israel, (1948). The truth differs, however, some commentator have described Israel as 'democratic for Jews and Jewish for the Arabs (Jerusalem Post, 2010).

Many Israeli Arabs frequently describe themselves as second class citizens (Nusseibeh, 2011). This is not only because their civic duty differs (they are exempt from compulsory military service). Allegations of discrimination have come from multiple entities, government and non-governmental organisations, within and outside of the UN (Human Rights Watch, 2012). All have been accused of bias, partisanism, and anti-semitism (Human Rights Watch, 2010). While true that Israel might be subjected to a more vigilant inspection than many of its neighbours (United Nation, 2006), the discrimination of its Arab population has been acknowledged both by domestic inquiries and by its very same indisputable allies. In 2003, the *Orr Commission*, a government inquiry appointed to investigate the events of the Second Intifada, in which 12 Arab Israeli and one Palestinian were killed by Israeli police amid several demonstrations. This demonstration concluded that 'government handling of the Arab sector has been primarily neglectful and discriminatory (Jewish Virtual Library, 2014). More recently, in its 2013 report to the Under-Secretary on Human Rights, Democracy, and Labor, the US State Department said Israeli Arabs face 'institutional, legal, and societal discrimination'; such discrimination materialises in terms of access to equal education and employment opportunities (Human Rights Report, 2014). In the annex to the report, the State Department analyses human rights problems related to Israeli authorities in the OTPs, and Israeli authorities' *vis-à-vis* the Palestinian population (including Arab Palestinians residents of Israel). The report acknowledges excessive use of force against civilians, including killings; abuse of Palestinian detainees, particularly during arrest and interrogation; austere and overcrowded detention facilities; improper use of security detention procedures; demolition and confiscation of Palestinian property; limitations on freedom of expression, assembly, and association; and severe restrictions on Palestinians' internal and external freedom of movement.

Besides the obvious violations of the right to life and personal freedom constituted by targeted assassinations and administrative detentions, Israeli check points daily violate Palestinian and Arab's rights to 'human freedom' intended in the Basic Law as freedom to leave and enter the country, consequently violating their right to an occupation, to an education, to proper health and to family life (Basic Law: Human Dignity, sec. 6). Night time Israeli's blitzes in Palestinian households, and the subsequent property confiscation, violate Arab Israeli and Palestinians' rights to privacy, to property and freedom from arbitrary searches. While namely justified by emergency regulations, the disproportionate concentration of such violations on Arab Israeli. Other Palestinian populations remain without justification, and contribute to the creation of a regime of separation and discrimination.

Applicability of International Humanitarian Law in the Occupied Palestinian Territories

- Alternative Legality and the Applicability of the Fourth Geneva Convention to the Territories under Israeli Control

It is widely acknowledged that humanitarian law applies to both situations of armed conflict and belligerent occupation (Fleck, 2009). As the occupying power in the West Bank and Gaza Strip, Israel's obligations are set out in The Hague Regulations annexed to the Fourth Hague Convention with respecting the Laws and Customs of War on Land (Hague Regulations), and the Fourth Geneva Convention Concerning the Protection of Civilian Persons in Time of War (Fourth Geneva Convention). While maintaining the applicability of the Hague Regulations (2014) due to their customary nature, Israel contests the inapplicability of the Fourth Geneva Convention to the OPTs. Although Israel ratified the Geneva Conventions in 1951, it indeed refuses to recognize their *de jure* applicability, maintaining that because they took the Palestinian territories back from other occupying forces such as Jordan, Syria and Egypt in 1967. These territories have no official status under the Geneva Conventions due to a lack of previous sovereignty, and do not therefore constitute a High Contracting party to the Convention. Israel, in fact, claims that the legal status of those territories has never been settled in any document agreed by both parties. Despite the settlement of this issue was part of the main agenda of the Oslo Agreements of 1995 (Jewish Virtual library, 2014). On the contrary, Israeli claims regarding the non-applicability of the Geneva Conventions have even increased following the signing of the Oslo Agreements: since Israeli military presence in the OPTs was progressively diminishing (Mideast Security and Policy Studies, 1994). Palestinians were assuming broadened responsibilities and powers with respect to internal affairs; Israel claimed. It could no longer be considered an occupying power with obligations towards the Palestinian territories and its civilian population (Ibid).

Israel, however, has *de facto* occupied the OPTs since 1967, as Working paper 42 of the Hague Regulations stipulates, a 'territory is considered occupied when it is actually placed under the authority of the hostile army', and that the occupation extends 'to the territory where such authority has been established and can be exercised' (ICRC, 1907). In the Hostagecase, the Nuremburg Tribunal held that, 'the test for application of the legal regime of occupation is not whether the occupying power fails to exercise effective control over the territory, but whether it has the ability to exercise such power' (Benvenisti, 2012). This test continues to apply to Israel's relation *vis-à-vis* the Gaza Strip and the West Bank. Repeated resolutions by both the UN General Assembly and the Security Council, and statements issued by governments worldwide, have all affirmed the *de jure* applicability of the Fourth Geneva Convention, and called upon Israel to abide by its obligations as an occupying power (UN Doc. A/RES/68/81). This has been the voice (almost at unison) of the international community when in 2001 High Contracting Parties to the Fourth Geneva Convention reaffirmed 'the applicability of the Convention to the OPTs, including East Jerusalem, and reiterate[d] the need for full respect for the provisions of the said Convention in that territory (Fourth Geneva Convention Declaration, 2001). This position was confirmed in July 2004 by the International Court of Justice (ICJ) in its Advisory Opinion on the Legal Consequences of the Construction of a Wall in the Occupied Palestinian Territory. The ICJ referenced the agreements between Israel and the Palestinian Liberation Organisation which resulted in the transfer of certain powers and responsibilities to the Palestinian National Authority, highlighting that these events, 'have done nothing to alter this situation. All these territories (including East Jerusalem) remain occupied territories in which Israel has continued to have the status of occupying power (REF World, 2004). In this regard, the Opinion also states that 'civilians who find themselves in whatever way in the hands of the occupying power' must remain protected persons 'regardless of changes to the status of the occupied territory. In reference to Israel's occupation of the West Bank and Gaza Strip in the 1967 War, the ICJ recalled working paper 2, paragraph 1 of the Convention noting that this convention applies 'to all cases of declared war or of any other armed conflict which may arise between two or more High Contracting Parties....' Once these conditions have been met, the Convention is deemed to apply 'in *any territory* [emphasis added] occupied in the course of the conflict by one of the contracting parties', including therefore all OPTs.

This should not come as a surprise, considering that the Israeli authorities had themselves initially recognised the applicability of the Fourth Geneva Convention. Working paper 35 of the Proclamation No. 3, promulgated shortly after the 1967 June War stated that: 'the military court...must apply the provisions of the Geneva Convention that took place in 12 August 1949 relative to the Protection of Civilian Persons in Time of War with respect to judicial procedures (IMFA, 2014). However, in October 1967, this military proclamation was amended by Military Order 144 to exclude the reference to the Convention's applicability (Israel War Source Centre, 1967). Since then, Israel has been claiming that its presence in the OPT as an *administrator*, and that despite, it would abide to the Fourth Geneva Convention by force of its 'humanitarian provisions (RULAC, 2012). That it officially maintained Israeli authorities non-accountable to their responsibilities under the Convention.

So far as Alternative Legality and the Applicability of the Fourth Geneva Convention to Persons under Israeli Control another knot of Israeli's alternative legality that extends beyond the issue of the *de jure* applicability of the Fourth Geneva Convention which is the status of Palestinian fighters, the legitimacy of their targeting. Admitting it would *de facto* respect the Geneva Conventions Israel seemingly agreed to respect the inviability of the principle of distinction. In the light of its 'alternative legality' interpretation and of its 'sovereignty argument', however, Israel refused to recognize Palestinian fighters their combatant status.

Conclusion

Israel-Palestine conflict is has its roots in the late 19th and early 20th centuries. The conflict is on-going between Israel and Palestine. The 1967 War (June War) is the crucial phase of Israel Palestine Conflict, which resulted most of territories under Israeli control. The populations whose are living in the territories are facing discrimination by Israeli's people. Even though, Israeli national law recognizes the value of man, the sanctity of his life and individual freedom.The Basic Law on Human Dignity and Liberty is Israel's domestic provision that protects human rights at the highest level of legislation. Israel's alternative legality invalid in justifying the human rights violations perpetrated against the Palestinian and Arab populations residing in the territories under its occupation. Israel's argument against the *de jure* application of the Fourth Geneva Conventions is invalid because of the *de facto* effective control exercised by Israeli authorities since 1967 on the territories under occupation. The claimed change of status of the contended territories after the Oslo Agreement (from occupation to administration) does not, as found by the ICJ, *de facto* change the status of the situation. Human rights law continues to exist and apply alongside humanitarian law. All ratified human rights instruments are, therefore, binding in all territories under Israeli jurisdiction, regardless of whether they contain or not territorial provisions on the scope of their application.

Works Cited

- 2013 Human Rights Report (2014), "Israel and the occupied territories, Bureau of Democracy, Human Rights, and Labor 2013 Country Reports on Human Rights Practices", [Online: Web] Accessed on 7 January 2015 URL: http://www.state.gov/documents/organisation/220568.pdf.
- Barak, Aharon (2006), "Human Rights in Israel", *Israel Law Review* 39 (12): 32-43.
- Benvenisti, Eyal (2012), *the International Law of Occupation, Cambrigdge:* Oxford University Press.
- Fleck, Dieter (2009), *the Handbook of International Humanitarian Law,* Cambridge:Oxford University Press.
- Human Rights Watch (2012), "Forget About Him, He's Not Here: Israel's Control of Palestinian Residency in the West Bank and Gaza" [Online: Web] Accessed on 4 January 2015 URL: http://www.hrw.org/reports/2012/02/05/forget-about-him-he-s-not-here.
- ICRC (1907), "Annex to the Convention: Regulations respecting the laws and customs of war on land, Section III Military authority over the territory of the hostile state', [Online: Web] Accessed on 5 January 2015 URL: https://www.icrc.org/ihl/WebART/195-200052?OpenDocument.
- IMFA (1948), Israel Ministry Foreign Affairs (Israel), "1948 Declaration of Establishment of State of Israel", Accessed on 2 January 2015 URL: http://www.mfa.gov.il /mfa/foreignpolicy/peace/guide/pages/declaration%20of%20establishment%20 of%20state%20of% 20israel.aspx.
- Jewish Virtual Library (1992), "Basic Law: Human Dignity and Liberty 1948", [Online: Web] Accessed on 3 January 2015 URL: http://www.jewishvirtuallibrary. org/jsource/Politics/Basic_ Law_ Human_Dignity_ and_ Liberty.html?MFAH00hi0.

- Jewish Virtual Library (1995), "Israeli-Palestinian Negotiations: Interim Agreement on the West Bank and the Gaza Strip (Oslo II)", [Online: Web] Accessed on 5 January 2015 URL: http://www.jewishvirtuallibrary. org/ jsource/Peace/interim.html.
- Jewish Virtual Library (2003), "The Official Summation of the Or Commission Report", [Online: Web] Accessed on 4 January 2015 URL: http://www. jewishvirtuallibrary. org/jsource/Society_&_ Culture/ OrCommissionReport.html.
- Jewish Virtual Library (2014), 'Vital Statistics: Latest Population", Accessed on 5 January 2015 URL: http://www.jewishvirtuallibrary.org/jsource/ Society_&_Culture/newpop.html.
- Nusseibeh, Sarih (2011), *What is a Palestinian State Worth?* Cambridge: Harvard University Press.
- Peleg, Ilan and Waxman, Dov (2011), *Israel's Palestinians: The Conflict Within,* Cambridge: Harvard University Press.
- Permanent Observer Mission of the State of Palestine to the United Nations, 'Fourth Geneva Convention and the Hague Regulations, [Online: Web] Accessed on 5 January 2015 URL: http://www.un.int/wcm/content/site/ palestine/cache/offonce/pid/11619;jsessionid=099EECCE67262BD AE364931 8C1A41625.
- REFWORLD (2004), "*Advisory Opinion Concerning Legal Consequences of the Construction of a Wall in the Occupied Palestinian Territory",* [Online: web] Accessed on 4 January 2015 URL: http://www.refworld.org/ docid/414ad9a719.html.
- Source: Government of Switzerland (2001), "Conference of High Contracting Parties to the Fourth Geneva Convention Declaration", [Online: Web] Accessed on 4 January 2015 URL: http://unispal.un.org/ UNISPAL.NSF/0/8FC4F064B9B E5BAD85256C1400722951.
- Tibi (2010), "Israel is Democratic for Jews but Jewish for Arabs", The Jerusalem Post, [Online: Web] Accessed on 3 January 2015 URL: http:// www.jpost.com/Israel/Tibi-Israel-is-democratic-for-Jews-but-Jewish-for-Arabs.
- United Nations Secretary General Address to the General Assembly, (2006), [Online: Web] Accessed on 6 January 2015 URL: http://www.un.org/ webcast/ga/61/pdfs/sgstatement_ to_the_ga06.pdf.
- Unknown (1978), "Amnesty International 'Administrative Detention in Israel/Occupied Territories", *Middle East Journal, 32 (3)*: 337-339.

  2013 Human Rights Report (2014), "Israel and the Occupied Territories, Bureau of Democracy, Human Rights, and Labor 2013 Country Reports on Human Rights Practices", Accessed on 04/01/2015 URL: http:// www.state.gov/documents/organisation/220568.pdf. http://www.state.gov/ j/drl/rls/hrrpt/humanrightsreport/index.htm? dynamic_load_ id= 220358 &year=2013#wrapper.

11

Patriarchy, Media and Making of Women Body Image

—Dr. Prem Anand Mishra

Violence against women has been perceived in many ways in the contemporary academic research. They generally tend to show that violence against women is more a kind of physical violence. Although, there is no denying of the fact that physical violence against women must be of prime concern, yet, what remains unnoticed is the other forms of violence committed against women. These other forms of violence are not only sporadic, occasional and personal in nature but they are also systematic and institutionalised.

This paper is an attempt to highlight the new forms of violence against women emerging in recent decades especially at the cultural front produced by media and market. There are several approaches to deal with this theme. The paper employs peace research approach to understand the nature and cause of violence against women and especially the cultural violence against women developed in recent decades. There is a reason as to why peace research perspective should be employed for the purpose here. In fact, peace research perspective gives us interdisciplinary insight to analyze the causes of violence. As it appears, the theme like cultural violence against women cannot be understood in isolation as they are the result of the deep rooted normative as well as socio-cultural structure of the society. Thus, it is appropriate to employ the peace research perspective to deal with the issue at hand as it provides a comprehensive framework to recognize the cause and nature of cultural violence against women through digging the variety of intellectual fields and using available intellectual tools.

First of all, it needs to be mentioned how peace research defines violence. Galtung (1969)-known as the father of peace research – argues that violence is present when the actual psychosomatic realisation of human being is below his/her potential realisation (p.168). Thus, in peace research violence is seen as a gap between the actual and potential psychosomatic realisation of the individual in the given time and space. Thus, violence is *not only an act* but also *a condition*. Galtung further points out that there are three types of violence; direct, structural and cultural which are interrelated with each other. Direct violence is actor generated violence which is personal, measurable and visible in nature while structural violence is structure generated, invisible and immeasurable in nature. Cultural violence is that form of violence that is inherent in our culture and that legitimizes both forms of violence-direct and structural. Galtung's typology of violence might be applied to analyze violence against women and especially cultural violence against women. Direct violence against women includes wife beating, dowry killing in India, female foeticide and rape. It can be noted that direct violence against women is related only with women's physical body. This kind of violence is measurable, it can be seen and its impact may be physically traced. However, direct violence against women draws attention only when it comes in public domain when it is reported in media or made public by other means in the case of its extreme severity. Besides direct violence against women, one can also trace structural violence against women which is not perceived and remains unnoticed because such violence is in-built in the structure of society. As one may note, by this criterion patriarchy is the most common form of structural violence that is prevalent in almost all the societies. At definitional level, patriarchy is a social system in which; males hold primary power; males predominate in roles of political leadership, moral authority, social privilege and control of property; and, in the domain of the family, fathers or father-figures hold authority over women and children. Consequences of patriarchy are difficult to measure but they are always noticeable on women as it puts certain restrictions on women and because of the restrictions women cannot fully realize their psychosomatic potential. It should be noted that patriarchy has developed in thousands of years of civilisation and only so-called biological reason of male supremacy is not alone in its development.

Cultural Violence against Women

There is a third form of violence called cultural violence that the paper wishes to focus. In general, cultural violence is a form of violence that is inherent in our culture, religion, tradition, scriptures, art and science and even in our world –view (Galtung, 1990, p.293). When we discuss cultural violence against women, it means those aspects of our cultural practices, religion and tradition that *justify* violence against women in some way - directly or indirectly. It *legitimizes* both forms of violence- direct and structural - against women by different subtle and rhetoric strategies. As social phenomenon seems quite normal, it is difficult to realize and recognize the forms of cultural violence against women. Moreover, culture also injects its value, thus, people are unable to detect the emphasis of male domination over women. However, through conscious reading of cultural attributes one may get the view how culture becomes a hindrance in realizing the psycho-somatic potential of women, thus, promoting violence against them.

In all social tradition, cultural violence against women may be seen in the forms of folklore, proverbs or regional idioms or religious sanctions in which woman is depicted in such a way that unconsciously tell us how women should be treated and what behvaiour are expected from them in the social life. These inform us how women have been subjugated in the society only because they are women. The consequence of such folklores, proverbs, and regional idioms prevalent in cultural and sub-cultural traditions and traits is that they close some of the significant avenues for women, for example their access to education in some part of India, because they are women. In general, cultural practices or some elements of culture define the boundary for women and they cannot go beyond that boundary. This shows the patriarchic structure of the society which is *legitimized* by the cultural traits in which women have no voice or little voice. This recalls us that feminist position that tells us that women are not born as women but they are made women by the culture and society.

At this point, it needs to be mentioned that although sex (male or female) is biological and natural but gender (masculinity or femininity) is a social construction. In fact, the social construction of gender assigns certain qualities for being a man (masculine) or woman (feminine). Further, the construction of gender is not static but dynamic in nature and it is influenced by our environment and socialisation. In this regard, Allard and Cooper (1995) assert that "our views on gender are not passively shaped by the larger societal forces but actively shaped by them, and in this regard schools and media play significant role" (p.24). This construction of gender identities that is also called subjectivities or in more specific way femininities or masculinities is also ongoing, changing and changeable. We may note here that although gender is a social construction, it has assumed such a status that it is hard to make a distinction between the gender and sex. In the discussion of cultural violence against women, it also needs to be pointed out that recently it has been suggested, after the advent of 'cultural studies', that culture is not 'given' but it is produced and reproduced by some agencies. In this context, one may observe that which kind of cultural is being produced and reproduced by the market and media in recent decades and how they portray women.

In fact, media and market as societal forces have produced a new 'body culture' in the society that constructs the femininities in a very discursive way. Moreover, they have constructed a typical body image of women that calls for perfection, thinness and fairness of the women body. These construct are represented as ideals and anything less than these ideals are portrayed as deviations. The constructions of such kind of body images of woman make impact on both men and women. As Garner (1997) points out, "body image actively influences much of our behvaiour, self esteem and psychopathology. Our body perception feeling and belief governs our life plan" (p.30). Thus, the media and market's construction of women body images cannot be taken lightly and they indeed make differences in our perception of personal and public life. In this regard, one might also question that to which extent the media's construction of women body images are realistic and attainable. It is in these theoretical underpinning the paper, first, traces that how market and media construct the different forms of women body images and then reveals that how they make a new form of cultural violence against women.

Male Gaze, Media and Making of Women Body Images

To unpack the question raised above, I would like to bring Foucault's notion of 'gaze' for present analysis. According to Foucault (1973), 'gaze' is way "by which one controls the behaviors of others by just looking" (p.xii). One may observe a 'male gaze' in society by which male tries to control woman's behaviors (especially her bodily behaviors) by just looking at her body. Although such male gaze is not permissible and accepted in society, especially in India, yet, patriarchy in subtle way attempts to inject a value in women by which she wants to be 'attention grabber'. Modern media (electronic and print both) and market culture produce an image in society that women must be 'attention grabber/maker' to such an extent that it sometimes seems that they are conveying a notion that as if such attention grabbing attributes were women's birth right.

In this regard, Fredrickson and Roberts (1997) argues that "most insidious way by which the media emphasize physical attractiveness of woman body is the 'objectification' of women's bodies" (p.175). The objectification of women body is represented in the media in a very discursive way. One of the major instruments of media that portrays women body as an object is advertisement. The logic used in the advertisements is fairly simple: beautiful women bodies or body parts of women can be employed to seize attention and create desire in both men and women, which would lead men and women to purchase manufactured goods. Yet, if one looks the media advertisements, one finds that often women are portrayed not in a whole but in fragments. The visuals show only legs, torsos, or an open mouth with rouge lip colour of women which is provocatively placed before the spectators. This reduces women to collections of parts, something less than human. Moreover, this objectification and sexploitation of women is made *normal* by constantly showing them to the viewers. This normalisation changes the attitudes of both men and women towards the female body. On the on hand, young girls and women internalize an observer's perspective of their own bodies; thus they think about their life in the third-person. In other words, such constructions encourage women to view their bodies as if they were outside observers. On the other hand, men compare the women in their lives to what they see on television screens, in magazines, and on billboards. Thus, for men the objectified women body becomes the ideal to be desired, regardless of the fact that they are fabricated. Recent studies show that the objectification of women not only induces states of shame and fear in women; it also promotes the treatment of them as inhuman playthings (Berberick, 2010, p. 7). Growing tendency of cosmetic surgery, reducing fats form stomach and thigh, are some of examples of this phenomenon. Thus, women's bodies are equated with commodities to be consumed. On the other hand, by inculcating the notion in men to regard women' bodies as objects, advertisements produce a culture that undervalue women as people, encourages sexual harassment, and worse (Jacobson and Mazur, 1995, p.84). Moreover, the more the women are presented as objects; more they are not connected to themselves. In other words, they are not for themselves but for male and their desires. Thus, the objectification of women body shows that women do not really have soul or spirit or voice.

In this regard, it is hardly noticed that the *normalisation* of the objectification of female body by media and market has developed and injected such a 'consciousness' in women mass that they think it normal to adorn herself to feel free, liberated and to be gazed and celebrated by men. Moreover, the process of objectification of women body has been made so normal that it is hardly understood as construction of media and market. It is quite interesting to note that in the market and media, the male body is taken as 'descriptive', while female body is expected to be 'performative'. This performative aspect of female body which is the part of new 'body image project' invented by the media and market as a new cultural production focus on two 'movements' in womenfolk –the 'white obsession' and 'culture of thinness'. Cindy Manyard (1998) has also pointed out that "such misperceptions of body images- whiteness and thinness- are so prevalent among women that it is almost considered normal" (p.3).

One may well argue that why women are accepting such objectification of their body and how it is becoming normal? As one scholar suggests, "Individuals create a personalised reality that is reflective of what they observe and identify as meaningful in their environment, and then they act based on those observations. Therefore, if women are observing images thrust at them through mass communication as a guideline of how to act, they naturally begin to act in that manner because it mirrors their environment" (Bandura, 1999, p.23). Thus, there is cultural pressure concerning the above mentioned two women body image project- whiteness and thinness. It needs to be mentioned that body image refers to personal constructions and public projections of our body and body parts, often in attempted conformity with parameters of 'beauty' established in socio-cultural or non-personal contexts as media and market. In other words, body image "involves our perception, imagination, emotions and physical sensations of and about our bodies in relation to values that are not necessarily innate but learned or expected culturally" (Lightstone, 2006, p.2). As noted above, media and market constructs woman body images through the representation of female body in the form of so called perfect female body that mainly focuses on thinness and whiteness.

Thinness

Many researchers have shown that women become/ can become part of an appearance-oriented culture developed by media and market that focuses on thinness (Berberick, 2010, p.12). Through print or electronic media, women learn the specific prescriptions for the ideal or perfect body. There is a huge market that sells sexualised clothing to imitate the thin ideal woman. Research has also found that there is social pressure for women to criticize their bodies in the form of 'fat talk' (Nichter and Vuckovic, 1994, p.109). In this context, it becomes socially acceptable, and even expected, for women to be obsessed with their bodies. There is growing tendency of body obsession among women that has become the synonym of thinness obsessions. One study found that between 30 per cent and 50 per cent of adolescent girls are concerned with their weight and many report dieting (Hogan and Starsburger, 2008, p.526). Recently, in one of the studies Grabe and Hide (2007) found that "girls as young as age 11 engage in self-objectification" (p.526). In another research of this kind, Kerr (2010) revealed the extent to which this objectification has been internalised by showing that merely reading words concerning body's physical appearance induced a state of self-objectification in women. These women reported significantly higher levels of body shame and appearance anxiety compared to men (p.21).

The idea and practice of looking thin among women, presented by media and market, has resulted in a kind of intra- personal violence that women commits on themselves. Repression of one's own body on the name of thinness has resulted in acute eating disorder and depression among women. In this regard, in one of the studies, scholar Kerr focuses on the relation between body image and depression in girls. Although Kerr's study provides the description of the Western society, however, his description does not seem away from the Indian reality also. Kerr argues that how 'not to be thin' presents a negative body image. In his words, "Negative body image in adolescent girls is of growing concern in modern Western societies. As girls go through their puberty, their bodies gain adipose and move farther away from the thin ideal for women. One must only take a look at a fashion magazine to see how the current ideal body is often asexual and childlike. Such a medium influences these girls and often causes them to become dissatisfied with their appearance" (Kerr, 2010, p.21).

Whiteness

There is a second construction of women body image by market and media that is whiteness. Media and market portray whiteness as the standard of beauty. When whiteness is considered standard or superior, white women are bound to be considered more attractive by definition. In our country, looking better has become synonym of looking fairer. Even the advertisements and store posters that use Indian women faces promote a look that depicts women having long, silky straight hair; a tall, thin body; and most importantly, a fair complexion. Moreover, in Asia, as Shome (2010) argues "beauty, wealth, and success are associated with fairer skin" (p.1). Because of this belief, whitening products are flying all over the markets in the world in general and India in particular. If one looks the consumption of beauty products, one may notices the Indians obsession with fair skin. Beginning with 1978 when Unilever launched Fair & Lovely cream, now market is full of fairness cream. In 2010, India's whitening-cream market was worth $432m, according to a report by market researchers ACNielsen; this was growing at 18 per cent per year. Last year, Indians reportedly consumed 233 tones of skin-whitening products, spending more money on them than on Coca-Cola (see. www.theguardian.com › World› India).

On the other hand, women who are not white or have not a fair skin develop a negative body image for themselves. As suggested by one of the studies, "the internalisation of body images in the form of 'whiteness as beauty' projected by media and market promotes body shame, body dissatisfaction, anxiety, and depression among those women who are not fairer" (McKinley and Hyde: 1996:196). At this point, it is important to note that though women suffering from a negative body image are a universal phenomenon, yet, there are cultural differences. For example, in Western culture where thinness is equated with success, happiness and wealth, women are generally obsessed with being overweight. On the other hand, in Asian cultures like India, apart from thinness, fairness is also equated with success and beauty. Women in our culture are obsessed with thinness as well as fair colour complexion.

Patriarchy and Objectification of Women Body as Cultural Violence

Objectification of women by media and market through constantly projecting the women body images in the form of thinness and whiteness reinforces the structure and value of patriarchy. Patriarchy is not only a static system of male domination over women but a dynamic structure and value also that operate in a very subtle way through different rhetoric. The rhetoric of patriarchy in cultural domain entails control over women by constantly defining and re-defining *what beauty is*, which, in fact exerts a new form of cultural violence against women as it constructs constantly new beauty norms that gradually transforms into social norms according to which women have to constantly adapt. In the context of our present discussion, it is significant to note that in the construction of woman body images by media patriarchy works in both explicit and implicit way. Explicitly men have the power to create women's body image, as they are the editors, directors, photographers and designers in media. In other words, they have the power to define and redefine women through images. With this power they make the particular images of women as universal and portray them as normal. This phenomenon is so powerful that even though women get the same power position in media, the beauty -

images does not seem to be changing. In this way patriarchy works explicitly through power and power position in a system like media.

On the other hand, patriarchy operates implicitly by promoting value which serves the male domination in subtle way. As women bodies are constantly under 'gaze' of men and their appreciation, women indirectly internalize the significance of her body which is in fact a value imposed by the patriarchy. This internalisation not only reinforces the idea and practice that women should view their body as commodity but also continuously should monitor it for faults and removes them if possible. What is not realised is that it is patriarchy that demands the perfection of female body. Moreover, in a very subtle way patriarchy also create, reinforce and inject the idea that women are incomplete and imperfect in themselves. Thus, what women need is to present themselves as perfect and complete as projected in the line of media projection of women body images. Thus, it is not surprising that women try to look nice, stay in fashion and presents themselves too lively, because they know they are being judged by their looks. On the other hand, through media images of women, young girls learn what should be the correct body size and weight. They internalize the message that thin is gorgeous and fat is careless and unattractive. Having perfect body shape is also taken as indicative of self-control for women. Thus, the body is understood as a pet animal that should be subdued and controlled at any cost with 'fit and fine' as motto. This dimension is not a personal one but it has social consequence also. On the social effect of such body images, Orbach (1986) has pointed out that "it is no coincidence that the more women demand their rightful place in workplace and society, the more subjugation of women takes place through their body image" (p.34). This is again a patriarchic strategy that reinforces itself in different way which is difficult to realize. Women get trapped in it and ironically they feel that they are free. Similarly, today there is more emphasis on conception of looking always young. As Julia Twigg (2007) points out, "while talking about body image one also needs to pay attention to thing like aging" (p.293). As one may notice in today's society, to 'look always young' is another demand, which really the patriarchy puts before the women and controls the body and psyche of women by its indirect strategy.

Thus, media and market employing patriarchic value have reduced women to being nothing more than objects to be won, prizes to be shown off, and playthings to be abused. It has also created a fabricated standard of beauty which is unrealistic and unattainable for women and women compare themselves to that standard. Also, men compare the women in their lives to what they see on television screens, in magazines, and on billboards. As a result, both the self and society has suffered because of the objectification of women. On the other hand, one may also see the cruelty of media projection of women body as it indirectly tells women to perform something for male even at the cost of their physical and psychological health.

Finally, it is significant to point out briefly how women body has been viewed in Women Studies and recent feminist literature. Feminists have generally accepted the biological attributes and differential qualities of female body but at the same time some feminists argue that women have rights to 'celebrate' this female attributes and qualifications. Thus, some feminists propose the celebration of female body, at least they do not consider it wrong, on the name of freedom of women body, yet, it can be argued that they fail to recognize that they are in very subtle way thinking under a patriarchic structure and values that they claim to oppose. Celebration of female body, in the view of some feminists, is not limited to its uniqueness and to the women liberation movement but they also identify it as a revolt against the patriarchy. However, as we have noticed that such 'celebration' is already trapped in the patriarchic way of thinking and structure of the society and 'celebration revolt' against patriarchy indirectly reconfirms the values of patriarchy.

Conclusion

Media has constructed a new culture that projects women body in particular appearances. This is a new form of cultural violence as it legitimizes and reinforces the value of patriarchy in a very subtle form. As noted above, women body images are not images of women by women but images of women by men or patriarchy. Moreover, women body images projected by media are not natural but fabricated for commercial purpose that employs patriarchic value as an instrument in a very subtle way that exploits both men and women's way of thinking. While men get victim of such body images and insist such images in real life, women internalizing such patriarchic value mimic the images in their daily life and suffer from eating disorder, anxiety and depression. Under the influence of patriarchy, media through women body images has reduced the women to an object. This objectification of women body by media through constructing women body images is a cultural violence against women at it reduces women to only as a crude body- a body that can be portrayed for male entertainment- a body that has meaning only in male society- a body that has always to perform- and finally a body that is devoid of its self.

Works Cited

- Allard, A and Cooper. (1995). Stages*: Steps Towards Addressing Gender In Educational Settings*, Melbourne: Curriculum Corporation.
- Bandura, Albert. (1999). Social Cognitive Theory: A Genetic Perspective." *Asian Journal of Social Psychology*. Vol.2. pp. 21- 41.
- Berberick Stephanie Nichol. (2010). The Objectification of Women in Mass Media: Female Self-Image in Misogynist Culture. *The New York Sociologist*, Vol. 5. pp.1-15.
- Cindy Maynard. (1998). *Current Health* 2, Weekly Reader Corp.
- Foucault, Michel. (1973).*The Birth of the Clinic: An Archaeology of Medical Perception*. London: Rutledge.
- Fredrickson Barbara L. and Roberts. (1997). *Psychology of Women Quarterly* Vol.21, No. 2, pp. 173–206.
- Galtung, Johan. (1969). "Violence, Peace, and Peace Research". *Journal of Peace Research*, Vol. 6, No. 3. pp. 167-191.
- Galtung, Johan. (1990). "Cultural Violence," *Journal of Peace Research*, Vol. 27, No. 3. pp. 291-305.
- Garner. David. (1997). Survey Says: Body Image Poll Results www.psychologytoday.com/.../survey-says-body-image-poll-results"ults.
- Grabe, S. and Hyde, J. S. (2007). Gender, Pubertal Development, and Peer Sexual Harassment predict Objectified Body Consciousness in Early Adolescence. *Journal of Research on Adolescence*, 17 , 723– 742.
- Hogan and Starsburger. (2008) Body Image Eating disorders and the Media. *Adolec Med.* 19. pp.521-546.
- Jacobson, Michael F. and Laurie Ann Mazur. (1995). *Marketing Madness: A Survival Guide for a Consumer Society* . Boulder, CO: West view Press, Inc.
- Kerr, Kara L. (2010). "Sociocultural Influences on Body Image and Depression in Adolescent Girls." *Priscilla Papers,* 24(2):21.

- Lightstone, Judy (2006). *Improving Body Image*. http://www.edreferral.com/body_image.htm retived on 23/11/2014.
- McKinley, N. M., & Hyde, J. S. (1996). The Objectified Body Consciousness Scale: Development and validation. *Psychology of Women Quarterly*, 20, pp.181–216
- Nichter, M., and Vuckovic, N. (1994). Fat talk. In N. Sault (Ed.), *Many mirrors: Body image and social relations* (pp. 109-131). New Brunswick, NJ: Rutgers University Press.
- Orbach, S. (1986). *Hunger Strike*. London: Faber and Faber.
- Shome, D. (2010). Skin Whitening / Lightening Treatment For Fairer, Lighter Skin? Retrieved on 10/12/2014. from http//: *deverajshome.wordpress*.com.
- Twigg, J. (2007). 'Clothing, Age and the Body: A Critical Review', *Ageing & Society*, 27, pp. 285-305.

12

Political and Economic Rights of Women in Democratic Iraq

—Priyadarshini Sahoo

Introduction

Iraq is one of the newly democratized states in the world where condition of women has become a matter of increasing concern. Iraq has become a democratic country after almost three decades of autocratic rule of President Saddam Hussein who was deposed subsequent to the 2003 US-led invasion. In the present day, women in Iraq seem driven not by the expectation of improving their status but by the determination to hold on to what rights they have in the face of growing insecurity, violence, religious fundamentalism and economic hardship. Women have seen significant gains in some areas since the 2003 invasion of Iraq, carving out an unprecedented space for women's political and public participation, such as they have largely been unable to capitalize on this position to improve women's daily lives due to a lack of political will, to place women in positions of leadership or to include them in fundamental decision making processes. Simultaneously Iraq exposes the considerable obstacles women face, in the quest to secure and safeguard their human rights. For example, women's access to healthcare remains restricted not due to discriminatory laws but due to a lack of implementation of legislation coupled with an increasing lack of resources. Likewise, the low participation rate of girls in primary education reflects the failure of the government to protect existing rights and the escalating security risks. In other areas, such as family and criminal matters, laws expressly discriminating against women set the framework for depriving women of their legal rights. The Iraqi Constitution of 2005 establishes the framework for equality in protection and enforcement of human rights. It remains to be seen whether those guarantees will be put into effect.

Surprisingly, under Saddam Hussein's early period of rule, status of Iraqi women was comparatively better and they were quite visible in the public sphere as well. The Arab socialism of the Iraqi Ba'ath party included in its ideology provisions for women's liberation and equality. It was however, only after the Iran-Iraq war, more particularly after the invasion of Kuwait that the status of women started deteriorating sharply. During the period of sanctions, more Iraqi women were refused to be allowed into schools. There was complete lawlessness and lack of security for women. They were subjected to increased harassment and abductions, as well as sexual abuse and rape. The collapse of Baghdad on April 10, 2003, brought Iraq and the women living in it into an uncertain transition period. The Coalition forces came to Iraq in March 2003 promising, among other things, to improve the lives of Iraqi women. In this vein, Security Council Resolution 1483 sought to establish a "rule of law that affords equal rights and justice to all Iraqi citizens without regard to ethnicity, religion, or gender" (United Nations Security Council Resolution 1483, 22 May 2003). But unfortunately, this has been, of course, easier said than done, the future of Iraqi women faces huge obstacles. Unfortunately, the most significant obstacles in this area appear to reside in the popular mind-set, the traditions and societal outlook of much of the Iraqi population.

The present study examines the condition of women in Iraq at three different levels: social, political and economical. The first section of this paper provides an overview of Iraqi women's situation under Baathist rule (1968-2003). The second section discusses the position of women in the immediate post-Hussein period, examining the role of the Coalition Provisional Authority (CPA), and also examines the current situation of Iraqi women, recent elections, and the impact the Transitional National Assembly (TNA) has upon women and the Final section of this paper highlighting the possible outcomes of a volatile security situation, indigenous challenges to women's rights (like the rise of Islamic conservatism), and of the transition to Iraqi sovereignty.

Women in Saddam Hussein's Iraq: Fluctuating Status

Iraq since its founding in the 1920's allowed its women far greater freedom than many other countries in the area. The Personal Status Law introduced in 1959 just after Iraq became a Republic, granted equal inheritance and divorce rights for men and women and included provisions concerning child support (Pina, 2006). The Ba'ath party, which seized power in 1968, admitted women into universities and the government and public employment sectors in large numbers, and in smaller amounts, into the private sector. In 1970, the Provisional Constitution was drafted, which declared men and women equal under the law. At one point during Saddam's 35 year reign, the percentage of women in the civil service even reached 40 per cent (Ciezadlo, 2003). In 1972, in line with the party's attempt to consolidate civil institutions under state control, the Baathists formed the General Federation of Iraqi Women (GFIW), also known as the Iraqi Women's Federation (Henninger, 2005). Despite the existence of the GFIW participation of women, within the national political discourse was fairly limited. Even though some scholars argue that there were some women in the Baathist Regional Command; however, in reality, men ran the state apparatus and filled most of the senior management positions as Iraq remained a largely patriarchal and tribal-based society (Henninger, 2005).

In 1980, one year after Saddam Hussein's ascendance, women were also given the right to vote and hold office (Brown and Romano, 2006). Furthermore, women's situation in Iraq degenerated significantly after 1990, when Saddam's war-weary regime sought support from neighbouring Islamic states. Saddam publicly acknowledged the moral authority of Islam and this acceptance led to an unfortunate reduction in women's rights that so often accompanies a patriarchal interpretation and implementation of the Koran (Congressional Research Service reports July 9, 2003). Men were allowed to marry additional wives and women lost what rights they had accumulated with respect to divorce, child custody, and inheritance. Rates of honour killings the practice of murdering women who, through "suspicious behaviour," pre-marital sex or by being the victims of rape have dishonoured the family's name rose dramatically when Saddam introduced Article 111 into the Iraqi Penal Code in 1990 (Office of International Women's

Issues, Washington, DC, March 20, 2003). Moreover, UN sanctions on Iraq and Saddam's mismanagement of 'Oil for Food' money' Female children were the first to be kept back from school when family finances were running short. The effect of this was stark: In 1987, 75 per cent of women were literate; by the end of 2000, this number had fallen to 25 per cent (UNOCHR, 2003).

The 2003 Iraq War and its Aftermath

The war of liberation has no doubt had an immediate effect on women all over the country. A majority of women expected the American overthrown of Saddam to deliver to them greater freedom from both the tyranny of the Ba'ath regime and the discrimination they faced in the home, society and the workforce. Unfortunately, Iraqi women soon realised that the Americans are not the ultimate harbingers of freedom from fear; they cannot deliver, immediately, all that they promised; and their declaration to offer greater rights and opportunities to women is not at the top of their agenda. The situation in Iraq differs from the north to the center and to the south of the country, where various political, religious, social and security forces are affecting the development of women's rights groups and their participation in civil society.

- **Position of Women in Iraqi Kurdistan (Northern Iraq)**

In the Kurdish north, while the government has promoted women's rights and the last 14 years of Kurdish, self-rule have allowed women's organisations and shelters to spring up in far greater numbers than elsewhere in Iraq, Kurdistan has still not thrown off a popular culture which relegates women to an inferior position in society. Although there has been much work among Kurdish elites and authorities dealing with women's rights, bottom-up civil society pressure for women's rights has not emerged as nearly as significant a force as the Kurdish administration's own initiatives on women's issue. The Kurdistan Regional Government has shown several significant advances regarding women's issues since its creation in 1991. Women are represented in the government and have become high-ranking judges. The KDP and the PUK, contrary to some reports, have typically been very supportive and even encouraging towards women trying to work themselves up in society (Mahmoud, 2004). The Penal Code introduced by Saddam in 1990, for example, which made honour killings legal, was renounced by the Kurdistan Regional Government in 2000, a giant step forward for women's rights in the area (Mahmoud, 2004).Unfortunately, both the KDP and PUK have still not done enough to enforce their new laws prohibiting honour killings, by meeting out severe punishments for those guilty of this horrendous crime. Furthermore, according to one report, female circumcision has increased to shockingly high levels in Iraqi Kurdistan, a region which has no history of this practice. Both honour killings and female circumcision are more rampant in outlying villages than in the more urban areas (Rashid, 2000). In addition, many Iraqi elites remain adamantly misogynistic. For example, the Shiite Turkmen director of the Iraqi Institute for Human Rights in Kirkuk expressed the following fear in a recent interview:

"There are no laws. It is true that the new constitution guarantees the rights of citizens, but this constitution is based on western models. Iraq is an Islamic country. This constitution will plant the seeds of rebellion between the different ethnic groups. Also they are using the example of women's rights to impose western ideas on us. How can the Iraqi man be a prisoner of the women! Islam has guaranteed many rights for women. They are planting the seeds of conflict between men and women" (Iraqi Institute for Human Rights, Kirkuk, 2004).

In Iraqi Kurdistan, the area's most positively affected by the American-led war were those who had been living under the control of radical Islamic Wahabi groups such as Ansar al Islam and the Islamic Group of Ali Bapir, both of which took control of a string of Kurdish mountain hamlets from the PUK and forced the local women's to cover themselves completely in black, stop attending school, throw out their televisions and radios and live with the knowledge that they were being watched constantly (Pina, 2006).

- **Conditions of Women in Central and southern Iraq**

Previously, the center of the country has seen much freedom for women whereas, since the American led war, the deteriorating security situation has confined many women to their homes. There has been a great push for greater attention to be paid to women's issues from the

International NGOs, the CPA, and some Iraqi elites. However, they are working against fierce resistance, wherein the threat of violence and general lawlessness seriously hampers any possible progress. Women working with NGOs, as well as individual female members of the general population, have been the targets of both random and targeted violence. For example, Yanar Mohammed, the outspoken leader of the Organisation of Women's Freedom in Iraq, has received numerous death threats. Average women in Baghdad and many other areas also fear rape or kidnap if they leave their homes. The increasing influence of Islamic groups in Iraq has also further restricted the movements and participation of women in the new society. Hence, the huge numbers of qualified women who are invaluable tools for societal advancement in general and women's advancement in particular, have been largely sequestered to their homes by lack of security in the south and especially the center of the country. The main problem facing women in the south since 2003 has been the strong influence of very patriarchal interpretations and practice of Islam. Women were even more fearful of such forbidden activities, however, because the punishment was much harsher for them their whole family could be taken into custody (Rida, 2003).

From the analysis above, it should be clear that both the policies of Saddam's regime and the Iraq war of 2003 had a mixed impact on the situation of women in Iraq. While Saddam's Ba'athist government policies introduced some progressive policies and legislation for Iraqi women, these were offset by the societal impact of ceaseless wars, domestic authoritarian control and repression, and a shift to more conservative patriarchal government policies after 1990. Although the removal of Saddam's dictatorship in 2003 has now ended his regime's oppression and allowed for the entry of a myriad of progressive NGOs, new pro-female emancipation government policies, and independent women's organisations, the current lack of security in Iraq as well as resurgent Islamic, tribal, and generally conservative forces in the country bodes ill for women there. In fairly stark contrast to the center and south of Iraq, however, the northern Kurdish autonomous region continues to make progress towards increasing women's empowerment, autonomy and integration into public life.

Democratisation of Iraq and Political Empowerment of Women

Since March 2004, several congressional Members have participated in the Iraqi Women's union, with the intention of improving Iraqi women's lives and supporting women to gain access to educational and professional opportunities. S. 2144, a bill introduced in the 108th Congress as the Foreign Affairs Authorisation Act FY2005, included a section expressing the "sense of Congress that the rights of women in Iraq, including their full participation in government and society, should be protected following the transfer of sovereignty to Iraq in June 2004" (Pina, 2006). Another bill, H. Res. 143 (also introduced in the 108th Congress), resolved that Congress encourage ongoing programs designed to support Iraqi women to participate more fully in democratic Iraq. The 1970 Iraqi Constitution issued by the Baathist regime declared equal rights for all Iraqis, regardless of sex, race, language, social origin, or religion. In 1980, Law No. 55 granted women the right to be nominated to the Iraqi National Assembly. Since the U.S.-led invasion of Iraq in 2003 and the formation of the CPA, the Bush Administration has stated its interest in ensuring that Iraqi women are involved in rebuilding and reconstruction efforts in Iraq. An August 2003 "Fact Sheet" issued by the Department of State indicated that:

"The U.S. is committed to helping the Iraqi people transition to a sovereign, representative form of government that respects human rights, rejects terrorism and maintains Iraq's territorial integrity without threatening its neighbors. We recognize that the women of Iraq have a critical role to play in the revival of their country and we strongly support their efforts. They bring skills and knowledge that will be vital to restoring Iraq to its rightful place in the region and in the world. The U.S. will engage with Iraqi women to secure and advance the gains that they have achieved so far" (Pina, 2006).

In the aftermath of Operation Iraqi Freedom, the Coalition Provisional Authority (CPA) paid little attention to women's rights and representation in post-war planning. When Iraqi opposition groups met in Nasiriyah in April 2003 to discuss self-rule, only four women all former exiles were among the approximately120 delegates (UNIFEM, 2003). Hundreds of women marched in Baghdad to demand women's inclusion in the Iraqi Governing Council (IGC), which was appointed by the CPA on July 13, 2003. Despite their efforts, only three of twenty-five IGC members were women. The CPA announced the appointment of twenty-five ministries in September 2003. Only the ministry of municipalities and public works would be supervised by a woman: Nesreen Berwari (UNIFEM, 2003). According to the U.S. State Department, the CPA approved a list of deputy ministers in April 2004.The list included seven women in the ministries of agriculture, culture, displacement and migration, electricity, environment, higher education, and transportation (UNIFEM, 2003). Two women were among eight appointed Iraqi members of the Independent Electoral Commission of Iraq (IECI), which was Political Participation by Iraq's Women established on March 31, 2004 to oversee the parliamentary elections of January 30, 2005. The INC was comprised one hundred members eighty-one newly selected and nineteen transferred from the defunct IGC. Once again, the membership of the INC reflected the twenty-five per cent target for women's participation stipulated by the TAL. Yet, women occupy less than twenty-five per cent of available positions at the ministerial level, as ambassadors, in the Constitutional Drafting Committee (CDC), and in the twenty-five INA committees that are tasked with designing and implementing Iraq's democracy. Among the thirty cabinet members appointed at the recommendation of Prime Minister Ibrahim al-Jaafari are six women, who currently hold seven ministerial positions. The Constitutional Drafting Committee (CDC), announced on May 10, 2005, was originally comprised of fifty-five members, and the subsequent addition of Sunnis Participants worked in small groups in December 2004 to discuss the January 2005 elections and determine avenues for women's participation in Iraq's new government brought its membership to seventy-one at least nine of whom are women. By rallying for the adoption and retraction of various legislations, women have influenced foundational positions on women's rights in Iraq. By being elected and appointed to governing bodies, women are empowered to bring about change within Iraq's leadership and facilitate democracy for Iraqi citizens.

The United States transferred limited sovereignty to an interim Iraqi government on June 28, 2004, with a new government and a permanent constitution to be voted on later. In June 2004, the United Nations formed an 8-member Independent Electoral Commission of Iraq (IECI), to assist in the election of a 275-seat National Assembly, a provincial assembly in each of Iraq's 18 provinces (41 seats each and 51 for Baghdad), and a Kurdistan regional assembly (111 seats). The elections were provided for in the TAL, and took place on January 30, 2005. Under IECI rules, every third position on electoral lists contained a woman's name. This calculus developed in response to the TAL's goal for at least 25 per cent female membership in the new Iraqi National Assembly. A new Elections Law was passed on September 12, 2005 replacing CPA Order 96. This law governed the December 2005 parliamentary elections. Article 11 of the elections law of 2005 says that "At least one woman must be among the first three nominees on the list and at least two women must be among the first six nominees on the list and so on until the end of the list". For many Iraqi women and outside observers, the elections results have been mixed. Iraqi women exceeded the baseline of 25 per cent Assembly membership to make up nearly 31 per cent of the Assembly (or 86 out of 275 seats). The winning Shi'i list, backed by the prominent Iraqi cleric, Grand Ayatollah Ali Sistani, has 46 women in its block of 140 seats (Bassoul, 2005). The fundamentalism of the government for women under occupation drastically undermined women rights. Women occupying 25 per cent (quota) in the Iraqi Parliament is only symbolic political representation which served to improve the image of the occupation. Only 62 judges operating in Iraq are women, out of a total of 1200 (UNAMI, 2010). Furthermore, there is widespread hope, among Iraqi women's groups, that a new constitution will continue to stipulate wide-ranging, liberal rights for Iraqi women. Although modern Iraqi history is replete with liberal views towards women, Iraqi Shi'ism and the wider culture of the country may create obstacles for women increasing their participation and visibility in Iraqi political and social life. Many critics argue that women hold no top positions in any of Iraq's 18 governorates or judiciaries. Women have participated actively in both sets of elections held since the fall of the Ba'ath regime. As documented in the press, women turned out in record numbers for the January 2005 elections, despite serious security threats to all voters. Despite provision for women's representation set forth in the

Constitution and put into effect under the Elections Law, women won only 19 per cent of the parliamentary seats in December 2005 elections. They ultimately reached the quota by allocation of compensatory seats to women such that women now make up 73 of the 275-member Council of Representatives (or 27 per cent). Moreover, women remain absent from leadership positions in the COR and political parties. No woman heads a political party or coalition list.

A number of security concerns affect not only the involvement of women in the developing Iraqi political system but also the access of ordinary Iraqi women to reconstruction programs. Some report that many Iraqi women, who work to advance political freedoms, do so under threat of violence, extortion, and kidnappings. The lack of security has been cited as a major obstacle in the progress of reconstruction efforts aimed at advancing women's rights. Religious and cultural factors in Iraq might also present challenges to reconstruction efforts targeting women. For example, there is a debate over the extent that Islamic law or Shari'a should play a role in a future Iraqi government. Some Iraqi groups including those represented on the U.S.-appointed Governing Council are interested in instituting Islamic courts instead of civil courts to oversee matters related to marriage, divorce, property ownership, and inheritance. These courts would be run by Muslim clerics - all of whom are male. Some recent studies indicate a degree of indigenous resistance to women's involvement in governance or to equal rights for women, particularly in the more traditional and Shi'i-dominated region of southern Iraq. One study of southern Iraq indicated that most Iraqi men and women do not fully support women's civil and political rights, "including freedom to move in public and to participate in government" (Amowitz, 2004).

The first democratic Iraqi government came into power in 2005. Despite a relatively successful parliamentary election, the process of drawing up a new constitution posed a major challenge for the new Iraqi state. There were widespread concerns about the future role of Islamic law, with question marks about the extent of its commitment to upholding human, and especially women's rights (Coleman, 2006; Eisenstein, 2013). However, when the Constitutional Committee was appointed to discuss about future women rights in Iraq, there was no single woman member amongst all nine member of this committee. This period also saw an increase in violence against women especially in the mixed Shia-Sunni area and East Iraq, with increase in the incidents of rape and abuse mainly by the Sunni insurgent groups, in order to create chaos and destabilise the current government. Even though most political parties talked about women rights and gender equality, eventually none of these parties took significant steps to improve the condition of women in Iraq (Cardsman, 2008; Leland and Mohammed, 2010). After the January 2005 elections, it was proposed that the Iraqi constitution would be made by the Transitional National Assembly (TNA). This constitution was highly important with respect to the condition of women in Iraq, mainly because it was to include various ordinances for upholding women rights, as well as development of a democratic and a stable Iraq. **Article 20** of the Iraqi constitution guaranteed equal rights to participate in public affairs and enjoy political right including the right to vote, elect and run for office (Iraqi Constitution, 2005). Further, **clause IV of Article 49** enshrined a provision for the reservation of 25 per cent of the total seats for women in the Council of Representatives (Iraqi Constitution, 2005). In 2006, a constitutional review committee was formed, which did not have enough representation of women; there were only two women in a body of thirty one. One of the major issues raised by this committee was to abolish Article 41, which gave the civilians right to speech, movement and other basic rights. They also enforced the personal status law- 137, which further curbed the rights of women in Iraq. This faced wide criticism from various women organisations like Iraqi Women's Leadership Institute in Baghdad, Organisation of Women's Freedom in Iraq (OWFI), the Iraqi Women's League and Iraqi Women for Peace and Democracy which demanded the abolition of this law and creation of more provisions for women's right in Iraq. Since the 2011 U.S. military withdrawal from Iraq, sectarian and ethnic divisions have widened, fueling a major challenge to Iraq's stability and to Iraq's non-Muslim minority communities. In October 2011, the COR passed legislation to lift Iraq's reservation to Article 9 of the Convention on the Elimination of All Forms of Discrimination against Women (Katzman, 2014).

Women's Economic Rights in Democratic Iraq

Women in Iraq had previous to the occupation made important advances compared to most countries in the region. Regeneration of the economy will be fundamental to the creation of available democracy in Iraq. Ensuring women economic rights and empowerment will be an important step toward economic recovery and toward ensuring equal rights for women in all spheres. By generating and controlling economic resources, women will gain respect and position in society. For the many women heads of household, economic empowerment will be a question of survival; it is imperative that post-war Iraq provide them with opportunities to earn an income so that they can maintain their dependents. Earlier laws ensured education for girls, family rights, and the right to serve in the government. However, present-day Iraq is plagued by insecurity, transforming the situation for women into a national crisis. Assassinations and abductions are rampant (United Nations General Assembly, A/HRC/19/NGO/145, 2012). Between 1960 and 2003, Iraqi women had successfully gained access to education, health care and employment, and their political and economic participation had significantly advanced (United Nations General Assembly, A/HRC/19/NGO/145, 2012). The women and girls of Iraq have borne the biggest brunt of this conflict and resulting in security after the 2003 invasion. "For Iraqi women, who enjoyed some of the highest levels of rights protection and social participation in the region before 1991, this has been an enormously bitter pill to swallow." U.S.-led coalition forces showed higher rates of indiscriminate killing of women and children than insurgents, as per a study in 2011 (Reuters, 2011). Hundreds of women have been targeted and killed as professionals or for their public role in Iraq. Over the past several years, women have increasingly been targeted with acts of violence, threats and abduction. Indirectly, continued insecurity has also greatly degraded the quality of women's lives across the country, no Matter their religious, economic or cultural identities (Al-Azzawi, 2007). Drawing on a comprehensive statistical survey, Dr. Souad Al Azzawi showed that the deteriorating security situation drove Iraqi women out of work. At least 85 per cent of educated women are unemployed. A 2011 World Bank report titled: "Confronting Poverty in Iraq", show that only about 11 per cent of adult women are employed, compared to about two-thirds of adult men (Al-Azzawi, 2007). Over the year 2006, numerous reports from various organisations working in Iraq established that the general rise in sectarian violence had a negative impact on women, restricting their mobility and opportunities, including educational and economic opportunities. February 19, 2007, wire reports detailed an account in which "a 20-year old Sunni woman accused three Iraqi policemen of raping her after she was detained during a search of her house in western Baghdad (Independent Women's Forum, 2007).

In Iraq, during conflict, women are particularly involved in the formal and informal economy, replacing men who have joined the fighting. Once war ends, these gains are often lost; much of the formal economy shrinks or collapses and the jobs that remain are generally given to returning male soldiers. There is often pressure for women to return to traditional roles. Though many instead move to the informal economy trading, small-scale food production and sale, and service provision), these women and girls lack access to more desirable opportunities (UN Secretary-General's Report, 2002). International aid projects often unintentionally perpetuate the problem by offering women opportunities in micro-enterprise initiatives rather than the mainstream economy. Additionally, these programmes often do not meet the needs of educated women with skills and experience (UNDP, 2003). In Iraq, it will be important to ensure that women are given the same opportunities for income and employment as men. Similarly, it will be necessary to create programmes that alleviate immediate need while creating the potential for longer-term sustainability and growth.

Conclusion

It is essential that Iraqi women continue to play a vital role in their emerging democracy. Through their active participation in their government and civil society, they must work to maintain their human right to be governed by civil not religious courts and statutes in matters of family law such as divorce, inheritance, and child custody. Since the very beginning, women in Iraq were deprived of various individual and civil rights. Many movements were launched to improve their existing situation but political instability did not facilitate them to improve their condition. In Iraq, wars, sanctions and occupation have pushed women's rights back to the dark ages, and political Islam and many other conservative norms and values have gained prominence in society. The Islamic groups believed that issues like marriage, inheritance right and divorce should be based on Islamic laws. They also believed that there should have been amendments in Personal Status Law and additionally demanded the abolition of 25 per cent reservation given to women in decision making bodies. Given women's predominance in the population at large, it is important to ensure that women are full and active participants in governance structures at the local and national levels for a true democracy to take root. In Kurdish Northern Iraq, women are included and have been making a significant contribution to the economic, social, and political development of society. But the other parts of Iraq (Central and Southern) the deeply conservative nature of society contributes to the discrimination and a very difficult situation for women in general. Many observers hail the representation of women in the political field as a positive development, while others note that women continue to lack leadership opportunities in local provincial, mayoral, and town posts.

Works Cited

- Al-Azzawi, Souad (2007), "Women Under Occupation," [Online: web] Accessed 10 January 2015, http://www.brussellstribunal. org/pdf/Women UnderOccupation.pdf
- Amowitz, Lynne et. al. (2004), "Human Rights Abuses and Concerns about Women's Health and Human Rights in Southern Iraq," *Journal of the American Medical Association* 29 (1):1-34.
- Bassoul, Joelle (2005), "Iraq Women Set to Take Almost Third of Seats in New Parliament," *Agence France Presse*.
- Brown, Lucy and David Romano (2003), "Women in Post-Saddam Iraq: One Step Forward or Two Steps Back?", [Online: web] Accessed 10 January 2015, http://www.hrw.org/legacy/backgrounder/wrd/iraq-women.pdf.
- Ciezadlo, Annia (2003), "Iraqi Women Raise Voices – For Quotas." *Christian Science Monitor*, [Online: web] Accessed 12 January 2015, http:/ /www.csmonitor.com/2003/1217/p01s02-woiq.html.
- Civilian death study rates "dirty war" in Iraq , *Reuters*, (2011) [Online: web] Accessed 12 January 2015, http://www.trust.org/alertnet/news/ civilian-death-study-rates-dirty-war-in-iraq.
- Fernea, Elizabeth (2000), "The Challenge for Middle Eastern Women in the 21st Century," *The Middle East Journal*, 5(4): 2-18.

- Henninger, Daniel (2005), "Muslim Women Seize Chance To Claim Rights," *The Wall Street* Journal.
- Human Rights Watch (2003), "Background on Women's Status in Iraq Prior to the Fall of the Saddam Hussein Government," [Online: web] Accessed 10 January 2015 [http://www.hrw.org/backgrounder/wrd/iraq-women.htm].
- Independent Electoral Commission of Iraq Report "Regime Change in Iraq and Challenges of Political Reconstruction", [Online: web] Accessed 10 March 2014, URL: http://www.ieci.org.
- Independent Electoral Commission of Iraq (2006) Update on 27 February, [Online: web] Accessed 20 March 2014, URL:http://www.ieciraq.org/English/frameset_english.htm.
- "Iraqi Constitution" (2005), [Online: web] Accessed 25 September,2013 URL:http://www.iraqinationality. gov.iq/attach/iraqi_constitution.pdfhttp://www.iraqinationality. gov.iq/attach/iraqi_ constitution.pdf.
- Iraqi Institute for Human Rights, Kirkuk, March 25th, 2004 — Interview with Mr. Moayeed, Director. Interview conducted in Arabic by Karim Khallaayoun, ICAMES Iraq Research Team – recording of the interview also translated to English and transcribed by Karim Khallaayoun.
- "Iraqi Women under Saddam's Regim: A Population Silenced," Fact Sheet, Office of International Women's Issues, Washington, DC, March 20, 2003, [Online: web] Accessed 11 January 2015, http://www.state.gov/g/wi/rls/18877.htm.
- Katzman, Kenneth (2005), "Iraq: U.S. Regime Change Efforts and Post-Saddam Governance", *Congressional Research Service*, [Online: web] Accessed 25 June 2014, URL:http://fas.org/man/crs/RL31339.pdf.
- "Iraq New Election and New Government", (2005), *CRS report for congress,* updated on April 7, 2005, [Online: web] Accessed 28 June 2014, URL:http://shelby.senate.gov/legislation/IraqElectionNewgov.pdf.
- "Iraq: Post-Saddam National Elections", (2005), *Congressional Research Service*, [Online: web] Accessed 30 June 2014 http://fpc.state.gov/documents/organisation/44121.pdf.
- "Iraq: Elections, Constitution, and Government", (2006), Congressional *Research Service, Library of Congress*, [Online: web] Accessed 28 June 2014, URL:http://digital.library.unt.edu/ark:/67531/metacrs9924/.
- "The Kurds in Post-Saddam Iraq", (2010), *Congressional Research Service*, [Online: web] Accessed 1 July 2014, URL:http://fas.org/sgp/crs/mideast/RS22079.pdf.
- "Iraq: Politics, Governance, and Human Rights", (2014), *Congressional Research Service*, pp.1-49, [Online: web] Accessed 6 July 2014.URL: http://fas.org/sgp/crs/mideast/RS21968.pdf.

- Mahmoud, Houzan (2004), "The Guardian", [Online: web] Accessed 11 January 2015,http://www.guardian.co.uk/comment/story/0,3604, 1164268,00.html.
- Manal Omar, "Women's Rights in a New Iraq: The Constitution and the Future," Councilon Foreign Relations Roundtable on Women and U.S. Foreign Policy, May 11, 2005.
- Mc Evoy, J. and Brendan O'Leary (2013), *Power Sharing in Deeply Divided Places*, Pennsylvania: University of Pennsylvania Press.
- Osgood, Charles (2005), "Iraqi Women Fear Setbacks in Civil Rights Because New National Assembly is Predominantly Shi'i," *The Osgood File*.
- Rashid, Nazaneen (2000), "DFID's Roundtable Conference on Violence Against Women in Iraqi Kurdistan," [Online: web] Accessed 11 January 2015, http://www.kwahk.org/index.asp?id=33.
- Rida, Usama Hashem (—) "Iraq: Women Join Shia Revival," *Iraqi Crisis Report* (ICR, No. 38, 3 December 2003) Institute for War and Peace Reporting (IWPR).
- The Coalition Provisional Authority, Fact Sheet on Deputy Ministers, [Online: web] Accessed 5 January 2015 www.cpa-iraq.org/government/ dep_mins.html.
- Transitional Assistance Law [Online: web] Accessed 10 January 2015, http:/ /www.cpa-iraq.org/government/TAL.html.
- UNAMI (2010), "Report on Human Rights in Iraq", [Online: web] Accessed 11 January 2015, http://www.uniraq.org/documents/UNAMI_HR% 20Report_ English_FINAL_1 Aug11.pdf.
- United Nations Development Fund for Women (UNIFEM), "The Impact of the Conflict on Iraqi Women", [Online: web] Accessed 10 January 2015www.womenwarpeace.org/iraq/iraq.htm.
- UNDP (2003), Iraq: Women in Public Life", [Online: web] Accessed 10 January 2015, <http://www.undp-pogar.org/countries/iraq/gender.html>.
- United Nations General Assembly (2012), A/HRC/19/NGO/145 "Violation of Women Rights in Iraq".
- UNOCHR (2003),"Occasional Paper: Situation of Women in Iraq," in Human Rights Briefing Paper, "Background on Women's Status in Iraq Prior to the Fall of the Saddam Hussein Government".
- United Nations Security Council Resolution, 1483 (2003), 22 May 2003.
- UN Secretary-General's Report (2002), "Women, Peace, and Security", pp. 117-118.
- U.S. Policy on Iraqi Women's Political, Economic, and Social Participation," August7, 2003, [Online: web] Accessed 8 January 2015, http:// www.state.gov./g/wi/rls/22492.htm.

13

Safeguarding Humanity during incidents of Communal Violence

—Abhijay Negi

Introduction

India gained independence in a much vitiated communal atmosphere. In the run-up to August 1947, when there was little celebration about the prospects of a free Indian nation with a unique national identity, given the multiplicities and diversities of cultures and traditions which it holds in itself as one; there were frequent rioting, and the newspapers of the day full of more and more stories of Hindus, Sikhs and Muslims killing each other as incidents of inhuman violence continued to rise. "*We are cleaning the mess of centuries*" was how the British Prime Minister of that time, Clement Atlee had explained to the House of Commons the rationale behind the withdrawal of Crown from the Indian subcontinent.

Almost parallel in the very next year, there was an interesting and noteworthy development on the global stage. As the scourge of colonialism was rapidly receding from the world space, almost simultaneously there was a growing international consensus on effectively protecting human rights and promoting the values which go along with it. Towards the end of 1948, the Universal Declaration of Human Rights with 30 articles was adopted by a number of countries including both India and Pakistan which had seen immense violations on their territories in the name of religion. It is only post 1948 that Human Rights jurisprudence acquired prominence.

An overview of Human Rights in India

While the slogans of India Shining, Make in India are making national and international headlines and vigorously marketing the Indian growth story; even a flimsy perusal of some of the basic human indices and statistics is enough to reveal the sorry state of affairs in which human rights are currently placed in India. In our nation, 47.4 per cent of the girl population has been married under the age of 18 and 18 per cent are married under the age of 15. Only 67 per cent women are literate. We must note that child marriage is concomitant with early pregnancy and hence leads to several problems. To look at some other statistics, 42.5 per cent children are malnourished. Gender-based violence is also on the rise. Child labour is common and corruption has developed like a very strong cancer throughout the social system. Laws like the Armed Forces Special Powers Act and the Prevention of Terrorism Act have questionable application. It is in this background that we will analyze the specific theme of communal violence and the role of human rights in an atmosphere where the urge to kill driven by the slightest of provocations overrides all basic rationality of human beings.

Communal Violence in India and the Role played by Human Rights

It has been rightly said that there is no evil which humans are willing to practice more easily and cheerfully than killing one another in the name of religion. Religion based rioting has been seen in almost all societies in different stages of their evolution to the point as they exist today; but in the context of India, it has dangerously become a recurrent feature and continues to be a reality even in today's time with 24x7 news channels and a very vibrant media community constantly criticizing such efforts but at times unwittingly encouraging the same.

Unfortunately, there can be many incidents in India's contemporary history which can be pulled out as an example to show the subversion of human rights in communal conflicts. However, for the sake of brevity and for a deeper analysis of the same, we shall discuss three instances of these national shames.

1. ***The 1984 Delhi Sikh Riots***: In the aftermath of the assassination of Prime Minister Indira Gandhi, the Sikh Community was singularly targeted as being the joint perpetrators of the heinous assassination. Massive rioting rights on the streets of Delhi had left over 3000 Sikhs dead. There was a long legal battle fought in a bid to punish those guilty of the brutal murders; but due to many political reasons and the shoddy investigations justice was not served. In the context of these riots, the understanding of human rights has been limited to the distribution of "fair compensation" as *ex gratia* to the kith and kin of the deceased. The issue is still kept politically relevant and very recently the Bharatiya Janata Party had organised an event where revised compensation amounts were distributed by Home Minister Rajnath Singh to the relatives of the deceased. However, the victims still demand punishment for the wrong doers and in the absence of the same; closure is unlikely to come to this case.

2. ***The 2002 Communal Carnage of Gujarat:*** It is remembered and invoked perhaps most frequently in any discussion regarding communal violence in India. There are disputed accounts of how the incident may have started. The District Court has held that close to five dozen Car Sevaks were burned to death in a train near Godhra which subsequently led to backlash and rioting in many parts of the state. As per Government records, close to 790 Muslims had lost their lives along with 250 Hindus. In an already adverse communal atmosphere, open funeral processions were taken out on streets which only intensified rioting and the prevalent communal discourse. Allegations of state machinery being effectively used as a tool to perpetuate the agenda of the rioters still continues to dominate the political mainspace of the country; even though the Special Investigation Team created by the Supreme Court of India had cleared the name of the then Chief Minister of Gujarat and the current Prime Minister Shri Narendra Modi. Given the constant media attention that those riots had elicited, there were many human rights activists who had taken up the cause of the riot victims in a very aggressive fashion. In fact, the judiciary has criticized this

kind of adventure activism and has cautioned against media trial which also in many ways violates basic tenets of human rights.

In the Gujarat riots, there were several individual cases of unimaginable brutality which had come to the fore, be it the Gulbarg Society Case or the Best Bakery massacre. Though it can be said that given a constant hot pursuit; the Gujarat riots have seen far more convictions (249 so far) and hence justice is being served in perhaps more than any riots in the country's past; the judiciary has also been sterner than required at a few instances. For example, in the case of Zahira Sheikh, a witness in the Best Bakery case who was constantly changing her statements and testimony; the court did not take a benign view of the obvious pressures which would have been exerted on the most unfortunate witness of such a high profile case and sentenced Zahira to prison for constantly changing her statements. The court could have been more mindful of the basic human rights which are guaranteed to every witness and should have first ensured that Zahira was given a pressure-free environment in which she could have testified without the fear and threat of facing consequences based upon her narration of facts. Instead, the Court chose to be strict on account of her changing statements while not going deeper into the problem. Having stated this, it must be noted that justice and values of human rights were indeed the guiding principles based on which the Court convicted the wrongdoers which also included an influential Former Minister and a sitting MLA Mayaben Kodnani. In the aftermath of these riots, human rights jurisprudence and a debate on its applicability has garnered much pace and significance.

3. ***The Muzzafarnagar Riots:*** Though at a much smaller scale when compared to the above two stated incidents of rioting, the Muzzafarnagar Communal tensions are the most recent right in the heart of the most populous state of the country. The Muzzafarnagar riots had created an acute human rights problem in Uttar Pradesh. While the incident of rioting was said to begin because of a clash between the Jat and the Muslim community after an incident of reported molestation

or a bike accident (as conflicting accounts of the same have been given), there were several incidents of rape which had been reported in the rioting. The biggest challenge to human rights emerged not just during the riots when police investigation was revealing the involvement of a number of senior local political leaders from across the political spectrum; but also in the aftermath of the riots as it had been stated that the relief camps which housed the displaced Muslim community was devoid of basic sanitation facilities in contravention of the salient principles of the Universal Declaration on Human Rights.

It was later reported that the State Government and the District Administration had planned to run over bulldozers on these relief camps; arguing that the residents of the relief camps were staying there as they were politically motivated to propagate the impression that the State Government had been failing to ensure proper rehabilitation of the victims. However, this apprehension of the State Government and the coercive tactics to vacate the camps was widely condemned. Moreover, what was also condemned was the fact that the State Government with much grandeur had organised a massive celebration festival at Saifai but had failed its basic duty of meaningful rehabilitation. This incident, hardly a year and a half old is one of the starkest reminders about the fact that the battle for upholding human rights is far from over.

The major issues and challenges during incidents of communal violence

The job of a human rights activist is such that he/she becomes the most hated person on the planet. That is because at times even against the sentiment of the society, the human rights activist, true to the job has to try and explain to the lynch mobs who now very easily congregate on the social media in a virtual way the simple message that every human has some basic rights. In this context, when we are to examine incidents of communal frenzy that only amplifies the difficulty of the job as a religious identity is one of the most sensitive aspects of a common Indian's personality. The following are the core issues which have a lot to do with human rights and strengthening the basic message which they seek to impart.

Compensation for Victims of Communal Violence

Although it is impossible to equate the loss of any human life with a lump sum amount offered to the grieving kith and kin as a "compensation" for the same; the act of providing this monetary relief becomes even more profound in the context that for any victim of communal violence, the State provides the compensation amount almost as a virtual certification of its own inability to have maintained law and order and as a token charge which it levies upon itself for the same. It may be noted that in India there is a Central Scheme for Assistance to Civilian Victims of Terrorist, Communal & Naxal Violence since 2008. As per the provisions of this scheme, the Government had disbursed Rs. 6.12 Crore as compensation to civilian victims in 204 incidents of terrorist, communal and Naxal violence in 2011-2012 and Rs. 3.99 crore to civilian victims in 133 such incidents in 2012-2013. However, what is most appalling is the fact that this scheme was practically rendered non-functional since there was no reimbursement which could be made to any civilian victim in incidents of terrorist, communal and Naxal violence during 2013-14 and 2014-14 (till July) as the State Governments had not sent in their proposals. Therefore, to uphold some of the basic tenets of human rights; there is an urgent and the most pressing need to remove some bottlenecks and allow the facilitation of such schemes.

In addition to making this scheme more workable and practically effective, what is noteworthy is the move of the new Central Government to enhance the compensation to civilian victims as covered in the aforesaid scheme from Rs. 3 Lacs to Rs. 5 Lacs. This scheme includes various terms such as assistance being provided to the surviving spouse in case of death or permanent incapacitation of the husband or the wife, as the case may be. However, in case both the husband and wife are dead in the same incident of violence, the family would be entitled to get assistance in such a matter. What is also clear is that the families of the victim would be eligible to get assistance under this specific scheme even if they have received any other assistance by way of payment of ex gratia or any other form of relief from the Government or any other source except when a similar scheme is already being implemented by the Central Government. In this context, it can only be vociferously reiterated that all the rosy benefits of this scheme will only accrue when its actual application is not subject to procedural delays as has been seen in the non-application of this scheme in the recent years even as the most brutal communal violence broke out in Uttar Pradesh as India's worst communal violence since the Gujarat riots.

A strong legislation specifically aimed at curbing communal violence and punishing its perpetrators.

While dealing with communal violence by a legislation is most desirable, the effort made by the National Advisory Council (NAC) to draft a Bill which came to be known as the Prevention of Communal and Targeted Violence (Access to Justice and Reparations) Bill, 2011 was definitely not a sincere step in this direction. This is because a sincere effort at combatting communalism cannot in any way mean assuming the same and a legislation which has a communal character itself and which seems to be inspired by one single communal incident. A political answer to one of India's major cancers can do little for this Nation. The first problem with the Bill is that an unelected body like the National Advisory Council cannot be said to be having the specific sociological expertise on matter of communal harmony and would definitely be far from national consensus.

The second aspect of the Bill is far more specific. According to an important definition (in the Bill) on the people who are presumably the focus of targeted violence, "group has been stated to mean a linguistic or religious minority in any State in the Union of India or Scheduled Castes or Scheduled Tribes" (SC / ST). If we were to take away the fact that religious minorities between themselves account for over 40 per cent of the total population, the Bill unwittingly is assuming that the other 60 per cent (which may include other backward castes, classes and upper caste Hindus are the only people capable of accentuating targeted violence). To conclude that 40 per cent of the individuals can never target 60 per cent of their own brethren in a scenario where numbers are widely distributed all over the country is something which is not correct. To take an example, if we were to assume a situation of rioting in Kerala where the Hindu population is around 55 per cent and when we take out the SC/ST population out of the Hindu total, Hindus according to this Bill would no longer remain the majority. Hence, a Bill which is not directly combating communalism and is only dividing people into majorities and minorities on unrealistic assumptions cannot be considered an adequate step in any regard.

A *third* aspect of the Bill is that it seems to have been inspired only by the Gujarat riots of 2002. It may be noted that the country has seen not just a single incident of communal rioting but the number runs up to many thousands and all of them had not been perpetrated and executed in such a uniform fashion that a legislation could be exclusively modeled on any one of them.

Fourthly, to say that law and order powers will vest only with the Indian Union and not with the States as regards incidents of communal violence is a perfect recipe for a political disaster as allegations of tampering with the Federal Structure of the Constitution will naturally be levied.

Fifthly, the National Authority of Communal Harmony, Justice and reparation, a body which has been proposed to be set up mostly includes political nominees which are nearly always going to have diametrically opposite views on the causes and consequences of religious violence. It is only more rational to have judicial and impartial bureaucratic appointments to this National Authority if there was a political will to make this political authority better.

In addition to all that has been stated above, the bottomline is that a law which differentiates between Hindu and Muslim victims and proposes separate courts to try Hindu and Muslim accused persons is only going to give a legal formal shape to communal polarisation which is unhealthy for the Indian Nation. Moreover, it must always be remembered that the majority–minority distinction which is at the bedrock of this proposed Bill is one of the weakest distinctions possible in a country as vast as India as majority and minority are nearly always contextual.

It must be noted that with the ouster of the UPA Government, this Bill has been put in cold storage. However, just because this Bill was a wrong way of dealing with the problem, there is no denying that rioting is an existing reality in our country where sporadic incidents of religion inspired violence can break out at the drop of the hat, a Legislation on this important and complex subject while safeguarding the basic rights of the accused as also serving and maximizing the interests of the victims as per the parameters laid down in our Constitution as also in several International Conventions is very desirable and hence, an effort to Legislate in this regard must necessarily be made.

An Out-Of-The-Box Societal Approach

Incidents of terrorism are by themselves enough to severely paralyze all human rights movements aimed at benefitting the victims. However, an out of the box approach to this problem could interestingly yield effective solutions.

To take an example, there were a number of cases in Bangalore where the ShriramSena was crossing all limits of moral policing and embarrassing youngsters who were sitting together, let alone celebrating Valentine's Day. In response to this moral policing and given that the State machinery was not taking much action against the wrongdoers, a campaign was initiated known as the "pink chaddi' campaign where pink colored underwear were sent to the office of the ShreeramSena Chief. It was quite on the lines of the Rose Campaign which has been shown in the *Lagey Raho Munnabhai* movie. Not only did this campaign severally and comically frustrate the perpetrators of the human rights violations but also in a very strong way brought the notice of the State Government to this pressing problem and action was initiated in a stark contrast to when the State machinery was doing absolutely nothing in the absence of the campaign. Similarly, if the extremists get a strong societal response and are made to feel the resilience of the society while also being shown that they themselves are essentially brainwashed individuals who can still be brought to the right path; human rights cannot only be protected but very effectively be universalised.

Conclusion

Article 18 of the Universal Declaration on Human Rights clearly states that everyone has the right to freedom of thought, conscience and religion and by virtue of the same; everyone also enjoys the freedom to change his religion or belief as well as to manifest it. Apart from Article 18; Article 26, Article 16 and Article 2 clearly state that no discrimination in the name of religion can ever be condoned in the human rights framework. Apart from this Universal Declaration, the ICCPR have further expanded the definition of Human Rights so as to include an entire gambit of empowerment oriented measures.

In today's time, communal violence is easily one of the most ardent challenges for effective human rights activists in this country. Communal harmony and equal treatment of all religions is at the very heart of the glue/cement which binds the Indian society. Throughout this paper, an effort has been made to calibrate the major issues and challenges facing human rights from the context of communal tensions, disharmony and related misgivings. The Chapter has been written in the backdrop of three major communal incidents out of the many thousands which have unfortunately been witnessed by independent India. An effort has been made to underscore the need of an effective legislation on the subject as well as to treat the compensation issue with greater sincerity while also exploring how best can some out-of-the-box ideas be used in combating this menace. Ultimately, the political, legal and social systems of this country would have to work in tandem to ensure that human rights and its essential values remain unfettered, justice is served and further incidents of communal violence and the violation of human rights which it can bring with itself are avoided.

Works Cited

- Ramachandra Guha, *India After Gandhi: The History of the World's Largest Democracy*, New York: Harper Perennial, 2008.
- L.K. Advani, *My Country My Life*, New Delhi: Rupa Publications, 2008.
- S.K. Kapoor, *International Law and Human Rights*, Allahabad: Central Law Agency, 2014.
- India Human Rights Report 2007, Asian Centre for Human Right, 2007.

- Khanna, D.P., *Reforming Human Rights* New Delhi: Manas Publications, 2000.
- Indu Singh & Ajay Saxena, *Human Rights in India and Pakistan*, New Delhi: Deep and Deep Publications Pvt. Ltd., 2004.

[Statutes]

- The Universal Declaration of Human Rights, 1948.
- The Constitution of India, 1950.

[Articles]

- *Accountability for Mass Violence-Examining the State's record*, Centre for Equity Studies, New Delhi, May 2012, available at: *http://centreforequity-studies.org/wp-content/uploads/2014/01/IDRCFINAL.REPORT.pdf.*
- Ram Puniyani, *Human Rights Violations of Minorities: Effects And Repercussions*, (2012), available at: http://www.countercurrents.org/puniyani201212.htm.
- Roshni Sengupta, Communal Violence in India: Perspectives on the causative factors, available at: http://www.sasnet.lu.se/EASASpapers/32Roshni Sengupta.pdf.
- Kalathmika Natarajan, *Riots in India: A Consequence of Democracy?* (2012), available at" http://www.e-ir.info/2012/07/18/riots-in-india-a-consequence-of-democracy/.

14

Human Rights in The Context of Good Governance

—Sangya Rai Meena

Introduction

All human beings are born free and equal in dignity and rights says Article 1 of the United Nations Universal Declaration of Human Rights. The concept of rights and liberty has always existed in one or the other since ages in all countries. While it existed then in the form of ethical values, the concept of human rights as such in its modern perspective developed in the aftermath of the world wars and subsequent abuse of human rights. The League of Nations was established in 1919 during the treaty of Versailles after World War I. Later, after the World War II, the United Nations Organisations came into existence and now human rights are seen as a sensitive subject and duty of every welfare state.

Though, the concept of human rights was criticized by great philosophers like Jeremy Bentham, Edmund Burke and even Karl Marx, human rights are now an essential part of good governance in democratic societies. Human rights enable a person to live a life of dignity. But no rights can be fully realised until and unless there is conducive and enabling atmosphere to facilitate their realisation. Rights can be protected only when good governance prevails so one may say that good governance is the prerequisite to the protection of human rights.

Good Governance

The idea of good governance emanated from the World Bank and it was part of its annual development economic conference way back in 1991. In the beginning, the term was initiated by the World Bank to ensure that countries seeking developmental assistance used the funds effectively and conscientiously. Later, its dimension gradually broadened to include socio-economic and political aspects. Since then, all countries have begun to see the importance of good governance in all fields whether it is managing economic or social resources or ensuring transparency or accountability. It is perhaps due to the indivisibility of human rights that economic, social and cultural rights as well as civil and political rights were included in the category of human rights by the United Nations Universal Declaration of Human Rights 1948. It is based on the obvious principle that different rights can successfully exist only in combination.

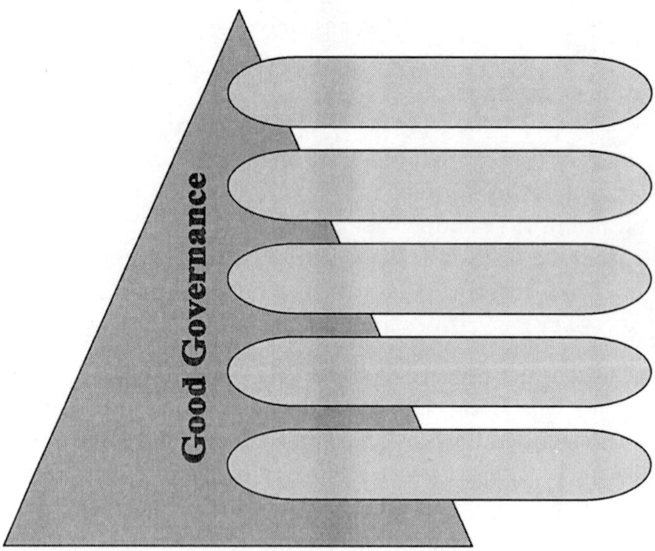

The UN Economic and Social Commission for Asia and the Pacific outlined major characteristics of good governance as Participatory, Consensus oriented, Accountable, Transparent, Responsive, Effective and efficient, Equitable and inclusive and Rule of Law. It is often summed up as five pillars of good governance.

Human Rights

Human rights are essential for existence, transcending all the barriers whether class, language, religion, nationality or race etc. Human rights are a must to ensure a life worth living because even the underprivileged and marginalised sections of society need to have some space in society. And that space must have some semblance of dignity. According to the UN Human Rights, human rights are "inherent to all human beings, whatever our nationality, place of residence, sex, national or ethnic origin, colour, religion, language, or any other status. We are equally entitled to our human rights without discrimination. These rights are all interrelated, interdependent and indivisible."

As mentioned earlier, the Universal Declaration of Human Rights made the pioneer attempt in codifying human rights, though the subject was taken up and discussed at several international conventions and forums. The Vienna World Conference on Human Rights 1993 took it a step further by saying that it was the duty of States to promote and protect all human rights and fundamental freedoms, regardless of their political, economic and cultural systems. It therefore outlined the principle of universality and inalienability of human rights, which is highly significant in terms of international human rights. The Indian Constitution gives its citizens fundamental rights and many other constitutions in the world promote equitable rights for the welfare of its citizens. Now the protection and promotion of human rights is seen as the pious duty and key objective of all democratic countries in the world.

Democracy and Human Rights

The crux of democracy is that it is for the people, by the people, of the people. That means all power lies with the people and peoples' representatives must exercise the power with their consent. Thus the core principle of democracy is that peoples' rights need to be protected and they must have a say in country's vital decisions. How can people have a say in decision making? In order to enable the people to allow realisation of their rights, certain freedoms are necessary and an atmosphere is needed where all sections of society, even minorities, women and weak can express their opinion without fear. The purpose of human rights as well as democracy is almost the same. In a democracy, every individual, even the weakest in society has the same right to express views. Or for that matter-freedom, equality and justice can be said to be the core values of democracy.

The Relationship of Good Governance and Human Rights

Human rights are very important in the context of good governance and have a crucial role to play to ensure freedom and develop a system which is fair, equitable and just in order to protect human rights. It is best done in an atmosphere of good governance where rights are protected and all individuals- big or small- are treated with the same dignity. It is an undeniable fact that the people cannot avail of their socio-economic or cultural rights unless their civil and political rights are protected.

Good governance, therefore, recognizes and protects human rights by eliminating the forces and challenges which interfere with the process of governance and consequently the availability of human rights. In a more precise way, the weakness in governance is reflected when human rights are violated and the weak, marginalised or minorities' rights feel unsafe or exploited. The element of non-inclusiveness has indeed a great volcanic force which can adversely influence good governance and human rights as well.

Good Governance also means that a government should realize that the three basic necessities- food, clothing and shelter- are made available almost freely and fairly to all members of society. The economic policy of a government needs to focus on the resources which would produce and protect the existence on sustainable scale. Food, shelter and clothes should be given a first and sincerest priority.[1] As everybody knows that only good economics result into good society, that is received wisdom if not ancient wisdom. Proper education shall be important at every phase and stage of human life that without recognizing and honouring the rights, good governance would never materialize.[2] It is for the good governance to identify and eradicate challenges and roadblocks at respective stages.

States are expected to "undertake, at the national level all necessary steps for the realisation of the right to development and to ensure inter alia equality of opportunity for all in their access to basic resources, education, health services, food, housing, employment and the fair distribution of income." In other words, developmental governance will be synonymous to right based social welfare. Effective measures need to be taken to ensure that women have an active role in the development process, and appropriate economic and social reforms are to be carried out with a view to eradicating all social injustices. The true test of "good" governance is the degree to which the promise of human rights, civil, cultural, economic, political or social is delivered.

International Guidelines on Good Governance

Since 1955, the United Nations Programme of Technical Cooperation in the field of human rights, administered by the office of the High Commissioner for Human Rights (OHCHR) has been providing rights based assistance to developing countries with the objective of strengthening governance. The primary focus has been on the domestic implementation of international human rights standards so that the serious imbalance between growth and distribution could be removed. OHCHR advocated a rights based approach to development as a conceptual framework for the process of human development that is normatively based on the international human rights standard and operationally directed to promoting and protecting human rights. Essentially, a rights based approach integrates the norms, standard and principles of the international human rights systems into plans, policies and process of development. The norms and standards are those contained in the wealth of international treaties and declarations.

Certain resolutions were passed by the Office of the High Commissioner for Human Rights (OHCHR) linking good governance to the enjoyment of human rights "prompting growth and sustainable human development". In sum, the declaration required states to take steps to "ensure the full exercise and progressive enhancement of the right to development, including the formulation, adoption and implementation of policy, legislative and other measures at the national and international levels".

Highlighting the importance of co-operation for securing good governance in countries requesting external support, the Security Council Resolution 2000 recognised the value of partnership approaches and development co-operation and the inappropriateness of prescriptive approaches.[3] The linkage of good governance to sustainable human development comprising principles such as accountability, participation, the enjoyment of human rights and rejecting prescriptive approaches to developmental assistance, the resolution stands as an implicit endorsement of the right based approach to development.

The Commission also requested the high commissioner to invite states to share success initiatives that have been effective in promoting good governance. The process began in the year 2000 and in the Resolution of 2001, the Commission on Human Right reaffirmed its earlier resolution.[4] The International Covenant on Civil and Political Rights requires its 148 stages parties "to respect and ensure.....the rights recognised" in the Covenant and to take the necessary steps....to give effect to the rights." In ratifying the international covenant on economic, social and cultural rights, 143 stages have undertaken "to take necessary steps... With a view to achieving progressively the full realisation of the rights recognised... by all appropriate means" (Art-2).

The relationship between human rights and good governance is now an accepted fact and an integral part of democracy and pro-poor development that "the scope of democracy must... be widened beyond elections, so that democratic institutions and processes facilitate, protect and reinforce; the full range of human rights." Good governance and human rights are complementing and mutually reinforcing; and human rights cannot be protected without good governance. Or one can say good governance is the precondition for protection and promotion of human rights. The importance of human rights, therefore, is immense to effectively run democracies and ensure pro-poor development. Mahatma Gandhi had said, "My notion of democracy is that under it the weakest should have the same opportunity as the strongest."[5]

Common Goals

If freedom from want and fear are the goals of human rights, these are also the essential aims of good governance. Governance is not restricted to simply running the administration of maintaining law and order in the country. The role of good governance is much wider and it is necessary to develop a system which is fair, equitable and just in order to protect human rights. It is best done in an atmosphere of good governance where rights are protected and all individuals-big or small-are treated with the same dignity. Everyone can live without fear and enjoy one's civil and political freedom only in a conducive environment. It is a fact that the people cannot avail of their socio-economic or cultural rights unless their civil and political rights are ensured.

Good governance can facilitate empowerment of the disadvantaged and marginalised people to defend their rights and enable them to participate in various activities. Good governance can promote and protect human rights in many ways. It not only encourages public participation in government or law making activities but it also ensures accountability of elected members. Thus marginalised and disadvantaged groups including women and minorities can be empowered to defend their rights.

The way in which good governance can be relevant to equality is to provide level playing field for industrial growth and social welfare for reducing poverty. Human rights empower individuals and communities by granting them entitlements that give rise to legal obligations on others. Provided the poor are able to gain access to and enjoy their human rights, the distribution and exercise of power within and between societies shall be equalised.[6] The Universal Declaration of Human Rights (Articles 21 and 28) recognizes the importance of participatory government and social and international conditions where rights and freedoms can be fully recognised. It means that governments should provide effective and fair remedies to people in case there is any instance of human rights violation.

Good Governance and Human Rights in Indian Context

The Indian Constitution gives its citizens fundamental rights and many other Constitutions in the world also promote equitable rights for the welfare of its citizens. A number of basic human rights are thus guaranteed to all Indian citizens irrespective of their caste, creed or culture. To protect these fundamental rights, the Indian Constitution has the provision of Directive Principles of State Policy. The Preamble to the Indian Constitution broadly highlights the goal "to secure to all its citizens justice-social, economic and political. "The Directive Principles cannot be enforced by any court but they are still fundamental to good governance in India.

In addition to the fundamental rights and directive principles, the 73rd and 74th Constitutional amendments have given constitutional status to panchayati raj institutions, thus promoting decentralisation of administration in the country. The immense success of panchayati raj and increased women's participation at grassroots level is sufficient proof to say that these steps have further strengthened democracy in India. Since good governance also means upholding the rule of law, India has independent judiciary and it is a well known fact that the judiciary has played a very active role in protection of human rights in the country.

Anti Corruption Movement

India in recent years has seen many big corruption scams and scandals unearthed. The Anti-corruption movement led by social activist Anna Hazare led to a new awakening in the country and mobilised people against corruption like never before. The Indian parliament has recently passed the Lokpal bill in order to control corruption at high level in office and due credit needs to be given to the Anna movement. The recent victory of Aam Aadmi Party (AAP) in Delhi state assembly elections is also a reflection against rampant corruption in the country and an awakening of the masses.

In this regards, transparency in execution of policies and programmes is of vital importance. The Right to Information, popularly known as RTI Act has proved a very effective tool in the anti-corruption drive in the country. It has empowered the general public to access public records which has proved very effective in tracking public spending.

Accountability in the use of funds and accountability to people's needs is an integral dimension of pro-poor governance. At the same time good governance strikes a balance between economic growth and social welfare. The defining attitude of good governance in development is the idea of accountability. All the partners in the development process—local, national, regional and international must accept higher levels of accountability.

It must now be seen that good governance shall recognize and protect human rights by eliminating the forces which interfere with the process of governance and consequently the availability of human rights. In a more forcible way, the weakness in governance is reflected on the existence and preference of poverty in all its multifarious forms such as economic scarcity, illiteracy, etc. The element of poverty has indeed a great force which has always adversely influenced good governance and human rights.

It is proposed in this article to deal with poverty and its impact on good governance and human rights. Poverty is generally linked with food and basic necessities for existence and in a sense rightly so, the natural resources should be tapped, developed and made available for consumption. The three-fold necessity, namely, *food, shelter* and *clothes* should be given a first and sincerest priority.

A government shall realize that these three necessities are made available almost freely to all member of the society. The other necessities for existence, namely, *luxury outfits* shall be given the next priority. The economic policy of a government shall focus on the resources which would produce the existence once. The attitude of the persons who govern, is almost deplorable when they concentrate more on the production of luxurious items under the guise of earning foreign exchange. This is because of the excuse that nation's security depends upon the strength of its armed forces, and to equip them with sophisticated arms, more foreign exchange is required and to accomplish the same, the production should be oriented towards acquiring more foreign exchange rather than consumer goods which cannot fetch any such foreign exchange.

Because of the mistrust between nations, the defence forces require to be equipped and to meet their demands, the production invariably goes towards that ultimate aim. Insecurity faced by every nation which suspects subjugation by other nation or nations subtly leads to production of unwanted goods at the cost of products necessary for human consumption.

It is suggested that all of the nations shall enter into a sincere and committed pact of non-aggression, every nation will have sufficient scope for the production of such goods which would satisfy basic necessities of life for the existence of human life. This would eradicate economic poverty to a very large extent unless impeded by natural calamities. The other kinds of poverty are varied which cause that deficiency in rational thinking and acceptance of the ideas which are necessary for abolition of Ideological confrontations and contradictions. Intellectual poverty is a dangerous phenomenon which would pose a real threat to human lives and can annihilate prosperity.

Now regarding the question of human rights, it is suggested that the government shall ensure that every citizen has the right sense and attitude both towards himself and others. Education shall be important at every phase and stage of human life that without recognizing and honouring the rights of fellow members of the society one's own such right would never materialise.

Conclusion

The great ideal of human beings enjoying freedom can only be achieved when human rights are protected. Without civil and political rights, people cannot assert their socio-economic or other rights. Similarly, in the absence of adequate livelihood opportunities, people cannot assert their political or civil rights. So let good governance not only nurse human rights but also marry them. Good governance is also important to achieve Millennium Development Goals since it will ensure equitable development allowing peoples' participation in a corruption free atmosphere, thus creating an enabling and conducive atmosphere for protection of human rights.

Notes

1. Arthashastra, book 1, Chapter XIX 39, as quoted in K. Kishore Government for citizens in CP Bartuwal (ed.) Good Governance in India (2003) page 23.
2. K. Sangeetha, paper presented at international law conference of jurists, at Vigyan Bhawan, New Delhi on November 24,2007.

3. Good Governance-Human Rights in development-OHCHR (www.ohchr.org).
4. Human Rights and Good Governance, chapter 9, K. Sangeetha page 128.
5. M.K.Gandhi, India of My Dreams, Page 20 (Harijan, 18-5-'40).

15

The Problem of Negotiating Rights in Mother of 1084

—*Richa Pandey Joshi*

While debates in human rights education have engaged popular imagination in both fictional and non-fictional spheres, the novel as enabling fiction bears the potential of recognizing human personality as both the primary agent and component of human society. The marginalisation and violent subjugation of women is a recurrent theme in contemporary Indian literature as much as it forms the basis of worldwide feminist critical inquiry. The fictive representation of the woman as mother and the mother as *subject* seeks to lend visibility and legitimacy to the Indian mother. However, representation is a problematic concept that could be either politically liberating or normatively contorting/constricting. While educational and value systems are culturally prescriptive, subject formation inevitably requires cultural negotiation. The culturally dominant representation of the ideal Indian mother—self-sacrificing and self-effacing—make important points of departure in the contemporary literary and social space where the personal is also the political. This departure from the traditional icons of motherhood cannot wishfully elude culture, even while the plea for subject formation gets louder. The current paper discusses Mahasweta Devi's novel *Mother of 1084* as a text that situates its female protagonist as the questing consciousness of Sujata—the mother of corpse number 1084—who finds no legitimacy for her son's unlawful killing even as she questions the wider morality of the society and its basic and more immediate unit—the family.

The Declaration of Human Rights (UDHR) identifies, first, the right to education and, second, to an education directed toward 'the full development of the human personality and to the strengthening of respect for human rights and fundamental freedoms.' However there is a sense of skepticism associated with this goal:

> While in principle virtually everyone takes for granted the benefits of HRE, such endeavors can be potentially costly from the perspective of a state. Human rights education is inherently revolutionary: If implemented effectively, it has the potential to generate social opposition, alongside rising demands for justice and accountability. (Cardenas qtd. in Bajaj 17-18)

The idea of Human Rights Education (HRE) must largely aim towards a participatory and empowering fabric of respect within society. Text books and school curricula along with grass root aspects of community education contribute in a bottoms-up manner in order to sensitize students towards this idea of respecting basic human rights. Literature is the vehicle of social change and an expression of the human predicament. While debates in human rights education have engaged popular imagination in both fictional and non-fictional spheres, the novel as enabling fiction bears the potential of recognizing human personality as both the primary agent and component of human society.

When 1974 saw the publication of *Mother of 1084*, Bandopadhyay avers "the more visible and widespread phase of the Naxalite movement was already over." (Devi vii). Mahasweta's novel has the evidentiary force of a document in the predicament of a mother whose Naxalite son is killed and the killing, along with several others like him, is cold, calculated, extra-judicial. The immediacy and urgency of her situation is striking right till the end of the novel when just like the realisation of an illegitimacy as paradigmatic of society, her own pain is an all encompassing one. The labour pain of Brati's birth, his killing and her inability to find any reprieve in the 'solitary cell' around her, commingle and congeal into rupture—a ruptured consciousness more painful than a ruptured appendix.

She writes the novel with a certain objective:

> In the nineties, in the Naxalite movement, I saw exemplary integrity, selflessness and the guts to die for a cause. I thought I saw history in the making, and decided that as a writer it would be my mission to document it. As a writer, I feel a commitment to my times, to mankind and to myself. I did not consider the Naxalite movement as an isolated happening. (Devi xi)

The novel continues to be read widely even today and continues to be sourced as material for feminist and subaltern literary research. The marginalisation and violent subjugation of women is a recurrent theme in contemporary Indian literature as much as it forms the basis of worldwide feminist critical inquiry. The fictive representation of the woman as mother and the mother as *subject* seeks to lend visibility and legitimacy to the Indian mother. The culturally dominant representation of the ideal Indian mother—self-sacrificing and self-effacing—in the figures of *Sita* and *Savitri* as revered icons make important points of departure in the contemporary literary and social space where the personal is also the political. This departure from the traditional icons of motherhood cannot wishfully elude culture while the plea for subject formation gets louder.

The novel *Mother of 1084* address the problem of representation of the mother as subject and instead of inventing a bogus and effete voice that is singular and universally representative, lend a situatedness to the mother-subject. Representation is not an unproblematic concept since it could be either politically liberating or normatively contorting/constricting. Sujata, mother of Brati, corpse number 1084, is the marginalised'other' in a family that refuses to legitimize her position as 'subject'. She is, as it were, a foil to Brati's own condition. Sujata is the alienated, unacknowledged part of a family, whose own morality is suspect. Her husband, Dibyanath, the elitenonchalant rake, only needs her as a 'womb' that must bear his children. The couple have little emotional connect, even as their physical connect is devoid of any real sexual attraction or fulfilment, rather as just the means to an end. Having never been treated as subject, liable to have her own desires and conflicts, she too has cared little to articulate herself, save for exceptional circumstances. But like in most of Devi's novels, Sujata, the female protagonist of the story, has her own way of exerting agency and subjecthood.

Nandini, Brati's girlfriend, on the other hand, is the woman subject who has suffered extreme torture of the solitary cell. She would most probably never get married nor experience motherhood—confining strictures of value current in the patriarchal hegemonic structure. In choosing the path she has—that of loyalty to her cause which is anti-establishment, she is Devi's epitome of the politically liberated woman, not because of her anti-establishment stance per se, but because of her loyalty to the cause and to Brati. Sujata, on the other hand has been educated into submission to patriarchal values right from her maternal home.

Sujata has been the stranger in the family, the irritant, unimpregnable "Other' who forms a silent discourse characterized by the assertion of an aberrantalterity marked by her momentous decisions. She refuses to bear any more children after Brati, having acquiesced to Dibyanath's desires until then. Having to conform to the mundane aspects of everyday life—put up by a patriarchy embodied by her mother-in-law, her husband and her other children, except Brati—Brati becomes her point of departure from such control. She clearly protects him from the 'rule of the law' exemplified by her mother-in-law and 'Boss'(Dibyanath) and for that matter, her other children—the household.

Even the child Brati's revolt—in getting up late, appearing late for the meals, and other such areas of potential 'discipline and punish'—become metonymic with Sujata's own oppositional discourse as she has herself been subjected to the same twin forces of social alienation and retaliation.The family meanwhile have no patience with either Brati or Sujata—her choice to work in a bank, since she does not typify, according to them, the woman in need of either 'finances' or 'fashion'. Brati alone is acutely perceptive to the needs and emotions of his mother. Him alone, she can question, "Do you need your mother at all? Do you ever try to know what your mother feels and thinks?" (42) It is only after his death, Sujata meets Nandini, who reveals Brati's knowledge of his father's illegitimate affair with the typist. This is when Sujata learns of Brati having confronted Dibyanath over the matter, while he was so keenly protective of her.

In Brati's death, Sujata is agonised not just because he is no more, not only because of the brutal manner of his killing, but also because she is alone in the family to acknowledge his death, while the others make the last ditch effort to occlude even his memory. If society has wronged him in not according him any ground for trial, his own people have been the worse in implacably glossing over it. "Sujata could see the design of an absurd play unfolding relentlessly" (30) As she slowly puts together the orchestration of his murder, she comes to the inexpressible realisation that while Brati has been the only legitimate reason for her to endure the ennui of an unresponsive world, he himself has found no redemption from a world of unjustifiable immorality and irrationality.

The very fact of such murderous violence leaves no room for alterity, dissent, retaliation or resistance. In keeping with its arbitrary nature, it has to destroy brutally, destroy in gruesome murder, as a logical recompense for its unjustifiablity. "It was not enough just to kill. It was an inevitable part of the pattern of killing to prolong the process of killing and watch with demonic glee the death throes of the man dying"(98). The act of killing here assumes a ritualistic orgy:

> shouting slogans they stepped out, darkness outside, a crowd of pitch-dark faces, loud laughter and yells, cries scattering the laughter all around, lights going off one by one in the neighbouring houses, doors and shutters slamming shut, scared faces drawing back, over there wolf whistles flung at the sky rending the sky as when Durga images are toppled over into the dark river,...Kill the Bastards!(65)

"Kill the Bastards!" resonates strikingly as a Kurtzian "Exterminate all the brutes!" (Conrad 138), "Ignore them. That's the way to exterminate them" (Devi 61) as the murderous dogma of a 'cadaverous' society strikes a parallel with Sujata's own extermination by her ever denying family.

Nandini tells Sujata about the gruesome near-death experience of the solitary cell. The performativity inherent in "living(ed) alone with oneself within four walls...trying(ed) to penetrate the world outside with a mind as keen and cutting as the knife of the surgeon in the morgue or the blade of a bayonet...the grating voice of the interrogation ...(holding) all the sounds within check" (73) is not alien to Sujata who feels the same hypersensitivity of the mind in her own situation of inert, unutterable grief.

There is no specific definition of torture in Indian law. The legal definitions of torture, and the less severe standard of inhuman and degrading treatment, are contained in a number of international instruments.Their prohibition is a fundamental principle of international law. A clear definition of torture is provided in the United Nations Declaration on Protection of All Persons from Being Subjected to Torture and Other Cruel, Inhuman or Degrading Treatment or Pnishment:

> any act by which severe pain or suffering, whether physical or mental, is intentionally inflicted on a person for such purposes as obtaining from him or a third person, information or a confession, punishing him for an act he or a third person has committed or is suspected of having committed, or intimidating or coercing him or a third person, or for any reason based on discrimination of any kind, when such pain or suffering is inflicted by or at the instigation of or with the consent or acquiescence of a public official or other person acting in an official capacity. It does not include pain or suffering arising only from, inherent in or incidental to lawful sanctions. (Tokyo Declaration quoted in Pelly 71)

Having suffered the irreparable agony of his killing, Sujata has refused to discuss Brati within the family, whose "charming social game" (Devi 30) of prudery, flirtations, cheating and deceit had no place for him. She flatly refuses to discuss Brati with Tuli, when Tuli levels against her dead brother the charge of anarchy or the absence of "beliefs" (28). Nor does she ask the questions that haunt her in Dibyanath's response to the Kantapukur killing "Do they all try to hush up things that soon? Even before the dead body is identified?...A father gets the message on the telephone and doesn't feel for a moment the urge to rush to see his dead son! The first thing that strikes him is it would be unwise to keep the car waiting before Kantapukur?" (29)

The society that has killed him has had to "burn as a rule" (39) Brati's books, papers and other revolutionary material—taboo to the world but potential memorabilia of a bereaved mother. The family and society having failed her in reducing the dead Brati into a nullity within the plot of trapping and killing him (though the narrative accords him a dignity in death as he risks his own life to save his friends- far lower in the social and class scale than him), the only sharing of her grief is with the utterly impoverished mothers of the dead Somu, Bijit, Partha and Laltu who along with her Brati have no "memorial tablets" (34) in their name, even as their families are ostracized.

Interestingly, at no point in the story does Mahasweta testify or condone Brati's ideology. What is most poignant is the agony of a mother whose unmourned son has been killed without a trial, in abysmal silence, as it spirals into a wider plea for basic human rights of all other sons. "To kill them one did not need any special sanction from the law or the courts of justice. Individuals and gangs of killers had equal right to kill these faithless young men. They could be killed with bullets, knives, hatchets, spears, with any weapon whatsoever. They could be killed any time any place for any audience present." (20) Their absence from the scrolls of law and medicine (the 'madness' or 'anarchy' ascribed to them, does not merit cure) is an attempt to delegitimize their suffering and torture, even as the cultural-intellectual milieu of Calcutta rhetorically espouses and agitates for remoter themes, for the rights of those across the border.

Susan Moeller uses the term 'compassion fatigue' as one that involves suffering from an overload of crisis stories where the audience, whose attention contributes to the network's power effects, simply refuses to receive or respond to any more stories. It may be that their receptiveness and reactions become duller as the number of narratives heaped upon them increases. In this case, the survivors have to suffer a jaded and lethargic response to such crisis stories. In Devi's novel, there is a poignant complete absence of compassion as a response to such stories. There is rather a deliberately cultivated "phlegmatic fatigue" where a jaded and lethargic response to mass torture and killing is unquestioningly accepted by a 'cadaverous' society.

This formulaic repetition of torture breeds a perverse social tolerance. However what Moeller says about 'compassion fatigue' may also be deemed true for Brati (and those like him) "It's a bit like that tree falling in the middle of the forest. If it falls and no one hears, it's like it never happened. The tree may lie on the forestfloor for years, finally to rot away, without anyone ever realizing it once stood tall" (Moeller 12).The social sensibility is desensitized and habituated to such killing. Just as the mother-subject is not offered a ground for institutionalised debate, so is Brati who has to pay for such a lacuna in the human rights debate with his murder.

The novel exposes illegitimacy as a paradigmatic condition of society at large where human rights are brutally violated just as the violent denial of the mother as subject. The individual body then becomes a metonym for the mother-subject's pain, rupture and liberation.The family remorselessly expunges every snatch of Brati's memory from their lives. The society has driven him to his cold and gory grave. Newspapers are cleared of his name. The only restorative space that may be offered to such gruesome violence of unspeakable and unsurmountable proportions then is fictional narrative. Fiction becomes the melting pot for the discourses that both Sujata and Brati have on offer. Mahasweta Devi's novel Mother of 1084 as a crucible of several debates—the feminist debate, the class debate, the debate on policing and last but not the least, the debate on human rights—has become iconic in having been read, appreciated and researched over the past several decades.

Work Cited

- Bajaj, Monisha. "Human Rights Education: Definitions, Histories, Ideologies." *Schooling for Social Change: The Rise and Impact of Human Rights Education in India.* New York: Continuum, 2012. Print.
- Conrad, Joseph. *Heart of Darkness and the Secret Sharer*. New York, NY: Signet Classics, 2008. Print.
- Devi, Mahasweta, and Samik Bandyopadhyay. *Mother of 1084*. Calcutta: Seagull Books, 1998. Print.
- Moeller, Susan D. *Compassion Fatigue: How the Media Sells Disease, Famine, War and Death.* New York: Routledge, 1999. Print.
- Pelly, Grace, and Jai Singh. "Torture in India." *State Terrorism: Torture, Extra-Judicial Killings, and Forced Disappearances in India: Report of the Independent People's Tribunal*, 9-10 February 2008. New Delhi, India: Human Rights Law Network, 2009. Print.

16

Impact of Sri Lankan Armed Conflict: Decoding International Legal Regime on Grave Violations, Victimisation on Children

— ***Devakumar Jacob***

"How can we tell what happened to us? There are no words to describe what we have witnessed. What we saw, what we heard, what we did, and how it changed our lives, is beyond measure. We were murdered, raped, amputated, tortured, mutilated, beaten, enslaved and forced to commit terrible crimes."—**Confession of a child victim to the Truth and Reconciliation Commission**

The Sri Lankan ethnic Conflict was the longest armed conflict in Asia. It was a conflict between the Government Forces and a rebel separatist group better known as the LTTE (The Liberation Tigers of Tamil Eelam). Demanded their rights as equal with Sinhalese, on the denial, they have organised a rebel movement with demand of separate autonomy to the Northern province where the majority of Tamil people lived. In course of times they were identified as terrorist .The LTTE was regarded as the most lethal terrorist group in the world. In the subsequent years, the LTTE was banned in UK, US and in Canada. Sri Lankan Army paid special attention, declared war on the rebel group. The LTTE attacked the Sri Lankan armed forces with modern high tech weapons. In addition, the LTTE used numerous unconventional methods to fight the Sri Lankan Forces using child soldiers and suicide bombers. In order to suppress the rebels Srilankan Army declared war on four occassions against the rebels which lasted for three decades.

The Sri Lankan military attack violated basic norms and left many-faceted consequences. The Northern conflict consumed many lives and caused damage to the property worth billions of dollars.

In Sri Lankan ethnic armed conflict, children, both girls and boys, are increasingly becoming the subject of military recruitment, targeted attacks, and sexual violence. The armed groups easy availability of small arms and light weapons have led to the recruitment and use of hundreds of thousands of child soldiers in the ethnic armed conflict. Children as young as eight are drawn into violence for a variety of reasons. Some are used by their commanders as front line combatants, while others carry out support functions. During armed conflicts, many children are forced to witness or to take part in horrifying acts of violence. They suffer from being orphaned, raped, maimed and manipulated to give expression to the hatred of adults. Many have lost their families, as well as education opportunities, a chance to enjoy their childhood, and to be part of a community.

World Scenario

It is estimated that children are being recruited to the armed forces in approximately 17 countries worldwide. Many are recruited by force and threatened with death; others join out of desperation when conflict breaks out leaving them without education, family or any coherent social structure.[1] Child soldiers are commonly abused and when hostilities end, many are left mentally and physically scarred, often stigmatised and unable to rejoin society. The emotional and physical strain the child soldiers suffer leaves them particularly vulnerable after the conflicts end. Many are left physically disabled and suffer post-traumatic stress syndrome in the form of anxiety, bedwetting, nightmares and hyperactive and aggressive behaviour, to name a few examples. The dehumanizing reality of child soldiers receives limited attention in some societies, as it is a taboo subject. This prevents the victims from seeking help and being able to rejoin society and reunite with their families. More generally, however, lack of awareness regarding what child soldiers are exposed to, such as sexual exploitation, leads to problems in regard to successful disarmament, demobilisation and reintegration of child soldiers. In 1996, the UN appointed a Special Representative to the UN Secretary-General for Children and Armed

Conflict to promote and protect the rights of all children affected by armed conflict. Furthermore, representatives from 58 countries committed themselves to putting an end to the unlawful recruitment and use of children in armed conflicts, as well as to ensuring that conscription and enlistment procedures for recruitment into armed forces comply with applicable international law at an international conference convened in Paris in 2007.[2]

In Gaza, over 500 children were killed and more than 1,300 injured, Ms. Zerrougui said, calling for a thorough investigation of the impact of the war on children. Thousands of displaced families are still living in schools and access to education for the children of Gaza is expected to remain limited. At least 244 schools were damaged or destroyed by Israel's armed forces during recent fighting. "We cannot afford impunity in the face of such grave violations of international law that in some cases may amount to war crimes," said the Special Representative. Many other situations witnessed grave violations against children in 2013 and face similar challenges today. Instability and rising tensions in Libya, Afghanistan, the Central African Republic, Mali and South Sudan continue to threaten children.[3] The Government of Chad has already fulfilled all the requirements and pledged to prevent the recruitment of children in its armed forces. In May, Yemen became the 7th country to sign an action place. Progress has also been achieved in South Sudan, Somalia, Afghanistan, Myanmar and the Democratic Republic of Congo.

Evidence indicates that the recruitment and use of children has become the means of choice of many armed groups for waging war. At root there are numerous and often interrelated factors that drive the recruitment and use of child soldiers. Children are either recruited by force or may voluntarily' join armed groups to safeguard themselves and their families. Many are compelled by poverty and lack of livelihood opportunities, domestic violence or lack of parental care altogether. Some children have seen family members killed in conflict and may be motivated by a desire for retribution or revenge. For some, the lack of legitimate avenues for political dissent and participation or ideologies of nationalism or ethnic identity become powerful motivating factors. Particularly in situations of protracted conflict that may have lasted for several decades and decimated the adult male population, the recruitment of children becomes a calculus of urgent demand' for fighters and ready supply' of children.[4]

The long-lasting war has had an enormous impact on children. Many children in the north and east were displaced and lived for years in camps before returning to their original homes after the war ended. Over the years they suffered from isolation and lack of basic services such as housing, health care and education. Many children struggled with the loss of family members, family separation and multiple displacements. Hundreds of children were forced to fight as soldiers. As a result of the war, many children did not experience a safe and secure childhood or receive support to develop to their full potential. Among them, the most affected children are those who lost one or both parents, or were separated from their families. These children often depend on institutions or extended families for better care and support. One of the remnants of the war is that communities are often unable to fulfill their responsibilities to protect children. Many children are engaged in informal labour activities, and face domestic and sexual violence and neglect. At times, poverty and traditional practices also lead to teenage pregnancies and early marriages.[5] Though there are no clear figures on the child soldier, child victims in the ethnic armed conflict, a serious attempt has been made to bring out the injustice enforced in the grave violations to the children at the time and after math of armed conflict.

Victimisation and Grave Violations Denial of Inherent Right to life and Killing and Maiming of Children

Children are brutalised, killed, taken as war captives and abused through the ages. Armed conflict in contemporary world is a perennial threat to the children. War is, and has always been, a dangerous place for children. This segment attempts to provide clear picture on the violations against children and victimisation in the course of conflict and its impact ever since the conflict originated and even during process of rehabilitation and resettlement of children in Sri Lanka. The changing nature of conflict and the use of landmines and unexploded ordnances pose a particular threat to children. The humanitarian principles of distinction and proportionality require fighters to distinguish between combatants and civilians, and they prohibit civilian damage beyond the scope of military advantage. However, in current warfare, this principle is eroding among armed forces and groups because of the changing nature of conflict. Children are often killed and injured in the course of military operations, including in cross-fire, aerial bombardment and shelling. Many girls and boys were killed and maimed during conflict.[6]

Another worrisome trend is the rise in suicide attacks, and the use of children to carry them out, that lead to death or serious injuries of children. Although thousands of children are injured and killed during military operations, many are also victims of landmines and unexploded ordnance. The right to life and the prohibition of killing and maiming civilians are principles enshrined in humanitarian law, human rights treaties, and jurisprudence.

Children Death toll in Peninsular Jaffana

The most worrying aspect in Sri Lanka's northern Jaffna peninsula was the traumatic effect it had on children due to incessant bombing of Tamil Tiger position by helicopters and aircrafts in Jaffna town by the government. They had nightmares and end up screaming in the night. The rest of the peninsula was under siege, the constant bombardments were having a devastating effect on the mental state of children. The level of sound and level of destructive power has really escalated to an unbearable level, many of those helicopters actually fired from areas where civilians were under the helicopter when it fired, the trauma experienced by children takes many different forms. Most of the places where children were trapped in the Ariel attack died or injured severely.

Child Death toll by Ariel attack and other means in Jaffna Peninsular

The CRC ensures that child has the inherent right to life and that state parties shall ensure the maximum extent possible to the survival and development of child (Crcart.6 1989). This is also a principle of customary international law which prohibits violence to life and person, in particular murder of all kinds of civilians and non-combatants

(Art.3 gc,1949). The bedrock standards of this law are principles of distinction and proportionally which requires the parties to the conflict to distinguish between civilians and combatants at all times, and prohibits military attack which might cause civilian death or injury (Unsc, 2009). According the Rome Statute of international criminal court, widespread killing or causing serious bodily harm to civilians may amount to a war crime, crime against humanity or genocide (at 6,7.8 rs icc). Despite these standing laws, the number of child causalities in armed conflicts has been considerably increasing. Responding to this injustice and unabated predicament, the UN SC designated the killing and maiming of children, as well as sexual violence, as priorities it in its resolution 1882 (Unsc, 2009)[7]

S. No.	*Places under Ariel attack*	*Death toll/ reported*	*Boys*	*Girls*	*Injured*	*Unreported death toll*
1.	Nachikunda	**17**	7	10	23	**11**
2.	Jaffana (Main)	**16**	9	7	18	**8**
3.	Navalay	**38**	20	18	32	**17**
4.	Kumarapuram	**7**	3	4	14	**5**
5.	Nagar Koil (Central school)	**42**	20	22	200	**22**
6.	Manalkadu	**8**	2	6	15	**3**
7.	Katkavalam	**13**	9	4	17	**6**
8.	Vadamacheri	**6**	2	4	11	**3**
9.	Jaffna	**42**	30	12	150	**44**
10.	Bindunuwa	**24**	14	10	35	**17**
11.	Donboscocenter	**40**	24	16	42	**15**
12.	Final war zone	**780**	400	380	1060	**400**
13.	1983 to 2009	**50.000**	23000	27000	35000	**15000**

Source: TCHR is an independent Human Rights organisation – not affiliated to any Tamil Federation or Association.

Due to limited access to the conflict area and unwillingness of government of Srilanka, there are no available statistics on exact figures of children killed or maimed during the final war. However, an available source clearly shows that large number of killing and maiming of children took place throughout the conflict. It was identified that death of an estimated 50000 children, including a large number of them under age of five in the three decades of armed conflict. According to the Secretary General's report on children on armed conflict in Srilanka, around 30000 maimed and at least 20000 killed in three decades.[8] During the final months of fighting, numerous civilians, including hundreds of thousands of children were trapped in the climax of war. The presence of LTTE among civilians in the no-fire zones put the civilians in serious danger. There is reliable evidence that civilians, including numerous children, were explicitly targeted by the GSL when it repeatedly shelled on the three no-fire zones as a part of its overall military strategy to defeat the rebel forces. Meanwhile, the little children trapped in these no-fire zones, prevented civilians from leaving the area, ensuring their continued presence as a human buffer. In the early period of conflict, numerous incidents of LTTE involved bombings took place which resulted in the death of many children. Attacks on places crawling with children in the Sinhalese dominated areas demonstrate that the forces had no regard for children's well-being.

The SLA commonly positioned its checkpoints and camps close to schools, and the LTTE unashamedly held children and elders as hostages at schools housing IDPS and no fire zones declared by the government. Such actions reveal that both parties mercilessly used children as human buffer between themselves and their opponent, and in doing so, intentionally exposed the children to harm. The conflict also witness that children are at great risk from the presence of landmines, both antipersonnel as well as anti-vehicle, and UXO that were extensively used by both parties before the cease-fire. The LTTE again increased the use of mines since 2006. It was as of July 2010, Srilanka had identified 1,469 contaminated by mines and UXO. Generally children are particularly susceptible to being killed or seriously wounded by land mines and UXO because they fail to recognise warning signs, they tend to confuse mines with toys and their small bodies succumb more readily to the wounds inflicted by mines.[9] Another alarming fact is that child recruits sustained horrific mine-related injuries while undergoing brutal trainings at the LTTE camps. The indiscriminate use of claymore mines has further resulted in the death of many children. Carrying claymore mines on buses by school children clearly shows that the force lacks concern for children's lives. The report of the UNSG on children and armed conflict documented 28 cases related to mine and explosive remnants of war in 2010.

Massacre of Tamil youths in a Detention and Rehabilitation Centre

There was a massacre of 24 unarmed boys in a Rehabilitation Centre run by the Sri Lankan Government international condemnation. This is a gross violation of International law and International Covenants to which Sri Lanka is a signatory. In accordance with International Law, authorities holding detainees are responsible for their safety and security at all times and in all circumstances. There are no exceptions. Tamil boys aged 14-23 were massacred by Sinhalese hoodlums at the Bindunuwewa Rehabilitation Centre, some 3 miles from Bandarawela town in the hill country of Sri Lanka. This Rehabilitation Centre is jointly run by Presidential Secretariate, Child Protection Authority, Ministry of Defence, Ministry of Rehabilitation and Reconstruction, National Youth Services Council and the Don Bosco Technical Centre.[10] The youths were detained under the notorious "Prevention of Terrorism Act", which breaches every international convention. A police unit and 12 home guards recruited from the neighbourhood, were in charge of security. It is important to appreciate that the young detainees were being held without charge or trial. They had been demanding that charges be filed against them or that they be released. They were denied the judicial process to which they have a right under the U.N. International Convention on Civil and Political Rights to which Sri Lanka acceded in 1980.

Around 2000 Sinhalese thugs stormed the Rehabilitation Centre wielding knives, machetes, axes and iron rods. They hacked to death some 24 detainees and set fire to the buildings. 16 detainees were seriously wounded and another 7 injured and 20 were missing. It is liked that the death toll will rise in view of the seriousness of the injuries and the refusal of the staff of the local Bandarawela hospital to treat the injured. The death toll has, in fact, already risen and currently stands at 29. It could rise further, government must take full responsibility for yet another blot in Sri Lankan history.[11]

Cold Blooded Murders of Tamil Children

Not counting Tamil children killed by Sri Lankan Air Force bombings and army shelling, how many Tamil children were killed in cold-blood by Sri Lankan soldiers and police by point blank shootings or by using knives and hatchets? How many cases were brought to the government's attention and in how many cases any action was taken? Is it less than 1 per cent? Will the Sri Lankan foreign minister provide a list of such massacres reported by international human rights organisations and identify governmental action in each incidence, such as cases filed against the alleged murderers, disposition of the case, number of convictions and punishment? To our knowledge, not a single soldier or police man is punished.[12]

Child Recruitment: A Serious War Crime

Hundreds of thousands of children are used as soldiers in armed conflicts around the world. Many children are abducted and beaten into submission; others join military groups to escape poverty, to defend their communities, out of a feeling of revenge or for other reasons. In many conflicts children take direct part in combat. However, their role is not limited to fighting. Many girls and boys start out in support functions that also entail great risk and hardship. One of the common tasks assigned to children is to serve as porters, often carrying heavy loads, including ammunition or injured soldiers. Some children act as lookouts, messengers, cooks or other routine duties. Girls are particularly vulnerable. They are often forced to serve as sexual slaves. Moreover, the use of children for acts of terror, including as suicide bombers, has emerged as a phenomenon of modern warfare.[13] Regardless of how children are recruited and of their roles, child soldiers are victims, whose participation in conflict bears serious implications for their physical and emotional well-being. They are commonly subject to abuse and most of them witness death, killing, and sexual violence. Many are forced to perpetrate these atrocities and some suffer serious long-term psychological consequences. The reintegration of these children into civilian life is a complex process.

In Asia, LTTE Recruited a large number of Children. Army of Sri Lanka violated all legal standards. The LTTE had recruited and used children as soldiers throughout the civil war in Sri Lanka. Prior to the 2002 ceasefire agreement, the LTTE routinely used children in combat, including for mass attacks during major battles. Children often suffered high rates of casualties. The LTTE used child soldiers in all capacities, including as infantry soldiers, security and intelligence officers, medics, combat and administrative support, and as trainers for other cadres. The LTTE also used children as suicide bombers, including girls, who may be less likely to undergo rigorous searches at government checkpoints. The LTTE gave cyanide capsules and grenades to its soldiers, including children, with instructions to ingest the capsule or blow themselves up rather than allow them to be captured by the Sri Lankan security forces.[14]

Table-2 Child Soldier Released by UNICEF

Age	*15 below*	*16*	*17*	*18*	*19*	*Total*
LTTE	293	207	256	285	247	**1288**
TMVP	44	34	24	18	6	**126**
SLGA/ Home guards	440	459	478	516	660	**2553**

(2006 alone 1387 children were released from Srilanka)

Table-3 Child Death toll in the Final war in the North East

Age	5 below	5-10	11-17	17-20	Total
Children	**365**	**494**	**4094**	**1289**	**6242**

The LTTE carried out vigorous campaigns in Tamil communities in LTTE dominated areas to promote their cause, often designed to attract children as new recruits. These campaigns included special events honoring LTTE heroes, parades of LTTE cadres, public displays of war paraphernalia, and street theater. In schools, LTTE cadres often gave speeches and showed videos, and gave teachers ¯history lessons on the LTTE to administer to their students. Many children were attracted to the perceived status or glamour of serving as an LTTE cadre, or were persuaded that it was their duty to join the nationalist struggle as part of the LTTE. Children from a disadvantaged background were particularly vulnerable to LTTE recruitment. Children, who were orphaned, were from poor or abusive families, or who had little access to educational or vocational opportunities often believed that joining the LTTE offered a positive alternative to their circumstances.

The events listed above are typical incidents in which a large number of children were killed. Saththurukondan massacre on 9 September 1990: Five infants under the age of 1 and 42 children under the age of 10 were killed. A total of 74 children under the age of 18 were killed after families were allowed back to resettle in their homes, the Sri Lankan armed forces surrounded the village and took 184 people. On that night, they raped and murdered several women; altogether, 85 women were killed. Twenty-eight men were chopped to deaths.[15]

Government abuses also fueled children‘s participation in the LTTE. During the conflict, many Tamil children in the north and east were directly affected by abuses carried out by government security forces, including torture, interrogation, unlawful detention, execution, rape, and enforced disappearances. A study of adolescents in Vaddukoddai in the north found that one-quarter of the children studied had witnessed violence personally, often against members of their own family. In response, many children joined the LTTE, seeking to protect their families and community, or to avenge past abuses. The LTTE also used coercion and force to recruit children into their ranks. LTTE recruiters abducted children on their way home from school or from their homes. Particularly in the east, the LTTE enforced one family, one child policy, informing Tamil households that each family was obliged to provide a son or a daughter for the cause. The LTTE‘s recruitment and use of child soldiers continued even after the ceasefire was signed in 2002.[16] LTTE routinely visited Tamil homes to inform parents that they must provide a child for the movement. Families that resisted were harassed and threatened. Parents were told that if they did not comply, their child would be taken by force, other children in the household or their parents would be taken in their stead, or the family would be forced to leave their home. In numerous cases, after a family refused to voluntarily hand over a son or daughter, a child was abducted from their home at night, or picked up by LTTE cadres while walking to school or attending a temple festival.[17] The LTTE typically targeted children of 14 to 16 years of age for recruitment, but in some cases it took children as young as 11 or 12. Girls were recruited in large numbers, and make up an estimated 40 per cent of the LTTE‘s child recruits.

The Karuna group and the LTTE are both in violation of international law for recruiting and using children as soldiers. The Sri Lankan government is also in violation of international law by facilitating child recruitment by the Karuna group and failing to take feasible measures to prevent such recruitment and secure the release of recruited children. International humanitarian law (the laws of war) and human rights law prohibit the recruitment and use of children as soldiers and in other combat-related roles.[18] Protocol II to the Geneva Conventions of 1949, which applies during non-international armed conflicts (civil wars), prohibits states and non-state armed groups from recruiting or using children under the age of 15 in armed conflict. This standard is also reflected in the Convention on the Rights of the Child (CRC), which Sri Lanka ratified in 1991. The prohibition on the recruitment and use of children below the age of 15 is now considered customary international law, and is binding on all parties to armed conflict. Sri Lanka is also party to the Optional Protocol to the Convention on the Rights of the Child on the involvement of children in armed conflict, which entered into force in 2002.

The protocol raised the standards set in the Convention on the Rights of the Child by establishing 18 as the minimum age for any conscription or forced recruitment or direct participation in hostilities. The protocol also places obligations upon non-state armed forces.

Article 4 states that ¯armed groups that are distinct from the armed forces of a state should not, under any circumstances, recruit or use in hostilities persons under the age of eighteen. It also places obligations on the state to ¯take all feasible measures to prevent such recruitment and use, including the adoption of legal measures necessary to prohibit and criminalize such practices.

The Optional Protocol does not set a specific age for voluntary recruitment by government forces, but requires governments to deposit a binding declaration establishing their minimum voluntary recruitment age.[19] The age set cannot be below 16. In the case of Sri Lanka, the government made a declaration at the time of ratification establishing that the minimum age for voluntary recruitment into government forces was 18.

Thus, in practice, the same age limits apply for all forms of recruitment by both state and non-state forces in Sri Lanka. In 1999, the member states of the International Labour Organisation (ILO) unanimously adopted the Worst Forms of Child Labour Convention (No. 182). It defines a child as any person under the age of 18 and includes in its definition of the worst forms of child labor. All forms of slavery or practices similar to slavery, such as the sale and trafficking of children, debt bondage and serfdom and forced or compulsory labour, including forced or compulsory recruitment of children for use in armed conflict.[20]

Sri Lanka ratified the Worst Forms of Child Labour Convention on March 1, 2001. The convention obliges the Sri Lankan government to ¯take immediate and effective measures to secure the prohibition and elimination of the worst forms of labour as a matter of urgency.

Under Convention No. 182, the government is required to take measures to prevent the engagement of children in the worst forms of child labor, remove them from these circumstances, and assist their rehabilitation and social reintegration; Recommendation 190 accompanying Convention No. 182 encourages states to make recruitment of children under the age of 18 a criminal offense. In 2005, the Sri Lankan penal code was amended to bring it into conformity with ILO Convention No. 182. Forcible or compulsory recruitment of children is a crime carrying a maximum penalty of 20 years imprisonment.[21]

Child Recruitment as a War Crime

The recruitment of children under the age of 15 or their use in hostilities is also considered a war crime under the Rome Statute of the International Criminal Court (ICC). The statute was adopted in July 1998 and considers such recruitment a war crime under its jurisdiction whether carried out by members of national armed forces or non-state armed groups. Even though, as of January 2007, Sri Lanka was not a state party to the ICC statute, individuals who are responsible for recruiting children under the age of 15 into armed groups may still be criminally responsible for acts amounting to war crimes under customary international law. In May 2004, the Appeals Chamber of the Special Court for Sierra Leone ruled that the prohibition on recruiting children below age 15 had crystallised as customary international law prior to 1996, citing the widespread recognition and acceptance of the norm in international instruments such as the Convention on the Rights of the Child and the Additional Protocols to the Geneva Conventions.[22]

The Special Court for Sierra Leone also found that the individuals responsible for recruiting children under the age of 15 bear criminal responsibility for their acts: The practice of child recruitment bears the most atrocious consequences for the children. Serious violations of fundamental guarantees lead to individual criminal responsibility. Therefore the recruitment of children was already a crime by the time of the adoption of the 1998 Rome Statute for the International Criminal Court, which codified and ensured the effective implementation of an existing customary norm relating to child recruitment rather than forming a new one. Both the Karuna group and the LTTE have recruited children under age 15 into their forces. Of cases reported to UNICEF where the age of the child was known, 17 per cent (1,012 cases) of children recruited to date by the LTTE were under age 15; 5 per cent (10 cases) of children recruited by the Karuna group were under age of 15.[23]

Abduction and Forced Recruitment

Generally, an armed conflict, disrupt and weaken protective structures surrounding family and community, thereby making children easy prey for abductors. Children were abducted for a range of purposes. It manifested in the form of recruitment by armed groups and participation in criminal acts, sexual abuse, forced labour, hostage taking and indoctrination. The UN resolution and armed conflict states that forced recruitment of a child as two separate violations: abduction and recruitment. Invariably both rebels and army abducted children for many reason. Rift rebel TMVP with indirect support of Srilankan government abducted quite a good number of children, forced them train in the government army camp. It was noticed that abduction of children aged between 8-17 were the common occurrences during the conflict. From 2006 to 2009 there were sudden escalation of child abduction, majority of them were taken from their homes during raids, and others were grabbed off the street to schools or in the public gatherings. In some incidences, abducted children were later found to have been killed.[24] During war climax, children at tender age were taken from IDPS camps. It was noted that forcing children to commit crimes during an armed conflict is in itself a war crime resulting in severe psychological harm, and is a violation to their rights.

In times of conflict, children are abducted from their homes, schools and refugee camps. Child abduction often leads to other violations against children such as forced labour, sexual slavery and recruitment. Many children also get trafficked across borders. Parties to conflict have used this practice in systematic campaigns of intimidation and reprisal against civilian populations. Abducting children against their will and the will of their adult guardians, either temporarily or permanently, is illegal under international law. It may constitute a grave breach of the Geneva Conventions and amounts to a crime against humanity and a war crime.

International humanitarian law prohibits all parties to armed conflicts from arbitrarily depriving any person of their liberty, including through abductions and forced recruitment. Article 3 common to the four Geneva Conventions of 1949 and applicable to non-internationalarmed conflicts, requires that all civilians be treated humanely – arbitrary deprivation of liberty is incompatible with this requirement.

On December 6, 2006, the government of Sri Lanka enacted new emergency regulations, the Prevention and Prohibition of Terrorism and Specified Terrorist Activities. The regulations prohibit any person from joining a group engaged in terrorism or taking part in any of its activities. The regulations apply to all individuals, including children, and make no distinction between individuals who may voluntarily join such groups and those who may join due to threats, force, or abduction. As a result, children recruited by either the LTTE or the Karuna group could be charged under the regulations, and if convicted, sentenced to prison for five to ten years.[25] The regulations do not specifically prohibit the recruitment of children into organisations engaged in acts of terrorism.

Child Recruitments and Abduction-1984-2009 -Age group from 10 to 17 in SriLanka

S.No	*Recruiters*	*Male*	*Female*	*Total*
1.	LTTE	2300	1700	4000
2.	TMVP (2004 onwards)	1400	600	2000
3.	GSLA	15000	12000	3000
4.	Home guards (GSL)	NA	NA	18000
5.	Deserters	NA	NA	75369

Source: TCHR is an independent Human Rights organisation – not affiliated to any Tamil Federation or Association.

Initially, GSL planned to recruit 15000 children to counter attack the LTTE in 2000. They were recruited and assigned as home guards in different places, like airport and government- controlled checkpoints. The Srilankan Military lists those 70,369 soldiers (most of them children) as deserted and appealed to get De-listed to lead normal life.[26] It was identified that GSL recruited children with bogus age certificate to justify their injustice on child recruitment from the international Law.

Sexual Violence against Children

Sexual violence is increasingly a characteristic of conflict and is often perpetrated against girls and boys in a rule of law vacuum. In some instances, sexual violence has been used as a tactic of war designed to humiliate a population or to force displacement. Children who experience sexual violence suffer from long-term psychological trauma, health consequences including transmitted infections such as HIV/AIDS and early pregnancies. Their reintegration is even a greater challenge as communities often stigmatize girls who have been associated with armed groups and are suspected of having been raped. Young mothers of babies born of rape often stay with the armed group because of the family ties and dependency that have evolved over time and to avoid social stigma in the communities at home. These girls and their children are particularly vulnerable to all forms of exploitation including prostitution and trafficking and need special protection.

Rape and other forms of sexual violence against children are human rights violations, and may amount to grave breaches of international humanitarian law. If committed as part of a widespread or systematic attack against a civilian population, sexual violence can constitute war crimes and crimes against humanity under the Rome Statute of the International Criminal Court. Under Security Council resolution 1882 (2009), the Council designated sexual violence committed against children as a critical priority and called on parties to armed conflict to prepare and implement action plans to address the violation. Sexual violence is also a trigger for the Secretary-General's list of shame of parties to conflict committing grave violations against children in armed conflict.[27]

The crimes remain one of the least documented violations of Sri Lankan armed conflict is rape and sexual violence. Fear of government stand and retribution by perpetrators among the people resulted in failing to register that sexual violence. There were young girls raped assaulted both in the rebels as well as in the army.

Children IDPS/Homes- sexually assaulted in the conflict

S. No	*Name of the Home*	*Girls*	*Boys*	*Total*	*Abused /assaulted*
1.	Kurukulam Children's home	275	225	500	79
2.	Senthalir Children' Home	38	42	80	18
3.	Kandaruban Arevucholai	121	101	227	15
4.	Chencholai Children's Home	98	152	250	47
5.	Iniya Vazhvu Illam (children with visual and hearing difficulties)	199	61	260	89
6.	Malarcholai	23	11	34	8
7.	Children home in Batticaloa	401	219	620	158
8.	Gandhi Children Home	130	117	247	79
9.	Baharathy Children Home	90	79	169	58
10.	Jayanthy Nagar Children Home	30	15	45	16
11.	Puneetha Pummee Children Home	89	31	120	45
12.	Vivekanantha Children Home	31	4	35	9
13.	Sakthi Mallar. Children Home	28	10	38	6
14.	Theruppalukammam Children	23	12	35	4
15.	Katheroli Children Home	32	20	52	23
16.	Maneekavasakar Children Home	15	25	35	12
17.	(There are many other children home in the NorthEast)	339	61	400	179

Source: TCHR is an independent Human Rights organisation – not affiliated to any Tamil Federation or Association.

It was identified that IPKF along with SLA women and young girls were sexually assaulted, final course of the war opened door for the army to increase the number of rapes before they shoot them. Forced marriages of young girls, girls were kept as sexual object by the rebels who were unwillingly undergone family life. There was no international agencies or NGOs, local government which took interest to study or to act on the issue. Through the conflict, women and girl children were being raped under threat, there is clear evidence that sexual violence was used as a weapon at the final war. In various IDPs Camps, both boys and girls were vulnerable to sexual abuse. It is important to note that in every reported rape, nine go unreported out of shame, fear and also because there is no official system to record these statements. There are 136000 IDP children in the northern part most of them are sexually assaulted either by officials or by the members of army.[28]

Parties to conflict are prohibited from subjecting children to rape and other forms of sexual violence. Children shall be the object of special respect and shall be protected against any form of indecent assault. Article 77(1), Additional Protocol I to the Geneva Conventions Rape and other forms of sexual violence against children, both boys and girls, are serious violations of international human rights law and may amount to grave breaches of international humanitarian law. Acts of sexual violence may constitute a war crime, a crime against humanity or a constitutive act with respect to genocide. In 2009, the Security Council, in resolution 1882, added sexual violence against children as an additional trigger for listing parties to conflict in the Secretary-General's Annual Report on Children and Armed Conflict.[29]

Rape and other forms of sexual violence during armed conflict are prohibited under the Geneva Conventions and their Additional Protocols. Child-specific provisions of these treaties specifically forbid sexual violence against children. The obligation of humane treatment under Common Article 3 implicitly prohibits rape or any other sexual violence, be it against adults or children. Article 27 of the 4th Geneva Convention explicitly prohibits such acts stating that:

Women [including girls] shall be especially protected against any attack on their honour, in particular against rape, enforced prostitution, or any form of indecent assault. The international tribunals for the former Yugoslavia and Rwanda, as well as the European Court of Human Rights and the Inter American Commission on Human Rights, have recognised that rape amounts to torture and is absolutely prohibited. Moreover, a number of international treaties prohibit the sexual abuse and exploitation of adults and children. These include the Convention against Torture (1984), the Convention for the Suppression of the Traffic in Persons and of the Exploitation of the Prostitution of Others (1949) and the Vienna Declaration of the World Conference on Human Rights (1993).

The ICCPR and the Convention for the Elimination of all Forms of Discrimination Against Women (CEDAW) (1979) affirm a women's right to liberty and security of person and to be free from discrimination. The CRC and its Optional Protocol on Trafficking and Exploitation unequivocally affirm that children must enjoy protection from torture, cruel, inhuman or degrading treatment, a protection broadly accepted as encompassing acts of rape and sexual violence. Regional human rights instruments such as the African Charter on the Rights and Welfare of the Child (1990) also explicitly forbid sexual violence against children. Rape and other forms of sexual Violence are International Crimes. International criminal law explicitly criminalizes rape and sexual violence during wartime and judicial recognition of its customary status in international law came in 1998 with a number of ground-breaking judgments by the ICTY. The statutes of the SCSL, ICTR and ICTY all cite rape and sexual violence as war crimes and crimes against humanity.[30] Sexual violence against civilians has been prosecuted by several international tribunals established to punish the perpetrators of international crimes. At the ICTR—the Akayesu (1998) and Musema (2000) cases. At the ICTY—the Furundžija (1998) and Kunarac (2000) cases, a number of accused have been convicted for rape, torture and enslavement. This was the first time in history that an international tribunal convicted individuals solely on charges of sexual violence against women and girls. In addition, the SCSL established that forced marriage is also an offence under international criminal law when it found three militia leaders guilty of crimes against humanity for forcing girls into marriage.

The Rome Statute of the ICC states that rape, sexual slavery, enforced prostitution, forced pregnancy, enforced sterilisation or other forms of sexual violence of comparable gravity may constitute war crimes and crimes against humanity. Jean Pierre Bemba Gombo, a former leader of a Congolese armed group, is currently standing trial at the ICC on war crimes and crimes against humanity charges resulting from allegations of rape and other abuses by troops under his command.

Other Relevant Security Council Resolutions

In 2008, The Security Council, in its resolution 1820 on Women, Peace and Security recognised for the first time that ¯sexual violence, when used or commissioned as a tactic of war in order to deliberately target civilians or as a part of a widespread or systematic attack against civilian populations, can significantly exacerbate situations of armed conflict and may impede the restoration of international peace and security.

Attacks on Schools and Hospitals

The most grave violation is attacking service utility centers especially schools and hospitals. A marked characteristic of the changing nature of conflict is deliberate attacks against education infrastructures, as well as the targeting of school children and teachers. Beyond the destruction and damaging of school facilities, there are also reports of the use of acid and gas attacks on girl students on their way to school, as well as shootings and suicide bombings on school premises. In some contexts, schools are also a prime recruiting ground for children. Elsewhere, school buildings are used as military bases that become strategic targets. Parties to conflict must not attack schools or hospitals, education or medical personnel.[31] Schools and hospitals

No. of Hospitals destroyed in final stage of war

S.No	*Type of hospital*	*No*	*S.No*	*Type of hospital*	*No*
1.	Teaching hospitals	2	5.	Maternity homes	5
2.	Rural hospitals	3	6.	Outpatient clinics	16
3.	District hospitals	3	7.	Peripheral units	4
4.	**other clinic**	**22**		**total**	**50**

Source: TCHR is an independent Human Rights organisation – not affiliated to any Tamil Federation or Association.

are civilian institutions that often provide shelter and protection, and tend to the needs of children during conflict. Attacks against schools or hospitals are, in principle, contraventions of well-established international humanitarian law, including customary norms, and may constitute war crimes and crimes against humanity.

Attack on hospitals and public health centers continued to hamper access to timely needed health care. Hospitals which are considered as necessary service centers were repeatedly shelled on frontline, raising the inference that they were deliberately targeted, nearly 35 attacks on hospitals in 2009, one of the deadliest shelling on Mullaivaikkal hospital where government declared no-fire zone killing 100 persons and many wounded. In the Northern Province, more than hundred hospitals were completely destroyed, educational institutions were targeted and deliberately attacked, access to education completely denied. Pandiyankulam Maha Vidyalayam School in Mannar was in the heart of the war zone. Currently, 375 students are enrolled in the school. The school serves several communities in the region. But, it is in dilapidated condition. Children do not have basic educational materials, classrooms are broken, there is no running water and only 1 toilet serves 375 children.[32] PTK hospital, Pottumattalaam, Vanni, Vallipuram, Iranipalai, Udayakadu,Valayanmadam, Mullaivaikal and Vellaimullaivaikal were the health centers attacked injured inpatient were again injured and died.

Attacks on Hospitals Child death toll in the Vanni (December 15, 2008 – May 2, 2009)

Date	*Hospital*	*Description/Damage/*	*Death toll*
12/20/08	MullaitivuGH	Mullaitivu General Hospital Shells hit inside hospital grounds.	18
12/15/08	Mullaitivu General Hospital	Shelling: 2 patients injured, damage to ward and medical equipment.	1
12/19/08	Mullaitivu General Hospital	11:30 a.m. Five shells hit hospital causing damage to operating theater, wards, and the Medical Superintendent's HQ: 2 staff wounded.	5
12/22/08	Kilinochchi General Hospital	6:20 a.m. Aerial bombing hit near hospital, causing shrapnel damage. No injuries reported.	5

(Contd...)

12/25/08	Kilinochchi General Hospital	Shells hit hospital grounds, narrowly missing staff. Damage to newborn nursing section, outpatient department, and reception.	6
12/30/08	Kilinochchi General Hospital	4 p.m. Shells hit hospital causing damage to the building. No injuries reported.	2
01/08/09	Tharmapuram Hospital	1:20 p.m. Shells hit Tharmapuram Junction 75 m from the hospital, killing 7.	2
01/13/09	PTK Hospital	10 a.m. Hospital hit by shells: 1 killed, 6 wounded. Patients fled to the wards to seek shelter from the shelling.	3
01/19/09	Vallipuram Hospital	Shell landed in hospital yard: 6 people in out-patient ward injured	1
01/21/09	Vallipuram Hospital	7 p.m. One shell hit hospital	2
01/22/09	Vallipuram Hospital	Morning. Shells hit hospital compound: killing 5 and injuring 22.	
01/26/09	UDK Hospital	Shells hit hospital: 12 killed, 40 injured.	6
01/31/09	PTK Hospital	Shrapnel from shells hit hospital.	4
02/01/09	PTK Hospital	Three attacks. First attack: 1 person injured by shrapnel inside the hospital. Second attack:1 shell hit the hospital: 1 killed, 4 injured. Third attack: 1 shell hit the women and children ward (no casualty information).	2
02/02/09	PTK Hospital	One shell hit hospital: 7 killed, including a nurse, 15 injured.	4
02/03/09	PTK Hospital	Two attacks – operation ward, staff head-quarters, and female ward hit. At least 2 killed and several injured,	NA
02/05/09	Ponnampalam Memorial Hospital	Shelling : 60 casualties inside and outside the hospital.	NA
02/09/09	Putumattalan hospital (make-shift hospital for PTK)	Around 10 p.m., one shell struck about 10 meters east of the hospital compound. No casualties, but the compound wall was damaged by shrapnel.	NA
02/10/09	Putumattalan	Shelling: 16 people killed.	3
03/16/09	Putumattalan hospital	Around 11 a.m. an RPG struck inside the compound, killing two people.	NA
03/23/09	Putumattalan hospital	An RPG hit in front of the hospital; at least one killed (a child); two shells hit close to the hospital, injuring at least 15.	NA
04/09/09	Putumattalan hospital and Putumattalan mother and child center	Several shelling attacks; 22 killed and at least 300 injured.	8

(Contd...)

04/20/09	Putumattalan hospital	Heavy shelling and gunfire attacks during the night; hundreds of civilians injured and at least 13 killed; 2 medical staff sustained gunshot wounds; hospital roof and surgery ward destroyed.	2
04/21/09	Valayanmadam make-shift hospital	Aerial attack; 4 or 5 killed; more than 30 wounded; one doctor killed.	NA
04/23/09	Mullivaikkal hospital	Three shells hit the hospital; no information on killed/wounded.	NA
04/28/09	Mullivaikkal Primary Health Center	Heavy shelling and aerial attacks; at least 6 killed (previously injured patients receiving treatment); 1 member of medical staff injured.	1
04/29/09	Mullivaikkal Primary Health Center	One shell; 6 patients killed.	1
04/29/09	Mullivaikkal Hospital	Shelling; roof of one of the wards significantly damaged; at least 9 killed and 15 injured.	2
04/30/09	Mullivaikkal Hospital	Shelling: 9 killed, 15 injured.	
05/02/09	Mullivaikkal Hospital	Shelling: two attacks, at 9 a.m. and 10.30 a.m.; 68 killed, 87 injured, including medical staff	7

Source: Human Rights Watch from interviews with aid agencies and witnesses.

Denial of Humanitarian Access to Children

Civilians, especially children, caught up in armed conflict are, undoubtedly, vulnerable to a number of hardships and violations of rights. Denial of humanitarian access can be a major obstacle in responding to the needs of the vulnerable population. Parties to the conflict may deny or delay humanitarian assistance to civilians or create a difficult security situation in order to force the withdrawal of a humanitarian organisation. Whether the goal is to protect humanitarian workers from harm or limit witnesses to human rights abuses, it ultimately deprives civilians of their basic rights, including the right to life (IBCR, 2010). Intentional attacks on a humanitarian assistance mission are considered a war crime under the Rome Statute.

Furthermore, the Statute states that using starvation of civilians as a method of warfare by depriving them of objects indispensable to their survival, including willfully impeding relief supplies may constitute a war crime or even genocide (Art. 8(2) (b) and (e), 1998).

The Fourth Geneva Conventions and its Additional Protocols, as well as customary international law reflects the principle that parties to a conflict must allow and facilitate aid to any civilian in need and protect humanitarian relief personnel and their equipment (UNSC, 2009). Several provisions under the CRC further necessitate the facilitation of humanitarian access to children in need, including ensuring that children seeking refugee status receive appropriate protection and humanitarian assistance (Art. 22(1), 6, 24, 27, CRC, 1989).

The denial of humanitarian assistance deprived Sri Lankan children of their right to food, water, survival, development and medication. As the armed conflict in Sri Lanka escalated, the humanitarian space for humanitarian actors in the affected areas began to shrink and all the parties involved showed an utter lack of respect for international humanitarian principles. Multiple displacements of civilians during the conflict deteriorated their living conditions and forced them to rely on humanitarian assistance for food and shelter. Unfortunately, continued restrictions on the transportation of supplies such as fuel, food, medical supplies, water and sanitation items, and construction materials into the conflict areas made the provision of humanitarian assistance extremely difficult. This particularly affected displaced children who were not only unable to continue schooling but were also increasingly the victims of undernourishment and diseases.

The government and LTTE blocked many important routes, both land and sea, that linked the high conflict areas in the northeast to the rest of the country, cutting off numerous people from aid supplies and exacerbating malnutrition and preventable diseases among children (Watchlist on Children and Armed Conflict, 2008). According to 2008 UNICEF figures, approximately 30.5 per cent of children, under five years old in conflict-affected districts of Sri Lanka suffer from chronic and 28.1 per cent from acute malnutrition or wasting (UNICEF, 2009a). The delay in the provisions of assistance due to cumbersome bureaucratic process that the humanitarian agencies were required to undergo further jeopardized lives.

The condition was made worse by the frequent killings, harassment and LTTE's forced recruitment of humanitarian aid workers that caused many NGOs to scale down their operations in the Northern Province, severely affecting the delivery of relief aids (2006, para. 50). According to the UNSG Panel of Experts report (2011b), in the period between 2006 and the end of the war, around 66 humanitarian workers, most of whom were accused of being Tiger sympathizers', were either killed or disappeared. Northern province of Sri Lanka which consists of all or part of five administrative district designated by the government – Kilinochchi and Mullaitivu districts in whole, and Vavuniya, Mannar and Jaffna districts in part (ICG, 2010). Humanitarian operations in the Vanni were restricted in the final phases of the conflict when the government ordered UN workers to leave the region for security reasons. Thereafter, with virtually no international witnesses to the gross human rights abuses, the government systematically deprived persons in the area; including thousands of children; of humanitarian assistance, in the form of medical care and food.[33] This led to severe shortages and greatly increased the suffering of the children and other vulnerable groups (UNSG, 2011b). Despite the end of war and the accessibility of many regions in the North and East of the country to humanitarian organisations, many areas and rehabilitation centers still remain out of bounds for NGOs, due to IDPs' past association with the rebel LTTE. This restriction amounts to violation under international humanitarian law.

Phases of Armed Conflict-Snapshots

Eelam war-I	Eelam War I' (1983-88) Rapid escalation of violent inter-communal attacks 1983, LTTE massacres of TELO and EPRLF members 1986,Arrival of Indian Peace Keeping Force (IPKF) 1987,IPKF leave Sri Lanka 1989-90.
Elam war-II	Eelam War II' (1990-94) GoSL forces launch attack in east & on Jaffna 1990,Tamil groups (other than EPRLF) ally with GoSL 1990, LTTE order all Muslims to leave the north, 120,000 flee 1990,GoSL imposes embargo on north 1991, LTTE assassinations of several senior politicians 1991-94.
Eelam War-III	Eelam War III237 (1995-)GoSL launche War for Peace , forces capture Jaffna 1995,LTTE kill over 1,200 GoSL soldiers in Mullaitivu Camp 1996, LTTE bomb Central Bank, Colombo: over 150 civilians dead 1996, GoSL forces launch major offensive in north 1997, LTTE step up bombing campaign in

(Contd...)

	south: Temple of the Tooth, Kandy partially destroyed 1998, GoSL offensive in north called off 1998, Series of GoSL attacks on LTTE positions 1999, LTTE capture Elephant Pass and almost reach Jaffna Town 2000
Eelam War-interim peace	Stage of peace talk- 2002 2007, split of LTTE, TMVP and GoSLA, Mass abduction of children, UNICIEF interventions and reliving of Children, Abduction of children below 10 years,
Eelam War-IV	Eelam War IV-2008-2009, Final stage and end of the armed conflict, Rape and sexual assault, war crime, attack on schools and hospitals, Denial of Humanitarian access, Total ethnic cleansing. Forced migration, IDPs, Refugee, attack on civilians 'Violation of International Humanitarian Law, Arrest, detention, torture, custodial deaths, and inadequate rehabilitation measures.

Conclusion

Every child has the right to grow to adulthood, peace and dignity. Young children are vulnerable and dependent on adults for their basic needs, such as food, health care and education. In many countries they are forced to fend for themselves, often at the cost of their full development and education. The United Nations Children's Fund (UNICEF) has estimated that 9.2 million children under the age of five die every year, mostly of preventable causes; 101 million children, a majority of whom are girls, are not in primary school; and 148 million children in developing countries under the age of five are underweight due to malnutrition. Children are obviously affected by more universal statistics: approximately 884 million people lack access to safe water and only 62 per cent of the world's population have access to adequate sanitation. UNICEF estimates that 4500 children die each day as a consequence of unsafe water and sanitation facilities. Child labour is another issue of concern - 158 million children between the ages of five and fourteen years are forced to work. Further, Human Rights Watch reports that children, in the tens of thousands', in approximately 15 countries, are actively participating in armed conflict. Ensuring the rights of children to health, nutrition, education, and social, emotional and cognitive development is imperative for every country and entails obligations for every government. Ensuring that children enjoy fundamental rights and freedoms not only advances a more equitable society, but fosters a healthier, more literate and, in due course, a more productive population. Clearly, children's rights are closely tied to women's rights; even before being born a child's survival and development is dependent on the mother's health and opportunities. Women are still primary care-givers for children, so ensuring women's rights is positively linked to children's enjoyment of human rights.

Though there were no specific laws relating to children in armed conflicts until the mid-1990s, many international conventions dealt with the issue of child soldiers, but not imposing a blanket ban. Article 38 of the United Nations Conveention on the Rights of the Child, 1989 and Article 77.2 of Additional Protocol I to the Geneva Conventions of 12 August 1949 relating to the Protection of Victims of International Armed Conflicts provides that state parties should take all possible measures to prevent the direct participation of all children below the age of 15 in hostilities. The wording of both these articles show that they do not prescribe a complete ban on the use of child soldiers but prevent their recruitment only to such a level as is possible for the state party in question. Also the use of the term direct indicates that children may be used in combat indirectly. Thus the provisions gave a wide scope for violation and exploitation of children. However Article 8.2.26 of the Rome Statute of the International Criminal Court (ICC), states that conscription and enlistment of children under the age of fifteen in an armed conflict is a war crime, thereby criminalizing the act under international law.

Though the protocol has increased the age limit of children taking part in direct hostilities from fifteen to eighteen, it only obligates state parties to take feasible measures to prevent such recruitment, again providing scope for violation. Though there are many provisions prohibiting the recruitment of children into armed groups, international law has not fully concentrated on the rehabilitation of these children and their reintegration into their families and society. Article 22(2) and Article 39 of the UN Convention on the rights of child are amongst the very few provisions of international law that concentrates on the same. Despite several attempts by the international community, there still remain many obstacles that prevent these rights from being appropriately enforced. International law provides treaties that are binding only on parties that have ratified them. Thus even with the existence of many conventions and treaties, every nation has an option to refrain from ratification and thereby escape the legal hassles. There are also various domestic problems that prevent the effective implementation of treaties. Unavailability of proper infrastructure and administrative system, financial instability, and the absence of a stable environment are some of the reasons generally cited in defense of the non-implementationof treaty provisions. Thus the mere ratification of these treaties will not lead to the improvement of the rights of the child. It requires strong political will, a change in the social outlook and strong administrative systems. In many of the third world nations, existing internal armed conflict, crumbling social and administrative structures and weak economy leads to the increase in the recruitment of child soldiers. In these countries where situation requires that these rights be strictly enforced, the very same reasons become major obstructions. Also the guardian of rights in the modern world, the United Nations does not have an effective enforcement mechanism. It lays down the guidelines in various conventions, but fails when it comes to its grass root level implementation. Even in the case of violations, it merely makes reports and provides advices which are not binding on any party, thereby diluting the effectiveness of the entire system.

As of May 2010, 568 children formerly associated with armed groups as child soldiers who were provided with protection and support in three Rehabilitation Centers, rejoined their families to revert back to a normal life. But many thousand still need to be taken care. Security issues and limitations on partnerships with NGOs were constraining factors in the Northern provinces resulting in lower than expected implementation rates. Although services are being rapidly restored for resettled populations, shortages of qualified human resources contribute to gaps in service delivery. On catch up education (CUE) and school dropouts provided the basis for merging Basic Literacy and CUE programmes in which 1,221 out-of-school children were enrolled in 2010. Still hundreds of thousands of children are to be taken care especially those who are under detention camp as suspects need to be rehabilitated.

In order to return to these children their childhood, international institutions should lobby for effective mechanisms including severe international pressure and sanctions on those countries that do not effectively establish and enforce national legislations for the rehabilitation of child soldiers and persecute their recruiters. Consistent support of national Governments and their cooperation with international organisations will go a long way in effectively rooting out this process. Until such cooperation and commitment can be achieved, every day one more children will die in the battle fields of Congo and another will take up arms in the mountains of Afghanistan. And longstanding peace will never be achieved without giving the children the means, skills, and education to re-build a society and institutions torn by armed conflict.

Works Cited & End Notes

1. Teddy Atim, International Conference; Children and Youth Affected by Armed Conflict: Where to go from here? Kampala, Uganda 25 – 27th Sept 2013, p.13
2. Children and Armed Conflict, monthly update.2014, p.18
3. Children and Armed Conflict, Strengthening the Impact of the Security Council Working Group on Children and Armed Conflict -May 2014,p.56
4. Report by the Special Representative to the UN Secretary-General for Children and Armed Conflict, A/63/227.
5. The Office of the Special Representative of the Secretary-General for Children and Armed Conflict (OSRSG/CAAC) was established following the groundbreaking report on the Impact of armed conflict on children (A/ 51/306 and Add.1) presented to the General Assembly in 1996 by Ms. Graça Machel, former Minister of Education of the Republic of Mozambique. p. 88.
6. The Six Grave Violations Against Children During Armed Conflict: The Legal Foundation October 2009 (Updated November 2013) p.89.
7. In 1996, the General Assembly adopted resolution A/RES/51/77 which called for theSecretary-General to appoint a Special Representative as a high-level independent voice on this issue. In April 2006, the Secretary-General appointed Ms. Radhika Coomaraswamy as Under-Secretary-General, Special Representative for Children and Armed Conflict. Children and Justice During and in the Aftermath of Armed Conflict September 2011
8. Strengthening legal protection for victims of armed conflicts 31st INTERNATIONAL CONFERENCE OF THE RED CROSS AND RED CRESCENT Geneva, Switzerland 28 November – 1 December 2011.
9. Report of the Secretary-General on children and armed conflict in Sri Lanka, report has been prepared in accordance with the provisions of resolution 1612 (2005). The report, which covers the period from 1 November 2005

to 31 October 2006, provides information on compliance and progress in ending the recruitment and use of children and other grave violations being committed against children in situations affected by armed conflict in Sri Lanka.

10. No Safety No Escape: Children and the Escalating Armed Conflict in Sri Lanka, April, 2008.p.
11. Dr. Brian Senewiratne,MA(Cantab), MBB Chir (Cantab), MD(Lond), FRCP(Lond), FRACP Consultant Physician - BrisbaneClinical Associate Professor of Medicine - University of Queensland, Brisbane. Australia.
12. Excerpt (—), Tamil Tribune, December 1997 – ID 1997-12-02 Jason Hart Ph.D refugee studies Centre, Oxford University, A discussion document prepared for UNICEF Regional Office South Asia.
13. Matthew Happold (—), protecting children in armed conflict: Harnessing the Security Council's ¯soft power. (Professor of Public International Law, University of Luxembourg.) This Article originated as a paper presented at the Minerva Center for Human Rights, Hebrew University of Jerusalem and the ICRC Delegation to Israel and the Palestinian Territories' November 2009 conference on–Securing Compliance with International Humanitarian Law: The Promises and Limits of Contemporary Enforcement Mechanisms.
14. Child Soldiers (—) : GlobalReporthttp://www.child soldiersglobalreport.org/files/country_pdfs/FINA L_2008_Global_Report.pdf.
15. Report of the secretary general's Panel of experts on accountability Srilanlka,March 31, 2011.
16. W. Andy Knight (—) Research on Children and Armed Conflict: Impact, Protection, Rehabilitation, Director, Children and Armed Conflict Project University of Alberta Security Council Report's fifth Cross-Cutting Report on Children and Armed Conflict analyses statistical information on children and armed conflict in country-specific decisions of the Security Council and trends in 2011 and early 2012.
17. The Secretary General, Report of the Special Representative to the Secretary-General for Children and Armed Conflict (—), para.11, delivered to the General Assembly, U.N. Doc. A/61/275 (Aug. 17, 2006).
18. *Ibid.*
19. N. Sivarajah, MD (—), Proceedings of the International Conference on Health, London, Sept., 1994) Today the infant mortality rate for southern Sri Lanka is 14/1000 (The Island, June12, 2002),(UNICEF, A Special Program for Assistance for Children and Women Affected by Armed Conflict in Sri Lanka 2000-2001, Colombo, Sri Lanka, March, 1999).
20. Aditi Pradhan, Sri Lanka's Armed Conflict (—): Children as Victims and Agents of Peace, Spring, 2012, Webster University Thailand..
21. Committee on the Rigts of the Child, (2010, October 19). Consideration of reports submitted by States parties under article 8 of the Optional Protocol

to the Convention on the Rights of the Child on the involvement of children in armed conflict, Concluding Observations: Sri Lanka. CRC. (2000, May 25) Optional Protocol to the Convention on the Rights of the Child on the involvement of children in armed conflict.

22. Harvey, R. (2003). Children and Armed Conflict: A guide to international humanitarian and human rights law. Retrieved November 1, 2011, from University of Essex web site:www.essex.ac.uk/armedcon/story_id/000044.pdf.
23. UNSG Panel of Experts report (2011b), in the period between 2006 and the end of the war, around 66 humanitarian workers, most of whom were accused of being Tiger sympathizers', were either killed or disappeared..
24. Wimaladharma, S., Silva, A. D. & Silva, N. D. (2005), Growing Up With War, Experiences of Children Affected by Armed Conflict in the Eastern Province of Sri Lanka. Colombo: Centre for Poverty Analysis (CEPA)..
25. TMVP/Karuna faction was established as an unregistered political party and a paramilitary group in March 2004 by Colonel Karuna, the LTTE's commander in the East, after splitting from the LTTE. TMVP became a registered political party on 24 January 2008 and fought against the LTTE..
26. Amnesty International. (2011, September 7). When Will They Get Justice? Failures of Sri Lanka's LLRC. Retrieved October 26, 2011, from Amnesty International web site:http://www.amnesty.org/en/library/info/ASA37/008/2011/en.
27. Northern province of Sri Lanka which consists of all or part of five administrative district designated by the government – Kilinochchi and Mullaitivu districts in whole, and Vavuniya, Mannar and Jaffna districts in part (ICG, 2010).
28. Dan O'Donnell (—), Dan Seymour of UNICEF, The Handbook benefited from the valuable input of members of the Inter-parliamentary Child protection A handbook for parliamentarians, UNICEF, 2012.
29. Samantha Wimalasuriya, Addressing the impact of war on women in Sri Lanka.
30. Wessells, M. G. (1998). Children, Armed Conflict, and Peace- Review Essay. Journal of Peace Research, Vol. 35, No. 5, 635-646..
31. Eyber, C. & Ager, A. (2004), Researching Young People's Experience of War: Participatory Methods and the Trauma of Discourse in Angola. In J. Boyden, Children and Youth on the Frontline New York: Berghahn Books (pp. 189-208).
32. Gow, M. (2002, September), 'Partnering with Children for Peace' in World Vison Discussion Paper 'Children and Peacebuilding: Experiences and Perspectives, November 30, 2011.
33. Hargreaves, C., Karlsson, M., Agarwal, S.,Tengtio, K & Hootnick, J. (2011). International Dimensions of the Sri Lankan Conflict, October 31, 2011..

34. Cammaert, P. (2009, December 05-11). Visit of Major General (ret.) Patrick Cammaert,Special Envoy of the Special Representative for Children & Armed Conflict, to Sri Lanka.

35. Human Rights watch (2007), Complicit in Crime State Collusion in Abductions and Child Recruitment by the Karuna Group.

36. The LLRC is composed of former government officials who have publicly defended the Sri Lankan government against allegations of war crimes and others who have worked for the Sri Lankan government in various capacities' (UNSG, 2011b).

37. Anderlini, S. N. & El-Bushra, J. (2004). Post-Conflict Reconstruction, Retrieved December 30, 2011.

38. Ayissi, A. (2002). Protecting children in armed conflict: from commitment to compliance. Retrieved November 25, 2011, from United Nations Institute for Disarmament Research (UNIDIR).

39. Camberlain, G. (2009, MAY 21). In Sri Lanka the war is over but Tamil Tiger remnants suffer brutal revenge. Retrieved November 20, 2011.

40. Dammers, T. (2010, September).The response of the international community to sexual violence in conflict-affected states, November 16, 20100.

41. Gnanadass, W. (2008, December 2011). Child Rights on the Firing Line, November 27, 2011, p..

42. Government of Sri Lanka, (2011, November)., Report of the Commission of Inquiry on Lesson Learnt and Reconciliation, December 18, 2011, from Govt. of Sri Lanka, p.

43. HRW, (2004, November), Living In Fear: Child Soldiers and the Tamil Tigers in Sri Lanka, November 5, 2011, IBCR, (2010), Children and Armed Conflict: Guide to international humanitarian and human rights law, October 31, 2011, International Bureau for Children's Rights.

44. Landmine Monitor Report . (2011, February 2). Landmine Monitor Report 2010, November 11, 2011, Landmine and Cluster Munitions Monitor.

45. Machel, G. (2001). The impact of war on children: A review of progress since the 1996 United Nations Report on the impact of armed conflict on children. London: C. Hurst & Co. Publishers.

Endnotes

1. The nature of this diffusion can be understood through an analogy with Foucauldian capillaries of power.

2. Young, Iris Marion. *Justice and the Politics of Difference.* United States of America: Princeton University Press, 1990, pp. 40-41.

3. Italics are added by me to emphasis on the multiplicity of the forms in which oppression manifests itself.

4. Young, Iris Marion. *Justice and the Politics of Difference.* United States of America: Princeton University Press, 1990, p. 40.
5. *Ibid.*, p. 39.
6. *Ignoring the systemic and interlocking nature of what I call complex systems of domination (e.g., racism, ableism, sexism, anti-Semitism, or homophobia) has misleading consequences. When the effects of sexism, for example, are not understood macroscopically as the products of systemic injustices, they are understood microscopically as the exclusive problems of particular women who have made bad choices, have poor attitudes, are too sensitive, or who are overreacting to a random incident. Failure to examine sexism, homophobia, racism, and anti-Semitism as harms produced by systematically related forces and barriers blurs the distinction between harm and oppression.* Bailey, Alison. "Privilege: Expanding on Marilyn Frye's "Oppression"." *Journal of Social Philosophy*, Vol. 29, No. 3, Winter 1998: 104-119, p. 105.
7. Frye, Marilyn. "Oppression." In *Gender Basics:Feminist Perspectives on Women and Men*, by Anne Minas, 10-16. United States of America: Wadsworth Publishing, 2000.
8. Bailey, Alison. "Privilege: Expanding on Marilyn Frye's "Oppression"." *Journal of Social Philosophy*, Vol. 29, No. 3, Winter 1998: 104-119.
9. I am using *symptom* in the strict Marxist sense as expounded by Karl Marx.
10. For the purposes of this paper, I am defining autonomy solely in the decision making power of making choices.
11. Hence the title of the paper- the spectral chains of oppression.
12. Frye, Marilyn. "Oppression." In *Gender Basics:Feminist Perspectives on Women and Men*, by Anne Minas, 10-16. United States of America: Wadsworth Publishing, 2000, p. 12.
13. Bailey, Alison. "Privilege: Expanding on Marilyn Frye's "Oppression"." *Journal of Social Philosophy*, Vol. 29, No. 3, Winter 1998: 104-119, p. 105.
14. Frye, Marilyn. "Oppression." In *Gender Basics:Feminist Perspectives on Women and Men*, by Anne Minas, 10-16. United States of America: Wadsworth Publishing, 2000, p. 12.
15. *Ibid.*
16. Young, Iris Marion. *Justice and the Politics of Difference.* United States of America: Princeton University Press, 1990, p. 44.
17. *Ibid.*
18. Michael Sandel criticizes liberal individualism for their theorisation of individuality as an unencumbered self.
19. Young, Iris Marion. *Justice and the Politics of Difference.* United States of America: Princeton University Press, 1990, p. 45.

20. Ore, Tracy E. *The Social Construction of Difference and Inequality: Race, Class, Gender, and Sexuality.* California: Mayfield Publishing Company, 2000, p. 5.
21. *Ibid.*, p. 15.
22. Bailey, Alison. "Privilege: Expanding on Marilyn Frye's "Oppression"." *Journal of Social Philosophy*, Vol. 29, No. 3, Winter 1998: 104-119, p. 106.
23. Ore, Tracy E. *The Social Construction of Difference and Inequality: Race, Class, Gender, and Sexuality.* California: Mayfield Publishing Company, 2000, pp. 6-7.
24. Hirschmann explains the three levels of its functioning: *Moreover, all of these happen in "levels" in another sense: at the micro level of individual practice, the meso level of institutional practice, and the macro level of conceptual categories. These levels cut across the three layers of ideology, materialisation, and discourse.* Hirschmann, Nancy J. "Response to Friedman and Brison." *Hypatia,* Vol. 21, No. 4, Autumn 2006: 201-211, p. 203.
25. Hirschmann, Nancy J. *The Subject of Liberty: Toward a Feminist Theory of Freedom.* New Jersey: Princeton University Press, 2003, pp. 77-81
26. Hirschmann explains this second level: *Guided by concerns such as pornography, domestic violence, prostitution, sexual discrimination, rape and abortion, feminists argue that such social expressions of male domination have produced and codified customs and rules that restrict women's opportunities and choices; women cannot be doctors, for example, if they are denied access to medical schools.* Hirschmann, Nancy J. *The Subject of Liberty: Toward a Feminist Theory of Freedom.* New Jersey: Princeton University Press, 2003, p. 80
27. Hirschmann explains this interplay of the levels: *What I like about "levels" is that it communicates the idea of a "deepening": Ideology is closer to the surface, coming from a loosely identifiable source and having a more or less specific target; materialisation goes more deeply into lived experience, but is still somewhat identifiable in terms of source and outcome, even if less than ideology; discourse goes more deeply, to the macro-structures that are incredibly difficult to identify, both in source and outcome, because they come from and end up everywhere at once.* Hirschmann, Nancy J. "Response to Friedman and Brison." *Hypatia,* Vol. 21, No. 4, Autumn 2006: 201-211, p. 202
28. Hirschmann, Nancy J. *The Subject of Liberty: Toward a Feminist Theory of Freedom.* New Jersey: Princeton University Press, 2003, Preface- p. ix.
29. Frye, Marilyn. "Oppression." In *Gender Basics:Feminist Perspectives on Women and Men*, by Anne Minas, 10-16. United States of America: Wadsworth Publishing, 2000, p. 13.

30. [...] two important comments regarding Frye's observations about group membership and its role in systems of oppression. First, because individuals are rarely members of one community, oppression is not a unified phenomenon. Group differences in race/ethnicity, sexual orientation, gender, or class cut across individual lives to the point that privilege and oppression are often experienced simultaneously. Bailey, Alison. "Privilege: Expanding on Marilyn Frye's "Oppression". " Journal of Social Philosophy, Vol. 29, No. 3, Winter 1998: 104-119, p. 106.
31. Patricia Hill Collins refers to this interlocking system as a matrix of domination. This model provides the framework for our efforts [...] in seeking to understand how categories of difference are transformed into systems of inequality and maintained as systems of oppression. Such a framework will allow us to move beyond simply describing the similarities and differences between various systems of oppression and will help us to focus on how they interconnect. [...] The matrix of domination also provides a framework that permits us to avoid additive analyses of systems of oppression (e.g., a black woman being viewed as twice as oppressed as a white woman). Such analyses are problematic in that they suggest that oppression can be quantified. Ore, Tracy E. The Social Construction of Difference and Inequality: Race, Class, Gender, and Sexuality. California: Mayfield Publishing Company, 2000, p. 16.
32. Bailey, Alison. "Privilege: Expanding on Marilyn Frye's "Oppression"." *Journal of Social Philosophy*, Vol. 29, No. 3, Winter 1998: 104-119, p. 104.
33. Ibid., p. 108.
34. Frye, Marilyn. "Oppression." In *Gender Basics:Feminist Perspectives on Women and Men*, by Anne Minas, 10-16. United States of America: Wadsworth Publishing, 2000, p. 14.
35. *Ibid.*, p. 16.
36. Bailey, Alison. "Privilege: Expanding on Marilyn Frye's "Oppression"." *Journal of Social Philosophy*, Vol. 29, No. 3, Winter 1998: 104-119, p. 117.
37. *Ibid.*, p. 110.
38. Ore, Tracy E. *The Social Construction of Difference and Inequality: Race, Class, Gender, and Sexuality.* California: Mayfield Publishing Company, 2000, p. 16.
39. Young, Iris Marion. *Justice and the Politics of Difference.* United States of America: Princeton University Press, 1990, p. 64.
40. Ore, Tracy E. *The Social Construction of Difference and Inequality: Race, Class, Gender, and Sexuality.* California: Mayfield Publishing Company, 2000, pp. 16-17.

17

Safe Guarding the Human Rights of Older People

—Aradhana Sethi

"The tragedy of old age is not that one is old, but that one is young."

Oscar Wilde

All human beings are inherent in certain human rights since birth, irrespective of nationality, place of birth, place of residence, sex, colour, creed and age. Human rights are essential component of sustainable development. These are vested in all human beings and everyone is entitled to the enjoyment of these rights without distinction of any kind. In fact they are part and parcel of life in society and they concern humanity. Human rights simply maintain that all human beings are born free and equal in dignity and rights. Human rights and fundamental freedom allows us to develop fully and use our human qualities, our intelligence, our talents, our conscience and help us to satisfy our spiritual and other needs. These are based on mankind's increasing demand for a life in which the inherent dignity and worth of each human being will receive respect and protection. When these inherent rights are respected, people are able to live with dignity and equality, free from discrimination.

Human rights does not vanish with the increasing age. Older men and women have the same rights as everyone else. We are all born equal and this does not change as we grow older. Old age is considered to be the inevitable stage of human life, which a man cannot escape except in case of untimely death. It is said that old age and childhood are natural conditions of life, where children depend on parents and vice versa. During old age, the mental and physical conditions of persons decline and they get dependent on others for their one or the other need. It is in fact the last phase of human life which is indeed problematic. At this stage, a person becomes dependent on others. A lot of problems confront an individual at the time of retirement, mainly loss of status, lowering of income, reorganisation of life activities and so on. The old person feels himself neglected and humiliated.

Scenario of Old People in the Modern Society

In the traditional Indian system, elderly were respected and they had a great decision making power in the family. Children felt duty bound to serve and respect the elderly and to contribute to the family resources. Elders used to take all the major decisions in the family. During the last century, this socio economic and value system has slowly eroded. In this materialistic age, couples are usually working full time, families have become smaller, nuclear, and migration and consumerism have become the order of the day. Due to modernisation and advancement of society, there has become the tendency to neglect and abandon the older people. Although there are some elder people who are well looked after, but we cannot deny the bitter truth that many of them are suffering from poverty, loneliness, neglect, abuse and abandonment and find it difficult to arrange resources for their most basic needs as their children are either unable or unwilling to maintain them. Problem of widows, widowers and the childless elderly is even more acute.

It has become a common phenomenon now that children force their parents to leave home. It happens when their so called children make their own family i.e when they get married, parents seems useless to them. Due to such circumstances, old people do not have any option left, but to take shelter in old age home. In India, unlike foreign countries, parents do not leave their children on their own after they turn 18, but children do not realise that their parent also want to relax and want their children to reciprocate their care. Every parent wants to see their child grow and be successful but no parent wants their child to treat them like an unnecessary load on their responsibilities.

Every day we find newspaper full of incidences where parents are being beaten up by their children, parents and in laws being forced to do the house hold chores, being made to live in small dungeon like rooms, their property are being forcefully taken over by over ambitious children. According to an estimate, nearly 40 per cent of senior citizens living with their families are reportedly facing abuse of one kind or another, but only 1 in 6 cases actually comes to light. Older people do not highlight all this as considering their family matter and due to fear of humiliation.

Case Study of an Old Man in Dehradun

This is a real incident of an eighty four year old man, having four sons, all very prosperous and well off, who was mistreated by the family members. The father seems to be burden to them and nobody was actually ready to look after them. He was ill-treated by his family members, confined in the four walls of the storeroom just like a prisoner. When he got seriously ill, he was just admitted in the hospital. Nobody even turned up to the hospital to him to ask about his whereabouts. Alone he used to lie in the hospital without any caretaker. He took it to heart, got mentally upset, considering that nobody needs him. Can a parent leave their children in such a plight. It is indeed very ironical that one parent can look after 4 children very well but 4 children when they grow up cannot look after their single parent. This is not the only case, it happens usually in families where family members don't take care of old people. According to NGOs incidences of elderly couples being misbehaved are very high. Children when they grow up, become more concerned about money and property. They are mistreated and misbehaved by their children. Many of them suffer in silence as they fear humiliation or are too scared to speak up.

Problems Associated with Old Age

Most of the old age people are surrounded with certain problems which are as follows.

- Harassment & mistreatment by family members.
- Economic problem i.e loss of employment, income deficiency and financial dependence.

- Problems related to ill health
- Other problems associated with old age i.e Alzheimer, loss of hearing, stammering, nutrional deficiency etc
- Psychological and social maladjustment

Human Rights of Old Persons

Ironically, in India older generations are not aware of their human rights due to high prevalence of illiteracy and lack of awareness. On the other hand, due to comparatively high physical as well as psychological vulnerability, their cries for help remain within four-walls, that's why only a few cases of violation of human rights of elderly come out. Ever-increasing numbers of distress calls from older persons clearly indicate disturbing condition of Human Rights of Older Persons in India.

The Universal Declaration on human rights states in Article 1 that "All human beings are born free and equal in dignity and rights" so this equality is bestowed to older people also. Such as right to equal protection before law, the right to own property, the right to education, the right to work and the right to participate in government. Some rights may have more relevance in older age than at other times in life, e.g. the right to social security in the form of pension, the right to access appropriate health and social care services.

The National Policy on Older Persons 1999 (NPOP) reintegrated the country's resolve that the older person's will not live unprotected, ignored or marginalised, that they will be given their legitimate place in society and they will be provided all help to "live the last phase of their life with purpose, dignity and peace."

Provision for Older People by the Government

In Article 25, paragraph 1, of the Universal Declaration of Human Rights, it is established that "Everyone has the right to a standard of living adequate for the health and well-being of himself and of his family, including food, clothing, housing, and medical care and necessary social services, and the right to security in the event of unemployment, sickness, disability, widowhood, old age or other lack of livelihood in circumstances beyond his control."

People above 60 years of age are claimed to be senior citizens and certain provisions have been made to them and approved by the National Policy for Older Persons on January 13,1999 in order to accelerate welfare measures and empowering the elderly in ways beneficial for them. This policy contains the following steps for the old people:

- Provision of old age pension
- Food grain through the Public distribution system to cover all persons 60+ living below the poverty line.
- Speedier settlement of pension, provident fund, gratuity and other retirements benefits.
- Special consideration to widows in the matter of settlement of benefits accruing to them.
- Pre-retirement counselling programmes.
- Better returns on provident fund accumulations.
- Long term savings instrument with attractive rates of interest or returns at the end of the stipulated period to take care of the likely erosion in purchasing power due to inflation. Life Insurance Corporation of India (LIC) has also been providing several schemes for the benefit of aged personal i.e Jeevan Dhara Yojana, the Varishtha Pension Bima Yojana, Jeevan Akshay Yojana, Senior citizen Unit Yojana, Medical Insurance Yojana.
- Concessions in the use of public transport system (road, rail and air), preference in reservation of seats.
- Construction of old age homes and day care centres for every 3-4 district.
- Former Prime Minister, A. B. Bajpai was also launched "Annapuranan Yojana" for the benefit of aged persons. Under this yojana, unattended aged persons are being given 10 k.g food for every month.

Transformation of traditional joint family system into nuclear or small family system is one of the main factors responsible for violation of human rights of older persons. In urban areas, cases of violation of human rights of elderly population is on rise in comparison to rural areas. Popularity of nuclear family system , lack of intergenerational interaction, less social interaction of older persons, age discrimination, non existence of inclusive social security system in the country are among the most important reasons of miserable condition of old age.

Measures to Safeguarding the Rights of Old People

In the modern scenario, it has become very important to safeguard the interest of old people. In order to make balanced development of the country, the rights of old people are to be protected. Development alone cannot bring peace and prosperity unless social justice and equality of older people are ensured. There are certain measures which can help to safeguard the rights of old people.

- **Awareness about older people rights**

In the modern scenario, although many rights have been bestowed to an old person but still there is a lack of awareness about Human Rights among older persons. Awareness of human rights of older persons in the society, particularly among older persons and protection of their human rights has become an uphill task for all of us.

- **Sensitisation of youth towards old people**

The elderly citizens are in need of urgent attention. It is our duty to see that they do not spend the twilight years of their life in isolation, penury and misery. There is a need to improve the quality of life of old people. Youth have to be sensitising towards the old people. Passing comments at an old man walking slowly on the road and disturbing the flow has become the ethics of youth. Youth themselves have to stand up against such injustice. Youth should never consider their parents as burden.

- **Education of older people human rights through curriculum**

In the fast changing circumstances, when the number of old people in every society is increasing at a very fast pace, we need to inculcate a sense of responsibility towards needs and rights of older persons through curriculum of school students and re-look at all the policy formulations and its implementation with a practical approach towards needs and rights of old people.

- **Respect for older people's rights benefits society as a whole.**

It is beyond doubt that older people make key contribution to society through their experience and wisdom. Violations of the rights of older people lead to exclusion, poverty, and discrimination of older people. Better protection of the rights of older people will allow societies to better capitalize on the potential that older people represent. When older people's right to social security is realised, there is a positive impact on reduction of poverty rates, restoration of older people's dignity, reduction of child labour and increased enrolment in schools.

Conclusion

It is high time that we, younger generation, think on moral grounds. Younger generation should never forget that their existence on this world is due to their parents. Rights of an individual in old age are considered as more of a moral responsibility of the family members. If we think and are concerned about the rights of old people, definitely there will be peace, success and prosperity and blessings all around. Old people should be given their due regard. Moreover old people should be aware of their life and live gracefully. In the end I would like to end by quoting the words of Andre Maurois.

"The art of growing old is the art of being regarded by the oncoming generations as a support and not as a stumbling-block."

Works Cited

- Chand, J.(2007). Education for Human Rights, ISBN: 978-818364-018-3, Anshah Publishing House, Delhi.
- Dhanoa, R ().Violation of Human Rights in India, Shiv Shakti, International Journal in Multidisciplinary and Academic Research, Vol. 1, No 4, ISSN-2278-5973.
- Kumar, S. (2012).Human Rights Education, KSK publishers and distributors, New Delhi.
- Sharma, B.L & Maheshwari, B.K (2006). Education for Values, Environment & Human Rights, S.S Computers, Surya Publication, Meerut.

- The rights of aged retrieved from http://www.hrea.org/index.php?base_id=162
- Strengthening older people right retrieved from http://social. un.org/ageing-working-group/documents/Coalition% 20to%20Strengthen%20the%20Rights%20of%20Older%20 People.pdf

18

Rigid Patriarchal Pressures on Women's Freedom, Sexuality, Reproductive Health & Women's Co-optation

— *Paritosh Singh*

Social scientists often define power as the ability to assert one's own will on others, regardless of the will of the others (Crosbie, 1975; Homans,1974). This definition of power emphasizes the relational aspect of the term. One cannot have power in a vacuum, without also having someone or something to have power over. The above definition also makes it clear that power is dormant; that means, it lies within the 'ability' of the power holder. He (sic) may act on this ability and translate it into action, at which time power becomes influence. He may force others to subjugate to his will disregarding all strong objections, at which time it becomes 'coercive power.' Nevertheless, it is often the case that the power holder does not need to translate his ability into action or force. Instead, the more perceived power the power-holder has, the less the need to turn it into action. Real and entrenched power is clearly known by all and very rarely challenged. Frequently, those who have no power of their own will go out of their way to appease the power holder, so that he does not act on his ominous ability to coerce, or even hurt them (physical power). It is also often the case that those who lack power themselves will become the foot soldiers of the powerful, enforcing the rules and regulations on their own kind and punishing the deviants. War-movies and psychological thrillers exploit these complex processes by showing prisoners taking on guard like behaviors and concentration-camp victims personifying the most ruthless characteristics of their captors. Of course, these are extremes and women are neither prisoners of war nor concentration camp victims. Nevertheless, patriarchal cultures do limit women's roles and choices to such an extent that, what little freedom is open to them can take shape only within the boundaries of roles that particular culture permits. Wife, motherhood and mother-in-law often define the acceptable and expected roles for women.

Patriarchal Power

At the micro level, the abuse of power is frequent in interpersonal relations, as millions of children who are beaten or sexually molested by parents or guardians can testify (Janko, 1994; Steed, 1994). At the macro level, some of the most toxic examples of abuse of power can be traced to mass pillage, rape, slavery and genocide, especially in times of war. More often than not, sexuality permeates power differences. For example, McKinnon (1982) maintains that sexuality is a form of power, where oppression takes sexual forms and where sexuality becomes the very "linchpin of inequality" (p. 533). Indeed, gendered power differentiations have been historically quite perilous. Gendered power differences occur between individuals or groups and advantage men. When they occur at the social and cultural levels, what we have is patriarchal power.

Most social scientists admit that of all concepts generated by contemporary feminist theory, patriarchy is perhaps the most overused and in many respects, the most under-theorized (Fox, 1988). The term captures the amorphous nature of male power and domination in a given society, which is so ingrained, so unquestionable and so effective that it penetrates all other social realities and institutions. Ironically, this amorphous nature of the term is its weakness as well as its strength. When male power and domination is infused into the workings of a social system, it becomes so taken-for-granted, so much a part of the values, norms, behaviour and even part of the socio-religious outlook that one can hardly challenge that power without creating a major reaction and turbulence. On the other hand, trying to dissect patriarchal power into observable/definable pieces will indeed miss the all encompassing and suffocating nature and the consequences of that power. It is due to this catch-twenty-two situation that feminists, themselves, have struggled to come up with a definition of patriarchy that all can agree on. It is because of the same reasons that most men have been able to dismiss altogether how they benefit from the existence of patriarchal systems.

Despite its conceptual difficulty, patriarchy has a life of its own. In its rigid manifestations, patriarchal power continues to exert dire consequences for women in different parts of the world. The type of patriarchy that has been particularly vicious is what Kandiyoti (1988) calls 'classic patriarchy.' Classic patriarchies can be found in geographic areas that include most of North Africa, the Muslim Middle East (including non secular Iran and parts of secular Turkey) and South and East Asia (most specifically, India, Pakistan, Bangladesh and pre-revolutionary or rural China). As one can see from the above list, classic patriarchy spans geopolitical regions and crosses over religious boundaries (Islam, Hinduism, Buddhism, Confucianism, Taoism, Sikhism and some orthodox pockets of Christian and Jewish faiths). Given the variation, it will be grossly naive to argue that a particular religion gives rise to classic patriarchy. It is more likely that in strongly patriarchal cultures, the interpretation and practices of any religion come to reflect the existing male domination, privilege and control.

A commonality amongst strongly patriarchal societies is that almost all are agrarian (pre-industrialised societies with labour-intensive farming). The labour-intensivity of the subsistence pattern makes large family systems as well as male labour a necessity. In such agrarian societies, the key elements to the reproduction and continuation of classic patriarchy are: patriarchal households where all decision-making power is vested in one man (often the patriarch, or his oldest son), patrilineal tracing of decent and inheritance (which manifest themselves as preference for male offspring produced in wedlock) and patrilocal extended households (where very young, sometimes childbrides are betrothed into the husbands' extended household). Taken together, these three pillars of classic patriarchy reproduce the skewed gender relations and give unprecedented power to men over women and to older people over younger ones (Fernandez, 1997; Kandiyoti, 1988). Walby (1989) theorizes patriarchy within six interrelated structures. These include the mode of production, relations in waged labour, the state, male violence, relations in sexuality and culture. What is important in Walby's conceptualisation is the strong link between patriarchal cultures and relentless control of women's freedom and sexuality. Violence becomes an overtly or covertly condoned tool of control. Men's obsession over male offspring translates into an unabated domination over women who give birth to these sons. This domination is infused in cultural norms, values and rituals. Women's worth is elevated through virginity before marriage and piety in motherhood. It observes, the three statuses open for women are being some man's virgin daughter, another man's pious wife and the self-sacrificing mother of sons. Under such cultural constructs, even younger men hold power over women much older than themselves. Moreover, deviation from rules can trigger severe forms of violence against women and girls.

This paper reviews some of the extreme forms of violence within which patriarchy manifests itself. In the following pages, female infanticide, dowry and bride-price systems, forced virginity tests and honour killings are also discussed. Although patriarchal rules vastly differ from region to region, what is noteworthy is in no place on earth and in no time in human history, can we find cultural rituals and practices that have similarly enslaved boys/men on the basis of their gender. In this paper it is described that how women themselves get co-opted into the patriarchal systems. The paper will end with suggestions for change from the international women's rights perspective and through local initiatives.

Female Infanticide

Classic patriarchies victimize girls/women (Kandiyoti, 1988; McKinnon, 1982; Millet, 1970; Walby, 1988). Generally, girls are not wanted, shunned, maltreated, controlled and/or deprived of opportunities that their male siblings freely enjoy. Often, girls are commodified. Historically, female infanticide (killing or exposing female children to natural elements, see was practiced within numerous classic patriarchies). Methods used to dispose of newborn girls include choking, suffocating, poisoning, starving, strangling and drowning (Hegde, 1999) and even injecting formaldehyde to the soft spot of infants' heads (Hom, 2001, p. 139). The executioners are mothers or other closely related female relatives who interpret their action in altruistic terms as 'freeing' their newborn daughters from experiencing life-long rejection and pain (Hegde, 1999). Sadly, women who have few freedoms of their own have much to lose from giving birth to daughters rather than sons.

Although on the decline, such ghastly practices are continuing in out of reach pockets of the developing world (Johnson & Johnson, 2001;). In China, the one-child policy has inadvertently exacerbated the risk for female infants. In rural India, female infanticide remains a dark secret. However, female infanticide is increasingly replaced by a more humane (but equally gendered) way of sex selection and selective abortions through the misuse of reproductive technologies (Lin, 1998; Luthra, 1994; Miller, 2001; Plechner, 2000). In regions where patriarchy is unchecked, girl children are still considered as a burden and their health and life still remain at risk (Hegde, 1999). Plechner (2000) argues that patriarchal states often collude with violence against women, either through acts of commission or through crimes of omission. The culling of the female unborn is an example to both patterns.

The low status of women in societies that practice infanticide has been extensively studied. However, what has often escaped analysis is the mental state of women who are socialised to devalue and despise their gender. How much worth and dignity can women attribute to themselves if they see their own infant daughters' lives as worthless?

Dowry / Bride-price Systems & Their Consequences

Even when girl children are allowed to live, most are considered to be a burden on their families (competition to the inheritance of their male siblings) because of 'dowry' practices. Dowry systems are generally defended as important cultural practices. It is argued that dowry is a form of transmission of some wealth to the female offspring, since patrilineal inheritance rules often bar women from inheriting from their male kin. However, most women never directly benefit since most or all of their dowry gets absorbed into the patriarchal household. In India, dowry is now illegal, but the practice is rampant. There are many sayings that compare 'raising a daughter to watering a neighbour's plant' which signifies the perceived futility of the investment (Hegde, 1999). Moreover, dowry has taken on crushing proportions since many grooms' families treat dowry as a life-long obligation. Women whose families are not willing or unable to fulfill these obligations are vulnerable to maltreatment: they are sent back to their families of origin (which is equivalent to becoming a social pariah), beaten or even killed (so called 'kitchen fires' or 'dowry deaths', see Mayell, 2002; Pratap, 1995; Sood, 1990; Shah, 1990; also see Anwary, 2003 for acid attacks). It is estimated that 15,000 dowry deaths happen in India every year. This estimate does not include murders which are successfully disguised as accidental deaths (UNIFEM, 2003b).

Other patriarchal societies practice 'bride price' or the lump sum payment of money/land/goods/livestock etc., required to acquire a wife. On the surface, the burden appears to be on the patriarchal and patrilocal households to pay brides' families the socially acceptable amount for the marital rights over daughters. On the surface, one may erroneously think that this type of a system will raise women's status. In its application, however, bride price system works similar to the dowry system where women are commodified. What they do, how they dress, where they go, whom they see, how they act, whom they marry... all become guarded, controlled and oppressed aspects of their lives. After all, from birth on, girls are commodities that must be prepared for marital sale and the potential buyers (patriarchal households) do not want unruly, unclean, unmanageable, tarnished or used (read: sexually experienced) women. Men who have no means to pay for the women they want may end up forcefully kidnapping them. In the latter case, women become damaged goods and may become vulnerable to crimes of honour, as will be later discussed in this paper.

Forced Virginity Tests

Sexual or reproductive control of women is rampant in classic patriarchies and often is closely tied to rules of honour and rules of marriage. One of the most blatant forms of these expectations is the insistence on virginity before marriage. In classic patriarchies, the constant surveillance of women's whereabouts, family curfews, complex chaperonage systems are the norm. Pre-marital girls are constantly guarded from participation in mixed-sex peer groups, at the cost of missing out on educational and/or work opportunities. Loss of virginity outside of marriage is considered a major catastrophe for the girl, her family, clan or tribe. Girls whose 'honour' becomes suspect can be subjected to 'forced virginity tests.' Grooms' families may require 'proof of virginity' as a condition of marriage (sale). The required proof may be in terms of a written statement from a physician (almost always a male) who examines the intactness of the hymen. Proof may also involve submitting bloodied sheets at the end of the first night of marriage. The extended family (mostly women) keeps vigil at the bedroom door throughout the first night. Moreover, the bride's body may be examined (again, by elder women) for fresh cuts in case she was not a virgin but tried to fool her examiners. These practices reinforce the cultural belief that women are not to be trusted. They also set women against women. Aside from the demeaning nature of these practices, more serious perils await girls/women who 'fail' such tests. They may be ostracized, sent back, replaced by a new wife, beaten or even killed (Cindoglu, 2000; Mernissi, 2000).

For those who have had the good fortune of being born in less oppressive cultures, it is quite difficult to imagine the stress young girls/women go through just prior to or during the first night of marriage. Even when they are virgins, it is possible that they may be subjected to false accusations, or due to the structure of their hymen, they may fail to bleed. Many young women attempt suicide, due to the heightened pressure during marriage. In societies where virginity at marriage is an obsession, there is a booming industry in hymen re-construction which exposes women to unnecessary surgical procedures. Such practices also engender dishonesty amongst marital partners.

Honour Killings

Caputi (1989: 438) points out that systematic violence against women, including murder, should be seen as sexually political murders or a "form of murder rooted in a system of male supremacy in the same way that lynching is based in white supremacy." Amongst all classic patriarchies, it is those that practice dowry or bride price that have developed the harshest rules to regulate girls/women's bodies and sexuality. Women are often socialised/cajoled/forced to wear various garbs that cover their bodies, limit their vision and interfere with movement. Most of the regulation stems from an elaborate conceptualisation of 'honour' where women's (especially young women's) behaviour and even attitudes are subjected to relentless evaluation (Duzkan & Kocali, 2000; Maris & Saharso, 2001). Honour (or the behaviours that are deemed to tarnish it) becomes a major social and family preoccupation. Honour is seen as much too important to be left to self monitoring by girls or younger women. Older men, older women and younger men (as potential purchasers) are all conscripted into controlling girls/women, around the clock (Fernandez, 1997). Those who are deemed to behave in ways that tarnish their family honour may be locked-up, severely beaten or even induced to commit suicide or killed. Going to movies, dating, getting married to someone without parental consent, or even being a victim of rape or incestuous molestation may be considered as an act of dishonour, punishable by death (UNIFEM, 2003a).Strong kin ties and social taboos about the privacy of patriarchal families deter witnesses from testifying even when murders take place in crowded public places.

In honour killings, usually the youngest son of the family is cajoled to carry out the gruesome deed. Usually, no one testifies, even though there may be numerous people who know about the crime. Most frequently, the murders are presented as accidental deaths or suicides and thus stay outside of the criminal justice system . Police and other branches of the criminal justice system may not be too eager to seek justice. In the unlikely event that a conviction ensues, the perpetrator's young age will assure leniency and a drastically shortened sentence. He will also receive a hero's welcome as the one who cleansed the family honour (Maris & Saharso, 2001; UNIFEM, 2003a).

WOMEN'S HEALTH AND HUMAN RIGHTS

Health Status Factors

1. Health considerations are important to women at different stages of their life cycle.
2. The need to determine the special impact on women of routine health procedures and products.
3. The importance of improving research on women's health requirements.
4. The need to consider women's health requirements and circumstances in the development of research protocols.

5. The importance of basing health policies on the most up-to-date scientific and technological knowledge.

Health Service Factors

1. The importance of treating women with dignity and respect, including the provision of adequate information so that women can make informed decisions on particular courses of treatment.
2. The rights of women as patients and the importance of confidentiality and privacy.
3. Conditions affecting the health and well-being of women.
4. The importance of ensuring a healthy and safe working environment.
5. The importance of eliminating traditions and practices that have detrimental health consequences for women.
6. The ability to identify and respond appropriately to women who live in abusive environments.

The above list is merely suggestive of the kinds of issues that could be addressed in order to incorporate human rights relevant to women's health into health policies and health care practices. Clearly, wider consultation is needed among women and those knowledgeable about women's health, human rights and medical ethics for the development of principles for the promotion and protection of women's health.

Discussion

So, the list of the dark faces of classic patriarchy goes on and on. One legitimate question is why do women who constitute approximately 50 per cent of all societies submit to these practices? A more intriguing question is why do women, themselves, become enforcers of the patriarchal rules? As we have seen in the preceding discussion, it is women who sacrifice their infant daughters to infanticide. Women have bound their daughter's feet in the past. Even today, women continue to mutilate their daughters' genitals. It is women who police the virginity of their daughters and daughters-in-law, chaperone them and report the observations/rumors to men. Women inspect the bloodied sheets after the first marital intercourse. It is also women who remain silent or actively serve as shields to protect their sons or husbands who murder their daughters in the name of honour. Although increasingly rare, a few women, willingly or not-so-willingly, still walk to their husbands' funeral pyres.

One answer to these puzzling observations lies in the relational aspect of all power relations (Crosbie, 1975; Homans, 1974). After all, those who lack power subscribe to the rules of the powerful and those who have power, try to hang on to it at all costs. However, a more insightful answer is found in what Kandiyoti (1988) calls 'the patriarchal bargain.' Patriarchal societies symbolically revere women's reproductive role within legitimate marriages and promise them respect, some power and prestige in becoming mothers (of sons) and mothers-in-law (Brown, 1997). For women, there are few legitimate alternatives for security outside of marriage. However, marriage is not a fundamental right. Instead, marriage is contingent on elaborate conceptualisations of honour, many restrictions on the physical body, complete control of sexuality and severe limitations on social and personal freedoms. Since deviations from rules of honour unleash unbearable pain and harm, most women learn to 'obey' the patriarchal boundaries and look forward to the future rewards their docile compliance promises. Moreover, they learn to make sure that their daughters also play by the rules, if they too, are going to gather the fruits from attracting a husband and bearing legitimate sons. In ancient China, it was the mothers who wrapped their daughters' feet in increasingly tightening loops. In Africa, it is the mothers who hold their daughters down when their genitals are being carved out. In the middle east and southwest Asia, mothers/mothers-in-law follow and chaperone every move of young girls and demand virginity tests. Mothers also participate, albeit indirectly, in decrees for honour killings and continue to protect their sons who carry out the execution. Women are the ones who seek selective abortions or snuff-out the life out of a female newborn, praying that the next pregnancy produces a son (Miller, 2001). In an ironic way, women collude with these practices in order to preserve the only life they know. To do otherwise, to change the rules in the middle of the game may mean that the suffering they, themselves, have endured may have been for nothing.

The above discussion should not be taken as blaming the victims. On the contrary, the intent is to show the extreme difficulty in breaking the chains of patriarchy which are so entrenched that only a few ever try. Dire consequences await those who dare to deviate. Patriarchal rules also make sure that women do not (can not) unite. They remain isolated in what appears to be individual struggles, while all women remain as the second class. Patriarchal rules set older women against the younger ones, rich women against the poor and women associated with the groom against women associated with the brides (Brown, 1997; Fernandez, 1997). Cast, class, race, religion further prevent women from seeking change as an indivisible group. Patriarchal practices even create unsurpassable chasms between mothers and daughters. Thus, like a mystical snake that devours its own tail, patriarchy re-produces itself within each generation.

What about the fathers, husbands, sons, brothers and the male kin? How is it that they do not raise up against the maltreatment and oppression of women whom they call mothers, sisters, wives and daughters? I think, the fact that they do not is yet another indication of the power of patriarchal rules. Even decent men are often silenced by the privileges the system bestows on them. They have a say in things, just by the fact that they are men. The exploitative balance works because even men at the bottom of the status pecking order can dominate some women, namely their wives and their daughters. Their gender brings men acceptance, recognition, and support of other men and servitude of women. Yet, ascribed power has its own drawbacks: In patriarchal systems, men never get to experience fulfilling egalitarian relationships with women because the system feeds on inequality. Some are conditioned/accustomed to seek mutilated women rather than cherishing the natural beauty of their partners. In company of other men, they may feel obliged to pass a decree to kill a wife, a blood-sister, their niece or daughter. In honour killings, often the youngest brother is chosen as the executioner, hoping that the legal system will be merciful on a child-killer. Yet, it is these young boys who will have to live with the nightmares of the evil they commit no matter what their patriarchal clan tells them. One day, they may have to force their own sons to duplicate their sins. Thus, classical patriarchy inflicts untold misery on women, but in a diabolical way, it also depraves its male benefactors.

Conclusions

What needs to be done to change the tide of patriarchal oppression which dates back thousands of years? What needs to change in order to break the cycle of women getting co-opted into the patriarchal rules? Of course, there is no easy answer to these questions. However, one thing which is clear to me is the necessity to see patriarchal violence against women as a continuum. If we fragment the perils women face by culture, by religion or by social or personal failures, we will lose our ability to see the destructive power of patriarchy in its amorphous and pandemic form. Fragmenting global forms of violence, women face also leads to the undesirable outcome of seeing the problems as 'us' (whatever us may be) against 'them' (whoever they may be). It is true that classic patriarchy is unique to certain parts of the world, as amply discussed in this paper. However, patriarchy and its negative consequences are manifested even outside of classic patriarchies. Fragmenting these issues also fragments our ability and resolve to confront and change the patriarchal rules and expectations that give rise to the problems. Since patriarchy is a global issue (despite the different faces it takes in different geographic locations or nation states), we must first seek its solutions at the global level. And since the different faces of patriarchy take on very unique forms, we must also seek solutions particular to that unique manifestation of the problem. The overall success lies in addressing multiple dimensions, not in truncated approach.

At the global level, concern for human rights became a beacon for many nation states that did not want to live through the atrocities of the WWII. In December 10, 1948, the Universal Declaration of Human Rights codified the principles of life, liberty, security and freedom from torture as indivisible and non-reducible rights for all people. Ironically, application of some of these fundamental rights to life conditions, specific to women and girl children had to wait another 50 years (Bond & Phillips, 2001). Even then, some of the United Nations declarations such as CEDAW (1979) and DEVAW (1993) mostly remain as guidelines without any means for international enforcement. Even when patriarchal states become signatories to these women's rights protocols, violations of women's rights continue to be overlooked or written off as cultural prerequisites (Abramson, 2002). If women's life, liberty, freedom of choice, and freedom from torture are truly going to be protected as fundamental and indivisible human rights, the individual states where violations of these rights occur must be held accountable for taking all necessary means to protect the victims as well as to persecute the offenders. If the states systematically fail either in their protection of women/girls and/or in the prosecution of the individual offenders of crimes against women, there should be an international body which strongly sanctions this failure. Sanctions should range from requests for specified changes, shaming, to political and economic sanctions. Notwithstanding the difficulty of developing internationally agreeable sanctions, what is important as a principle is that the states themselves must be made to feel moral, political, legal and economic pressure from the community of nations in order to protect their own citizens (especially women and children).

Within the local levels, especially in classic patriarchal regions, top down, direct foreign interventions do not work because traditional societies are suspicious of the ideas and ideals associated with the west. Given the deep-rooted suspicions, the existence of either national or international laws/treaties/agreements are not, by them, sufficient to eliminate the dark patriarchal practices. On the contrary, in an effort to preserve the religo-cultural identities within an increasingly westernizing world, orthodox patriarchies may even respond with rigidification of their practices (comparable to resurgence in religious extremism). Thus, although international interventions are absolutely necessary at the state level, they are useless or even counter-productive at local levels. Within the latter, solutions may involve working within the positive aspects of the individual cultures. The aim will be to allow and encourage the positive aspects to strip down the legitimacy attributed to violent practices. For example, in patriarchal societies, the concept of 'honour' and its link to women is so entrenched that it will be futile to attempt to dismantle it. Instead, the importance of honour can be reconceptualised as honour in not hurting women and children, and the honour of forgiving perceived misdeeds. Elders should be able to see a role for themselves and find face-saving mechanisms for discontinuing historically binding rituals (i.e., honour killings). Another example would be in terms of a culture that is transfixed on dowry. Maybe, expectations about elaborate gifts to flow from the bride's to the groom's side can be altered slightly, by seeing, for example, the formal educational attainment of the brides to substitute for dowry. This transformation in thinking may work by making the brides more independent and in a stronger position to productively contribute to the finances of their household while at the same time, gaining economic self-sufficiency and bargaining power. This will preserve the system of investment, without enslaving women.

Education and job opportunities, better standards of living for all (including men/women of all ages), incremental replacement of the need for only male labour with need for male and female workers through technological development will go a long way in breaking down patriarchal walls. The states also must invest into the future of their citizens through reform of inheritance and land-ownership laws. Perhaps more than any other dependency, economic dependence is the one which increases vulnerability. States must also be beckoned to invest in health-care and educational programmes to curb high birth rates.Women who have no control or say about their own reproductive capabilities are more saddled by the traditional views which define them exclusively in their reproductive roles. Without dismantling the reverence for the motherhood role, creating alternate pathways for respectability for women will be a key in breaking the patriarchal choke on their lives. In this transformation, it is crucial to enlist the help and authority of the local elders (both men and women) into the process of social change where change will come along with them rather than despite them. Without eliciting the help and cooperation of the elders, the age-based patriarchal systems will sabotage any and all efforts to create positive change.

Works Cited

- Abramson, A.T. (2002). Nation States are responsible under international law to take measures against domestic violence. Paper presented at Halifax, Nova Scotia for the HSSFC Congress Meetings (June 1, 2003).
- Al-Dawla, A.S. (2000). The story of the FGM task-force: An ongoing campaign against female genital mutilation. In P. Ilkkaracan (ed.). Women and Sexuality in Muslim Societies. Istanbul: Women for Women's Rights.

- Anwary, A. (2003). Acid violence and medical care in Bangladesh: Women's activism as casework. Gender & Society 17(2): 305-313.
- Barstow, D.G. (1999). Female genital mutilation: The penultimate gender abuse. Child Abuses & Neglect 23(5): 501-510.
- Bond, J. & Phillips, Robin (2001). Violence against women as a human rights violation: International institutional responses. In. C.M. Renzetti, J.L. Edelson & R.K. Bergen (Eds.). Source-book on Violence Against Women (pp. 481-499). Thousand Oaks: Sage.
- Brown, J.K. (1997). Agitators and peace-makers: Cross cultural perspectives on older women and the abuse of younger wives. In A. Sev'er (ed.). ACross-Cultural Exploration of Wife Abuse. New Jersey: Mellen.
- Caputi, J. (1989). The sexual politics of murder. Gender & Society 3(4): 437-456.
- CEDAW (1979). Http://www.un.org/womenwatch/daw/cedaw (Last visited, Oct. 2003).
- Chen, P-C. (1984). China's other revolution. International Family Planning Perspectives 10(2): 48-57.
- Cindoglu, D. (2000). Virginity tests and artificial virginity in modern Turkish medicine. In P. Ilkkaracan (Ed.). Women & Sexuality in Muslim Societies. Istanbul: Women for Women's Rights.
- Crosbie, P.V. (1975). Interaction in Small Groups. New York: Macmillan.
- DEVAW (1993). Http://www.un.org/womenwatch/daw/cedaw.
- Dorkenoo, E. (1995). Cutting the rose: Female genital mutilation-the practice and its prevention. London: Minority Rights Group.
- Duzkan, A. & F. Kocali. (2000). An honour killing: She fled, her throat was cut. In P. Ilkkaracan (ed.). Women and Sexuality in Muslim Societies. Istanbul: Women for Women's Rights.
- Dworkin, A. (1974). Women Hating. New York: Dutton.
- Fernandez, M. (1997). Domestic violence by extended family members in India: Interplay of gender and generation. Journal of Interpersonal Violence 12(3): 433-455.
- Fox, B. (1988). Conceptualizing patriarchy. Review of Canadian Sociology & Anthropology 25(2): 163- 180.
- Hegde, R.S. (1999). Marking bodies, reproducing violence: A feminist reading of female infanticide in South India. Violence Against Women 5(5): 507-524.
- Johnson, P.S. & Johnson, J.A. (2001). The oppression of women in India. Violence Against Women 7(9): 1051-1068.
- Luthra, R. (1994). A case of problematic diffusion: The use of sex determination techniques in India. Knowledge: Creation, Diffusion, Utilisation 15(3): 259-272.

- Maris, C. & Saharso, S. (2001). Honour killing: A reflection on gender, culture and violence. The Netherlands' Journal of Social Science 37(1): 52-73.
- Mayell, H. (2002). Thousands of women killed for family honour. National Geographic News (Feb. 12). Http://news.national geographic.com/news
- McKinnon, C.A. (1982). Feminism, Marxism, method and the state: An agenda for theory. Signs: Journal of Women in Culture and Society 7: 515-544.
- Miller, B.D. (2001). Female selective abortion in Asia: Patterns, policies and debates. American Anthropologist 103(4): 1083-1095.
- Paratap. A. (1995). Women: Killed by greed and oppression. Time Magazine 146(11). Http://www.time.com/time/international/1995/950911/women. india.
- Plechner, D. (2000). Women, medicine and sociology: Thoughts on the need for a critical feminist perspective. Health, Illness and Use of Care 18: 69-94.
- Shah, G. (1990). Crime against women: Dowry-divorce-bride-burning. In S. Sood. Violence Against Women. New Delhi: Arihant.
- Sood, S. (1990). Violence Against Women. New Delhi: Arihant.
- UNIFEM (2003a). Violence Against Women Around the World. Http:// www.unifem.org/www/newsroom/events/not_a_minute_more.
- Walby, S. (1989). Theorising patriarchy. Sociology 23(2): 213-234.
- Walker, A. & Parmar, P. (1993). Warrior Marks: Female Genital Mutilation and the Sexual Blinding of Women. New York: Harcourt Brace & Company.

19

Surrogacy or De-Personalised Motherhood: A Human Rights Perspective

—Aparna Dixit

This paper aims at the psycho-social mapping of surrogacy what has been occasionally termed as virtual motherhood or may be understood as de-personalised motherhood as well. Surrogacy as a modern day debate has been criticized on many grounds. There are intellectual circles who maintain that it involves the wrongful commodification of persons and relationships. Even masses sometimes brand surrogacy as baby-selling business that is harmful to the children born to surrogates, analysts also believe that it's also harmful to all children, whose sense of security is undermined by the practice, and on the whole harmful to women as a class[1]. Not only in its meaning but surrogacy is believed to be exploitative in its nature and attitude and that such subjugation is grounds in the patriarchal set up of society, where "purity of blood" is important as a concept of identity. There is another line of argument that says; this exploitation depends on whether it would be harmful to the exploited party or there can be mutually advantageous exploitation, because some have argued a transaction cannot be exploitative unless the exploited is coerced (or perhaps defrauded). Sometimes a surrogate bargain form patriarchal society and chose her womb to rent out for her (Family) own financial security that she justifies as comparatively "Respectable contract" for her stability.

Whether the (surrogate) herself chooses to become mother for the other, or coerced by her family members or society, pays for that in terms of her health, psycho-social condition and as a women on whole. Gupta (2006) argues, the impact of surrogacy on women is multilayered: "while for some women use of these technologies has meant a shift from being 'objects' and 'victims' to 'knowing subjects' and 'agents' of control over their own bodies, for others they have brought more outside control and expropriation."

Conceptualizing Surrogacy

Surrogacy is a "*form of third party reproduction in which a woman agrees to create and/or maintain a pregnancy for another person or couple, typically for monetary compensation*"[2] Surrogacy, a practice in which a woman agrees to carry a baby for someone else who then keeps the child as her own, has mostly been a conversation about moral and ethical debates that very often argues as subjugation.

Surrogacy as exchange of motherhood is itself patriarchal in nature. As Erving Goff man famously argued that *bodily signs that depart from the ordinary can be deeply discrediting*. In case of motherhood, if it's a normal pregnant woman, she gets support and respect from family and society but if she is a surrogate gets nothing but of humiliation and discretion and in general society never respect her.

In contrast Everett Hughes invoked the term "dirty work" to refer to tasks and occupations that are likely to be perceived as degrading. A work can be "dirty" because it is perceived as physically disgusting (like janitorial work and butchering), because it wounds dignity by requiring servile behavior (like domestic work or shoe shining), or it offends moral conceptions (as does sex work, topless dancing, and surrogate mothering). Surrogacy resides in this sticky area. Surrogates are described as "true angels" who "make dreams happen," but surrogacy is also surrounded by controversies about the "ethics of selling mother hood" and "renting wombs[3]."

In societies like India, Surrogacy is still unacceptable. Surrogates are seen as "Bad women" of society, who sell their womb for their personal interest and discredit motherhood for money only, however this 'Self interest' is still debatable that cost a big loss of these hired mothers.

Traditional versus Gestational Surrogacy

In situations where the wife is infertile, surrogacy refers to the fertilisation of the egg of another woman by the sperm of the husband. In such cases, the surrogate mother provides both the genes and a womb for gestation. The infertile wife or female partner has no biological connection to the child. This type of surrogacy is known as "Traditional Surrogacy" because biological motherhood remains intact (Pollitt, 1990; Newsweek, 1990).

"Gestational Surrogacy" (or "pure surrogacy") relies more heavily on reproductive technology, for it involves the separation of genetic and gestational motherhood, (Newsweek, 1990: 66; Raymond, 1993). Gestational surrogacy, as the more radical yet now preferred and more common type of surrogacy, opens the door for both husband and wife and/or two partners to be genetically related to a child who is not born by the wife or female partner (Benardo & Benardo, 2007; Ali & Kelley, 2008). The "infertile" couple provides both sperm and an egg (either their own or ones they have purchased). A fetus is conceived via IVF and implanted into the surrogate's uterus. The surrogate mother is not genetically-related to the child she carries, and is therefore only responsible for the gestation of the fetus (Benardo & Benardo, 2007).

Surrogacy arrangements have been relatively rare until recently. Because of its rarity, surrogacy comes with many legal, ethical, economic, moral, and social issues (Markens, 2007; Benardo & Benardo, 2007). Surrogacy challenges the traditional process of reproduction and also long standing definitions of parenthood and motherhood. There is also an Intersections perspective that suggests surrogacy allows us to examine how motherhood is defined today, and how changing definitions affect the lives of mothers in different caste, class and community. Because of their different position in society, some groups of women/mothers will be affected favorably and others unfavorably, despite a common gender location. Those privileged by caste or class can maintain this privilege through the use of surrogacy, and those who disadvantaged by their caste, class and community may only confirm a lesser position in society when participating in surrogacy arrangements. So this arrangement holds a matrix of subordination (Collins, 1990; Weber, 2001).

Surrogacy: An Indian Perspective

In India it's not new but still a growing business to rent out womb. For foreigners it's most attracted place to get a surrogate because of cheap labour. Unfortunately, there has not been any public debate on moral, ethical or social aspects of this hired pregnancy. In legal terms to understand surrogacy, one has to look upon Transplantation of Human Organs Act, 1994. According to this, the sale of human organs, organ loaning is banned in India but on the other hand an equally dangerous business is not only promoted but growing that is paid surrogacy.

There is another shocking fact that the incidence of total infertility in India is 8 to 10 per cent approximately and in majority of cases it's preventable as this infertility is result of poor nutrition, maternity services, high levels of infections and bad health of individual. There are only 2 per cent women who are facing 'primary infertility' that is also curable by ART[4] (Assisted Reproductive Technologies), hardly 1 per cent need surrogacy arrangements for getting their 'OWN' baby even though ART itself has its complications like high possibility of foetal anomalies, low rates of success and multiple pregnancies.

The medical industry keeps rising because of this attractive reproductive venture but the cause of the attraction is deep rooted in the concept of "Purity of Blood". One has comparatively progressive, easy and safe option of adoption but it comes with the feeling of "Other" that is not associated with the privatisation of relationship and for a family keeping baby, means replicating so called familial traits that are bestowed by biological parents (especially father) only. So the concept of surrogacy is only to maintain purity that cost exploitation of mother (Surrogate, child intended) and motherhood as whole. In India, unfortunately besides many obligations for women to become a mother society easily justify surrogacy as a "Charity of Motherhood".

Exploitation through Surrogacy: The Interplay of Class, Caste & Gender

Gender discrimination on any ground can never be understood without analyzing class and cast within it. Richardson defines combination of Class, gender and caste as a new form of exploitation (Richardson, 1987; Weber, 2001; Collins, 1991). In this regard, as far as the surrogacy is concerned, women's wombs can only be "rented out" due to the devalued role that women play in the reproductive process. Bringing class into the business, the majority of women only rent their wombs in financial crisis; poor women are more likely to become surrogate mothers on contrast the wealthier women are more likely to be the intended "mothers". So women's class affects gendered experience of pregnancy and motherhood and that particular class location outline individual experience simultaneously. Majorly, the 'lower caste' women come from lower economic strata (Weber, 2001), that's why the effects of this combination make women more vulnerable to get entered in to surrogacy arrangements. The very combination of caste and class is also safe for child intended mother so that the gestational mother never claims for the gestating baby more often because of her caste and class effects.

Women from lower caste and class are hardly seen in position of child intended mother, this is of course because of their caste-class intricacy. Though it is generally presumed that all women face exploitation as surrogate mothers, but poor or working class and lower caste women may be exploited more than upper caste and class women within third party reproductive arrangements. This subordination is a outcome of the interplay of caste, class, and gender. The position of father in this matrix is very much debatable, he is always in better position even than child intended mother. So as Collins (1990) and Weber (2001) maintain that the effects of any social location or inequality (Gender) are mediated by other locations or inequalities (class and caste) at all times.

The Psycho-Social State of a Surrogate

The concept of parenthood is grounded largely in biology and not in an arbitrary agreement even though surrogacy comes with some legal norms and terminates one's parental rights and duties prior to conception. So this arrangement compels a mother (gestational mother) to relinquish her child on legal ground but is it possible on emotional or psychological ground? Throughout the process of pregnancy and delivery a psychosocial pressure works against her genuine motherhood in order to break the natural, biological and maternal bond that she has with her child. It's to make it easier to relinquish the child she has nurtured in her womb.

On psychosocial ground an agreement can't dissolve existing motherhood bonds that are grounded in biology, between the gestational mother and resulting child. To rent a womb does not mean to rent out one's motherhood. So in surrogacy arrangements, gestational mother must go through the process of depersonalisation, that's practically not possible and as Rosalie Ber argued that, The question of whether the suffering of a childless woman is greater than that of the gestational surrogate, who "abandons" her baby, is "solved" when the surrogate mother is de personalised, and looked upon solely as a "womb for rent". This is to place a surrogate a greater risk of exploitation. In surrogacy she is just like a commodity for conceiving and producing child she is mere a means to get child. Ciccarelli in a study described, surrogate mothers were asked to report their feelings or concerns about relinquishing the child. One mother reported emotional distress over the relinquishment and two others reported a strong instinctual urge to bond.

According to Gresham M. Sykes and David Matza, when individuals are engaged in stigmatized occupations that threaten to spoil their identity, they do remedial work to manage and neutralize the stigma associated with the deviant occupation. This "management" can work out worldly but their own position is still a subject of debate. A psychologically and physically exploited woman is like a 'waste product' of this baby manufacturing business and the feeling of commodification disturbs women psychosocial position on whole.

Epilogue

The objectification of women that surrogacy necessitates leaves a surrogate vulnerable to exploitation and coercion and its worst in case of commercial surrogacy. The Ethical dilemmas related to the surrogacy are still debatable because of legal diversities throughout the world. In any condition, a surrogate always face greatest challenges because of her intimate psychological and gestational relationship with the child.

As Markens (2007) suggests that there are still very few macro-level analyses of what surrogacy means for our definitions of motherhood and family indicates that there is a lack of empirical research on surrogacy from a social problems perspective (Markens, 2007). So this is the time to pay close attention to how the separation of genetic, gestational and social motherhood affects the definitions of individuals and their families, and in what sense class, caste and gender affects the very definition and experience of surrogacy. For example Jyotsna Agnihotri Gupta (2006) is very clear about multilayered effects of surrogacy as she argued, for some it may be straightforward exploitation but for others it's like a shift from being "other" or "victim" to "knowing subjects". Amrita Pande in her paper argued it as method of resisting stigma of commercial surrogacy. Markens argument of social problems perspective to address the surrogacy must be seen in broader sense and it should be dealt with the very stand point perspectives of surrogates (as victim, agent, angel or knowing subjects). This analysis will never be rational if one would not analyze it in class, caste and gender frame. However, the minority and transgender section is also very much important to bring in the research in surrogacy arrangements. So in this case practice of social justice is only possible if research see the issue in diverse social structure with surrogate's point of view.

Works Cited

- Anderson, E. (1990)."Is Women's Labor a Commodity?" Philosophy and Public Affairs 19, no. 1,71-92
- Andrews, L. (1987). "The Aftermath of Baby M: Proposed State Laws on Surrogate Motherhood," Hastings Center Report 17 (October/November): 31-40.
- Benardo, S. M., & Benardo, K. (2007). "Assisted Reproductive Technologies: Egg Donation and Surrogacy Arrangements in Law and Practice" (Bloomberg Corporate Law Journal 2: 406-414).
- Ber, R. (2000). "Ethical Issues in Gestational Surrogacy".

- Ciccarelli, J.C &Beckman, L.J. (2005). "Navigating Rough Waters: An Overview of Psychological Aspects of Surrogacy". Issues; 61:30-1.
- Collins, P. H. (1990). "Black Feminist Thought". (New York: Routledge).
- Goffman, E. (1963). "Stigma: Notes on the Management of Spoiled Identity" (Englewood Cliffs, N.J. Prentice Hall).
- Gupta, J. A. (2006). "Towards Transnational Feminisms: Some Reflections and Concerns in Relation to the Globalisation of Reproductive Technologies," European Journal of Women's Studies 13(1).
- Hughes, E. (1951). "Work and the Self," in Social Psychology at the Crossroads, ed. John H. Rohrer and Muzafer Sherif" (New York: Harper & Brothers).
- Markens, S. (2007). "Surrogate Motherhood and the Politics of Reproduction". (Berkeley, CA: University of California Press).
- Pollitt, K. (1990). "Checkbook Maternity: When is a Mother not a Mother? The Nation" December 31. pp. 839-46.
- Pollitt, K. (1994). "Reasonable Creatures: Essays on Women and Feminism" (New York: Alfred A. Knopf).
- Raymond, J. (1993). "Women as Wombs: Reproductive Technologies and the Battle over Women's Freedom" (San Francisco: Harper,).
- Richardson, H. (Ed.). (1987). "On the Problem of Surrogate Motherhood: Analyzing the Baby M case. Lewiston". (NY: The Edwin Mellen Press).
- Sykes, G. M. and Matza, D. (1957). "Techniques of Neutralisation: A Theory of Delinquency," American Sociological Review 22, no. 6, 664-70.
- Weber, L. (2001). "Understanding Race, Class, Gender and Sexuality: A Conceptual Framework". (New York: McGraw Hill Publishers).

Notes

1. See Hanne Anderson's (2014).Choice or Enslavement? Psychological Damage in Surrogacy. Available Online.
2. Benardo & Benardo, 2007. P. 409.
3. See Adrienne Vogt's (2014).The rent-a-womb boom. Inside Story. The daily Beast. Available Online.
4. Assisted reproductive technology (ART) is the technology used to achieve pregnancy in procedures such as fertility medication, artificial insemination, in vitro fertilisation and surrogacy.

Index